Windows PCs in the Ministry

STEVE HEWITT

Author

THOMAS NELSON
Since 1798

NASHVILLE DALLAS MEXICO CITY RIO DE JANEIRO

Published in Nashville, TN, by Thomas Nelson. Thomas Nelson is a trademark of Thomas Nelson, Inc.

Thomas Nelson, Inc., titles may be purchased in bulk for educational, business, fund-raising, or sales promotional use. For information, please email SpecialMarkets@ThomasNelson.com.

Book Interior: Stephen Ramirez

Editor: Gabriel Hernandez

Series Editor: Michael Lawson

Produced in Association with Lawson Music Media, Inc.

Library of Congress Cataloging-in-Publication Data is available upon request.

ISBN: 1418541737

ISBN-13: 9781418541736

Acknowledgements

I would be incredibly remiss if I didn't take this opportunity to thank my Savior for all of the opportunities I have been given to serve Him, including the writing of this book. One of my favorite scriptures is I Cor 1:27, where God declares he can use the foolish and weak to confound the wise and the strong. For, I know how foolish and weak I really am, and I am always humbled by any opportunity to be used by Him.

Along those same lines, I must acknowledge the help of my loving wife Gina, who has provided me the inspiration to accomplish things I never thought possible. Her love and support allows me to stay focused on serving my Lord, and I know she is one of the many blessings He has bestowed upon me.

I also need to thank all of those that helped me during the writing of this book, including Gregory Fish who has served as my consultant in the area of video production, and Kevin Purcell who also serves as my consultant, consistently keeping me up to date on the latest features that emerge in the area of Bible study software. During the course of writing this book, I've been blessed to have had the opportunity to consult with more people than I could ever list. My sincere thanks go out to each for patiently helping me gain a clear understanding of the many products and services that I've been able to include in the writing of this book. I appreciate the host of friends and colleagues that have helped keep me abreast of the continuously changing technology landscape.

Contents

Preface

The ministry of the church has not changed over the centuries, but the methods and tools used to accomplish today's ministry certainly have! Computers have evolved into today's communication centers, allowing us to take the message of salvation, hope and love as mandated in the Gospels and present it in exciting and vibrant ways, both to the masses, and on an individual basis. This is vital for the church, since we are a people with *The Message*! The good news is that technology has not only made it possible for anyone to make major enhancements to their ministry, but they can now do it using free or inexpensive applications or services as well. You no longer need an expensive, powerful computer with high-cost software to produce quality media. Now, as a result of the Internet, thin-client and cloud computing services, you can produce and distribute exciting media to your congregation and community, as well as to the nation and the world.

Introduction

This book will present a variety of ways to use technology to enhance and expand ministry using Windows programs and Internet services. If you are reading this book, then hopefully you're seeking to learn how to use computers and technology to expand and enhance your ministry opportunities. Every church has a mission and ministry. And while the methods have changed over the centuries, the message remains the same: Jesus is the way, the truth and the life, and He is the answer for many who are seeking. The church, in general, is losing its opportunity to get that message out to our nation. This is due in part to changes in technology, which often reflect new methods of communication. Unfortunately, most churches have failed to willingly use these new communication tools, and thus have passed on various opportunities to share the Gospel with many in our nation.

Why? In the book, *The Blogging Church*, written by Brian Bailey with Terry Storch, a good job is done of defining this problem. They state, "Although churches are necessarily grounded in technological traditions, this commitment often becomes a commitment to methodology as well. There is a firm resistance to change within a typical church, and technology is certainly an agent of change. New technology often redefines staff roles and processes, many of which have been in place for years. With change comes conflict and perceived loss of control."

So, while some churches still sing about telling the "old, old story", we are faced with the challenge of using modern tools to reach new generations. I do not believe that the advancement of technology is happening by accident. Nor do I believe we are clever if we use these tools supposedly designed for the purposes of the world and adapt them for our intention. The fact is, during my last 20 years in the industry of reporting on technology and its use by Christianity, I have discovered that some of the brightest minds working in the highest levels of technology today are brothers and sisters in Christ. I have met those that are creating the fastest chips for Intel, and they are Christians. I have met leading officers at our nation's communications companies, and they are Christians. Those that pioneered the ability to give our television and cable networks the ability to broadcast live camera shots and commentary of events happening around the world are Christians. I am not saying that everyone working at the highest levels of technology is a born-again believer, but I am no longer surprised when my connections bring me face-to-face with people who are working at our nation's top technology companies; only to find out they are Christians. I believe that the advances in technology that we are seeing are not only being created for the world's marketplace, and to boost the stocks of large companies, but also for the purposes of God and for his people to use to spread his Word around the world, and to allow us to minister to our local congregations in fantastic new ways.

Walt Wilson, in his book *The Internet Church*, states, "The dramatic and startling changes seen through the lens of technology indicate that God is doing something tremendous at this moment in history. These developments are changing society, economies, and politics at an increasing rapid pace. It is important for the positioning of the church and the delivery of God's message in the 21st Century that we understand the direction and speed of these changes." (pg 43)

Throughout the book I will also reference specific products, and in some cases provide feature lists with descriptions of what the products can accomplish, specifically as they relate to ministry. I am aware that in spotlighting particular products or services offered by various companies, other companies that provide similar products or services might feel overlooked. It is simply impossible to provide a list of every product or service available in the areas I will cover. Please know that I am merely mentioning the programs that I am aware of, and will try to provide additional information about other products when possible. New products enter the market all the time, and I am certain they provide services that are fantastic. In fact, I am sure something was launched as I wrote this paragraph! The purpose of this book is to introduce the reader to the many ministry concepts and Internet services available to them in a Windows-based computer environment. Let me apologize in advance if I have failed to mention your favorite product or service.

Special Note about the Title

The title of this book, *Windows PCs in the Ministry*, should be defined. With each passing year those that use computers on a regular basis should notice that there are more and more online services available to them, as opposed to programs that have to be installed on their computers. Computing is quickly moving toward what is known as "cloud computing," which means users are accessing programs that are available online. For example, Google has recently designed and released a collection of online applications that include a spreadsheet, word processor, and other useful, everyday programs. Regardless of the operating system you use (Windows, Macintosh, Linux, etc.) you can easily access and use any of these services.

In this book, I talk about the use of both programs and services. And obviously those using various operating systems (OS) will be able to take advantage of the services available through online application services. However, the distinction in the title of this book is designed to help readers understand that program suggestions will be based upon the Windows OS.

CHAPTER 1

What Does Technology Have to Do with Ministry?

Technology is more than gadgets, shiny monitors, fast computers, cool programs and other services on the Internet. The computer, and the many applications that have been developed since their introduction into our society, have become the leading way for many in our society to communicate. Thus, it has become the glue that binds relationships, the source for growing friendships, and provides the connection tools that help keep families together. In essence, the ability to communicate via the Internet and mobile computing devices has begun to bury traditional mass media communications.

Newspapers and those who have lived by the barrel of ink for the past century have had to adapt. Television has not been able to increase its audience, and those that provide our national news have had to adapt to the new tools in order to broadcast their message or face the reality that their message will go unheard. Even those running for the presidency of the United States have realized the power of personal communication options and have made great use of tools like texting. In fact, President Barack Obama may have obtained the highest office in the land because of his willingness to expand into new ways of spreading his message. Yet, many of those with the greatest message—and the most pressing need to communicate that message—have held back. The church, by far, is one of the last institutions in America to press forward and effectively use technology, and especially the communication opportunities that come with it, for their own purpose.

What does technology have to do with ministry? Maybe everything!

"Christians are now making up a declining percentage of the American population."

The statement above was published in *Newsweek*, April 4, 2009, in an article entitled "The End of Christian America" (by Jon Meacham). It wasn't intended as an attack on Christianity. It also wasn't "spin" by those hoping to discourage the church, nor was it a proclamation from a victory party held by those who have worked hard to remove the visible symbols of Christianity from public view. Instead, it was a simple fact. The church is declining in America, and frankly, at an alarming rate.

According to the American Religious Identification Survey, the percentage of individuals in America that identify themselves as being a Christian has fallen by 10 percent since 1990. That means the population in America that *admits* to being Christian is around 76 percent. Some would blame other religions that have experienced some growth in America during the last decade. However, the number of people who state they are not affiliated with any particular faith has doubled since 1988, going from 5 to 12 percent of the American population.

In addition, the overall number of people that identify themselves as members of a Protestant denomination in America has declined over the last 10 years by 9.5 percent, while the national population has increased by 11 percent.

Why is the number of Christians declining? Around half of all Christian churches in America did not receive a single addition to their membership as a result of someone having a conversion experience. The Hartford Institute for Religion Research believes there are 300,000 churches in America. If this number is correct, that means 150,000-plus churches opened their doors each and every Sunday to hold services, yet went the entire year without seeing the result of one person coming to a conversion experience and beginning a walk with Christ. They sang hymns which gave testimony to the glory and majesty of God, served as verbal testimony to those sitting in the pew around them as they declared their desire to "serve the Lord with gladness," and wished they had "a thousand tongues to sing of their great Redeemer's praise." Following these musical outbursts of dedication and testimony, someone stood in the pulpit and preached a message, with most using passages from the Bible. Many of these attendees found themselves surrounded by stained glass, pipes that were connected to air bellows and an organ, and a large wooden cross. Yet with 150,000-plus churches doing this week after week, 52 weeks per year—and many holding not one, but *two* services on Sunday—not one person who'd been living without Christ decided to convert and become a Christian.

With those statistics and track record, it should be obvious as to why we are declining in numbers. We're simply not getting our message out to those that need to hear it. America is not hearing the testimonies we are singing as we sit in our pews on Sunday. Why are they not impressed as we sing about God's power, his "sweet Holy Spirit", and his "joy, joy, joy, joy, down in our hearts"? Could it be that they are not hearing our songs? Maybe they're not aware that we put steeples on our roofs because they are symbols that the church is the place to come to find God. It could be that when they drive by our church signs and see that we're having an "organ recital" on Sunday afternoon that this is our way of inviting them to come to Jesus and have a life-changing experience. It could also be that the lines of communication have broken down somewhere!

OK, THIS IS GOING TO HURT A LITTLE
. . . .

I know that my words might sting a little, and that my sarcasm might seem harsh. But we are losing the opportunity to win our nation to Christ, and Christianity is dying. So, while some of what I have yet to say will hurt, my intent is not to harm. There is a difference. Dentists hurt, but they do so in order to help us have better teeth. Doctors have to hurt, but they do it because sometimes it is necessary to prevent real harm. I hate it when my doctor says, "Ok, this is going to hurt a little," but I know that sometimes I have to endure a little pain in order to experience the overall benefit.

In reporting about church growth in America between 1990 and 2000, George Barna and Mark Hatch reported in their book, *Boiling Point*, that "More than 80 percent of the adults who get counted as new adherents and thus as a part of the growth statistic are really just transplants from other churches—religious consumers in search of the perfect, or at least more exciting and enjoyable, church experience. Disturbingly little church growth is attributed to new converts. All in all, it was not a good decade for church growth." (pg. 236)

Some point out that all is not lost. While the overall number of churches in America is declining, there are also many new mega-churches popping up across the country. Willow Creek, Saddleback and other mega-churches are commonly known names in Christendom. They give us hope for the chance to turn around this slide away from Christianity that American seems to be going through. Yet only two percent of churches in America have 1,000 or more adults attending in a typical week.

THE "WHY" BEHIND THE WHY?

There are many articles on why America is moving away from Christ. Some believe it is because of the messages sent by Hollywood to our movie theaters. Others believe it's because of efforts to remove God and Christ from the public view. Some might claim it's because public prayer has been removed from our schools. Frankly, I don't believe that any of these can be blamed for the decline in the number of Christians in America. I am a firm believer that anytime the church is ready they can bring their light out from under the bushel, and that nothing will be able to hide it. We know that Christians can thrive in the midst of persecution. Christians started and spread across the known world during a time of worldwide persecution, leading to the martyrdom of the very apostles that helped spread the Word. From pulpits across America, I have heard people declare different reasons for the decline of Christianity in America, yet I believe most are missing the real reason for our decline

I don't believe we're losing the battle because the world has overcome us, and in fact the Bible declares this will never happen. I don't believe that people are turning away from Christianity because we suffer such great persecution here in the United States. If something or someone is to blame for the decline of Christianity in America, it is the church itself. Most churches simply do not set a high priority on using the tools available to them to bridge the communication gap that separates the way we used to do things from the way we need to do them today in order to communicate the Gospel to our nation.

The tools already exist for churches to reach their communities, and we just need to use them. We need to recognize that we're not just talking about computers, computer programs and Internet services; we're talking about communication tools and opportunities.

I have seen them. I have seen them in churches up north, out east, and even down south in our nation's Bible belt. Over the years I literally have visited hundreds of churches in my travels across the country while speaking at conferences. I have visited Churches of all denominations, flavor and size, and I have heard from church leaders who share with me their frustration in dealing with church memberships that purposely stand in the way of their church using the necessary tools to communicate the Gospel to their communities. I have heard the excuses and the illogical reasons. I have been invited to speak at churches across the nation on how to use the many new tools available to help expand the ministry of churches in our nation, and everywhere I've been I always find those that resist the chance to look at new technology tools to advance their ministry. They simply don't want to change and they do not want to be uncomfortable with anything that takes them out of their comfort zone.

We are failing because too many of our members, and too many of our leaders, don't want to be uncomfortable. They don't want to try something new, or learn a new technique. They are happy to have become keepers of the fish bowl, instead of fisher's of men.

DO YOU LIKE TO FISH?

I love to fish. I love to fish for bass, crappie and catfish, all native to my native state of Missouri. I also love to fish for trout.

In Missouri, trout fishing is different. In our state we have to go to special trout farms since trout are not natural to our state. Normally our lakes and rivers are too hot for trout. But there are a couple of places where we have large natural springs where the water is ice cold.

Since I love to fish for trout, I've discovered a perfect place down at Bennett Springs State Park. There is this one spot in one of the streams where I know there is a hole. And while the water goes by swiftly at the surface, the hole itself is a great place for the trout to drop in and feed. There are different fishing rules for different areas in the park. Up near the spring, you can fly fish only. A bit farther down the stream, you can use spinners and lures. My favorite hole is in an area where you can use live bait, and if you put a minnow on a hook in front of a shinny spinner and wade out into that cold water and drop your bait just above that hole and let it drift down, you will normally catch your limit in about an hour or so.

A couple of years ago, I took some friends down to Bennett to fish. The night before, in anticipation of everyone in our group catching their limit, I told them all about my favorite spot and what to do. I even drew a picture of where my special hole was. We all got up at 5:30 a.m. to be sure to reserve our spot on the side of the stream so that when the whistle blew we could all wade out and catch some trout. Well, when the whistle finally blew, my friends followed me and we all waded out into that cold stream, grabbed a minnow and were ready to go. I noticed everyone in my little party was standing around me ready to learn exactly where to cast except for the wife of one of my friends. When she hit that cold water she decided it was too uncomfortable for her, so she decided she was going to fish on the side of the stream. I tried to tell her that from where she was standing she would never be able to cast out far enough to reach deep enough water to catch anything. We were fishing with very light tackle and two-pound test line, so were very limited in how far we could cast. She informed me that she really didn't care as the water was simply too cold, and it was more comfortable for her to sit in a folding chair on the bank rather than wade out into the cold water. She also had an issue with using minnows, and decided to fish with a bare hook and spinner. After a couple of hours everyone else in the group had a nice stringer of trout . . . all except one. And you can guess which one it was, right? She hadn't caught anything. Now, the point could be made that everyone had an equally good time, and she actually seemed to enjoy the morning on her lawn chair casting out into the water near the shore. She never got a bite, nor caught a fish, but she made it clear that she wasn't disappointed and as good a time as any one of us did.

My point is this: She didn't catch any fish. And she was happy about not catching any fish. This is a great example of what is happening in many churches today. They are not willing to do anything uncomfortable, and are happy with the appearance that they are trying. As long as they maintain that appearance, continue to be a part of the group and are comfortable, then the end result doesn't really matter.

But when it comes to the mission and ministry of a church, results *do* matter. Many years ago, steeples on the buildings, organs with pipes, and stained glass were all the allure we needed to let seekers know that the church was the answer and the way to find God. Today, this simply doesn't work.

The fish are biting, but we're not using the right bait. You might say that I'm wrong, that we're not catching anything because the fish simply aren't biting. If you look around you will see that this simply isn't true, and here are two glaring examples to prove it.

First, visit any bookstore and you will find a large selection of books under the heading of "Spirituality." People are seeking spiritual things. They have become disillusioned with a church that insists on trying to reach them without answering their questions. The Bible is applicable to today's problems and does have the answer to the questions people have. It's just that most churches refuse to wade into the cold water and bait the hook with the items that men and women are seeking.

Barna and others report that the search for spiritual answers is on the rise, although church attendance is on the decline and there are less and less Christians each year. Why? Barna reported in 2001 that within this decade as many as 50 million individuals may rely solely upon the Internet for all of their faith-based experiences. And what do they find if they visit a church Web site? They find a picture of the church's pastor, maybe a picture of the building, a church services schedule and, if they're really innovative, a map to help find the building. This is not what people are looking for when they're up late at night, sitting in front of their computers desperately surfing the Internet for answers.

IT'S TIME TO GET UNCOMFORTABLE AND WADE INTO THE COLD WATER

Churches that are made up of older adults (yep, those of us 50 and over) will die if they don't recruit new members in their 20's, 30's and 40's. It's a fact . . . they don't have a choice. So the choice is to get a little uncomfortable and wade into the water, or just hold on to the illusion and convince yourselves it's enough. This doesn't mean that church members who don't like to text *must* start texting. It does mean, however, that the older members of the church—normally the financial backbone of a church—need to commit to supporting new ways, new ideas and new methodology in order to expand and enhance their churches' ministry. They can't just sit it out. All of us need to be held accountable for our part in the evangelistic impact of the churches we belong to and attend.

I love to observe people, and since I'm in my mid 50's and a techno-evangelist seeking to encourage churches and Christians to use the latest technology tools, I am aware that I must grow old gracefully, but not be a hindrance to those younger than me. I see many older people in churches that are all about their own comfort zones. They don't want change, and I find some who can't tolerate young people. Thankfully, I also see many that are in their 70's and 80's who are fantastic supporters and cheer leaders for their church's efforts to use new communication tools and methods to reach their community. It's all a matter of attitude and priority. I know some who are in their 80's that complain how tired they get after getting up from their nap. They talk as if their life is over. Yet as I write this book, former President George H.W. Bush just celebrated his 85th birthday by jumping out of an airplane to skydive, and I just finished watching an interview with a 100 year old male tennis champion with plans to head to Holland for an international tennis tournament. Don't let your age prevent you from changing with the times, and don't discourage your church from using new technology. Instead, step up to the task, wade out into uncomfortable waters, lead by example, and invite and inspire your church's leadership to use the tools before us to reach the community, and our nation for Christ!

IS IT ABOUT CONTROL?

While some people decry that they don't like change, I suspect in many cases it is about control. Most churches have to deal with control issues and conflict. As I mentioned earlier, many churches are dependent on the contributions of older members, which makes it hard for them to justify the need to invest in technology services and tools designed to reach out to a younger generation. I believe, however, that you *can* make the case if the church is sincerely seeking to follow the leadership of the Lord. I honestly believe it's time we quit blaming the world and start taking responsibility for our failure to minister and evangelize. We need godly men and women to stand up and lead our churches.

I have been a pastor, and I understand how difficult it can be to introduce change and new techniques to an established congregation. In addition, as editor of Christian Computing for the last 20 years I have had the opportunity to meet and communicate with literally thousands of pastors that are frustrated with many of the technology tools that have reached the market. Yes, it *can* be frustrating, but there is hope. But even though it can be discouraging, don't give up. (If you get too anxious or discouraged, skip to the last chapter of this book and read it before you continue with the rest of the book.) There are ways to implement new technologies that are not threatening to your present membership. And while I go into greater detail later in the book, the basic rule for success is to introduce new technology methods without eliminating the current methods in use today. For example, you can introduce an email newsletter without eliminating the print version. Over time, it will be obvious that the new digital newsletter will save the church money, and provide greater—and better—features like videos and hyperlinks for additional information.

IS MONEY REALLY AN ISSUE?

For many years I've heard pastors tell me that they would like to use new technology tools to expand and enhance their ministry, but they just don't have the funds. In fact, surveys reveal that most churches will tell you that they place evangelism as a high priority for their church, yet the same surveys show that most churches budget a very small amount for evangelistic efforts and communication tools that could be used for evangelism.

I have seen small churches (100 adult members on a typical Sunday) that could raise $50,000 for a new organ, yet were unwilling to purchase a new computer for the church office, or invest more than $100 to host a Web site.

I was a pastor for about 15 years, and during that time I learned a thing or two about churches. One of the things I learned was that they will always have the funds to do the things they deem really important. It has never been about the money, It *has* been, however, everything about priorities.

I became the pastor of my first church as soon as I graduated college. The church was a little church in a small country town that was about four blocks wide by five blocks long, and surrounded by farmland. The church was over 100 years old and had never operated with a formal budget. On many a Sunday the church treasurer would hand me my paycheck and tell me that I should check with her later that afternoon to be sure it was good, depending on the morning's offering. I understand serving a church with limited funds. However, this usually happens due to a lack of vision!

While serving at that church I lived in the housing they provided, which was a small trailer behind the church. The trailer was old and needed many repairs. I remember one night as I was sitting inside watching the television, a cat—not belonging to my wife or I—pushed up the heating vent and crawled into our living room. We obviously had some holes in the heating ducts!

After living in that little trailer for a couple of years I called for a meeting with my three deacons. I told them it was time to build a house, and I presented my case in such a way that I was sure they couldn't turn it down. I told them that if they had a better house for their pastor to live in that they could probably get a much better pastor than the likes of me! They seemed to like that logic and decided to call a meeting of the church and see what everyone else thought. Understand that they *had* a building fund set aside to raise funds for a new parsonage, but in the three years I had been their pastor they had only raised about $1,000.

We had the meeting and one of the deacons (the one charged with doing the constant repairs needed on the trailer) and I presented the idea. I have to be honest: I was actually hoping they would consider a newer trailer, as my faith wasn't very big back then.

But I learned something that night: if God's people get a vision, the money will always be there. People started pledging some pretty large amounts of money right then and there during that meeting if the church would vote to build a new house. We raised half of the money in that first meeting then the following week went to a bank to secure a 15-year loan for the rest. Much to my surprise, however, we couldn't seem to get the money to stop! By the time we drew up the plans and were ready to break ground, ALL of the money to build the new house had been donated, with even a little extra amount that allowed us to make the entire house two feet wider and increase the size of all of the rooms by a little bit.

On a good Sunday this little country church would see just 60 kids in Sunday school, yet it raised enough money to build a new home in less than 60 days!

It was, and always will be, a matter of priorities. Churches will always come up with the funds to do whatever it is they *want* to do. They just need to want to do it.

The interesting thing about computers and technology is that the cost for either continues to decline every year. In 1988 I remember paying $5,000 for my 286z IBM computer and $5,000 for the toner printer that I purchased to go with it. That was $10,000 for a computer and printer. Now you can walk into a store and buy a computer that is 100 times better, faster and easier to use, for less than $1,000 and they will *give* you the printer!

So why don't more churches take advantage of the software programs available that can connect them with a professional-looking content management system designed to provide the connection and content to help seekers find that God is the answer to the questions that have been plaguing them all of their lives? Does anyone really want to try to convince me it's because they don't have the money? Of course, you can show me your budget, but if most churches are given the inspiration, the challenge, the encouragement, and even the opportunity to give and sacrifice to reach their community for Christ I believe they would rise to the challenge and do what it takes to raise the money, find the talent, and volunteer their time and expertise to meet the need.

Also note that money is no longer an excuse to use and apply many of the solutions mentioned in this book because many are free! In the last chapter I give several examples and explanations on how churches can begin to take advantage of many new ways to communicate and use technology without spending a single penny.

COMMUNICATION METHODS HAVE BECOME "AGE" SPECIFIC

Most churches that have ceased to grow and are declining are made up of congregants that are 50 years old, or older. I am over 50 myself, so I'm talking about my generation. Those of us over 50 usually start falling out of the latest technology trends, and unfortunately technology adaptations for new methods of communication are commonly viewed as "trends".

Computers and technology have translated into communication. Most people over 40 use computers to communicate via email. And unfortunately even then most Christian ministries and churches don't adapt the use of email as a tool to reach new prospects, but rather as an administrative tool to communicate and broadcast information to their present membership.

Most of those under 40, however, use computers to communicate using email, text messaging, instant messaging, watching and posting videos, creating and using personal Web sites such as those provided by social networking sites like Facebook and Myspace. They also typically blog and leave comments and enter into discussions on a variety of Web sites. All of these items are considered new ways to communicate, to stay connected, to share information and experiences, and to spread messages.

Pew Research has released a report stating that we are experiencing the greatest generation gap since the 1960s. The reason the generation gap had such an impact in the 1960s was a result of communication differences adopted by young people. At the time, adults didn't understand what young people meant when they said something was "cool." However, the generation gap lessened when it was discovered the importance of adopting new terminology. This report shows that the problem is back, and while the reason is the lack of communication it is not a matter of terminology, rather technology. Young people are using technology tools to communicate, and adults over 50 have failed to keep up. This gap has overlapped into the church's ability to spread its message to a younger generation.

For over two years now, there are more text messages being sent from cell phones than voice calls, and one-in-five homes in America no longer has a landline phone (and this number continues to decline by 10 percent per year). Yet there are many churches that still believe they are on the cutting edge of technology by sending voice messages to their membership, despite the fact that many congregants under 40 prefer a text message.

Throughout the last year, I attended several conferences where I had the opportunity to ask other attendees if they were interested in group texting tools for their churches. These conferences were not non-technical in nature, but were actually user group conferences for some of our nation's leading church management software companies. I imagine that I spoke with more than 250 different church staff and leaders about texting. The most popular responses were, "I don't text," or "my congregation is too old to be interested in texting." Only a few were actually interested in taking a few minutes to talk about the opportunity to use broadcast texting as a tool to help achieve their ministry's goals.

In 2008 I led two sessions at the National Association of Church Business Administration. In both sessions I discussed the "hot topics" that were important for churches to adapt in order to enhance their membership. I told them the No. 1 thing to watch, and to learn to use, was texting. The attendance at both sessions numbered approximately 300 church leaders. I asked them two questions. First, I asked them if anyone was there under the age of 40. Then I asked if they preferred using text messaging as their primary use of technology communications. Out of the 300 in attendance, only one person was under 40. And, guess what? Out of the 300, 299 were avid email users, with only one admitting that he used email only for work, and texting to communicate with family and friends. You guessed it: he was the only one under 40. The good news is that when I asked the same question of those that attended my sessions at the NACBA in 2009, about 80 percent were now beginning to use text. However, few had yet to begin using texting as a communication tool for their church.

If we really want to reach those under 40, we have to stop doing things the old way, and start stepping out and using what's new. Of course, this doesn't mean you have to like rap music or body piercing, but it does mean you have to use whatever communication tools are most popular with those that are younger. We are a people about communication. We have to reach out into new areas or we risk losing the chance to be heard. And since our message is about Christ—that is a risk we can't afford to take.

Web sites, texting, social networking services, videos, instant messaging, blogs, and online chats are all communication methods. Churches must use them if they wish to stay connected to those they need to reach.

Church ministry is about relationships, and the core of relationships is communication. Imagine two people—a man and a woman—meeting, and one speaks English and the other French. In our imaginary story, let's say they both had taken a first-year Spanish class 20 years earlier in school, although they never had a need to use the language since then. Sure, some communication could take place as they both awkwardly try to connect with a few common words, and of course some communication can take place through hand gestures. But frankly do you think they could fall in love and begin a deep relationship with such a communication barrier? I doubt if they'd even be able to develop a friendship, much less a meaningful relationship. Today, face-to-face communication is rare. We may not like it, but most people are now choosing to communicate with their friends and family via electronic communication means, such as those listed in the paragraph above.

COMPUTERS AND THE COMMUNICATION TOOLS THEY REPRESENT ARE VITAL TO MINISTRY

With a computer and access to the Internet, anyone can now post articles on the Web for anyone to read and respond to with comments (typically called blogging). With a computer and the Internet, anyone involved in the ministry can also post audio files for anyone around the world to access and listen to. Through podcasting, people can actually subscribe to receive future audio files from their favorite speakers, teachers, or musicians. With the advent of digital cameras and camcorders (some costing less than $100) anyone can now create and upload video files to the Web. And this just scratches the surface.

Recently I had the opportunity to hear Terry Storch, co-author of *The Blogging Church*, speak at a Christian conference. He said, "Using technology for ministry is no longer an opportunity, but a responsibility." Many churches seem to look at technology as a tool for the church administrator or other office personnel. They feel that ministry is about one-on-one attention, and that the use of the latest technology tool, program or service can just get in the way. In reality, nothing could be further from the truth. If you want to really think about one-on-one personal ministry, let's take a look at today's hospitals and emergency rooms.

My wife was recently involved in a car wreck as she was returning from a woman's meeting at our church. She had been run off the road by oncoming traffic, and was able to call me immediately after the dust settled a bit. She told me that someone had called for an ambulance, and then said she felt some pain. That's about all I remember from the phone conversation. Within a few seconds I was in our second vehicle and rushing to the site of the crash. When I arrived I was only briefly allowed to speak to my wife because she was already in the ambulance being connected to all kinds of electronic monitoring equipment. You could see she was receiving some very intense personal attention. At the same time you could see that the emergency personnel were using the latest technology to monitor her situation, and the latest wireless communication tools to send that information to the hospital so that they could receive treatment advice, as well as prepare the hospital for our arrival. I did some sincere praying, asking for God's protection and healing as I followed the ambulance to the hospital. When we arrived, she continued to receive some very personal one-on-one attention, which pleased me. But I was just as pleased that this hospital was fully equipped with hundreds—if not thousands—of the latest technology tools to assist those helping my wife perform their job to the fullest. They took x-rays and cat-scans, and quickly ran blood tests through computerized analysis machines. Can you imagine going to a hospital without computerized medical equipment? Without question, their attention to my wife's needs was direct, personal and one-on-one. But personally I appreciated a bit more all of the technology they used to assure my wife was going to be fine. Oh, and she was . . . praise God!

I can't imagine someone going through the same experiences my wife and I did that night, and decry the money spent by the hospital on technology. On many occasions churches decry the expense of using technology with the excuse that their ministry is "personal" and "one-on-one," and simply do not make the connection that technology tools can enhance the overall ministry experience. It's simple. The church of America needs to implement technology tools for their ministry. Those that do will be able to communicate the Gospel to their community and do a better job of enhancing their ministry to the present membership. Both are vital for a church to sustain life and encourage growth. Besides fast computers, great programming, and the acceptance of computers in the average home in America, we have been blessed with the Internet. It is a gift from God that allows us to network, develop new relationships and broadcast our messages to individuals, businesses, communities, our nation and the world.

I count Walt Wilson as a friend, and one of those that "get it" when it comes to understanding the need to use computers and the Internet to spread the word. In his book, *The Internet Church,* he gives the following example of how the use of the Internet is vital:

"We are all familiar with the evangelistic tent meetings of days past. They were designed to reach people in the community, especially those who were not attending church. People were saved in those meetings because they heard the claims of Christ on their lives. The tent was an outreach tool that integrated people into the church by conveying information. Today, however, except for an occasional stadium crusade, the tent is gone, and we have nothing to replace it. Or do we? The Internet and the results we see from using it represent the new tent, an Internet tent, if you will. Like the tent meeting of old, the Internet church is the provider of information that is leading people to the foot of Calvary's Cross. More and more, we hear people saying that they are finding Jesus on the Internet. The tent is back. Only this time it's not in atoms; it's in bits.

"Nothing substitutes for one-on-one relationships, however. Thus we need to recognize two things about today's society: (1) many people feel isolated and do not have churchgoing friends and (2) many think the church is irrelevant to their lives. People who will not go through the door of a church, though, will go to the electronic tent in the quiet of the night. They will go to the tent in the midst of a chaotic business day. Some will be in pain, others will just be empty. All will be seeking answers." (Page 23)

Each local church must decide its mission. Are they fishers of men, or keepers of the fish bowl? The fish bowl is brick and mortar, and about half of the churches in America have concentrated their efforts on retaining a suitable and comfortable building for its congregation. These churches were started with a great purpose and mission, but have slipped into caring only about the maintenance their aging membership and the upkeep of a building.

Hopefully, some will be inspired after reading this book to either begin a concerted effort to launch the use of technology in the expansion of their present ministry, or to turn the tide of decline in their church and begin to see the growth, discipleship, increased ministry and new conversions possible through the use of the many tools and services outlined in this book.

If I have offended or discouraged you in my rant about the failings of over half of the churches in America, it was not my intent. My intent is to expose a problem, issue a warning and offer a solution.

The rest of this chapter, and the rest of the book, will explore a long list of opportunities to use technology to expand your church's ministry and outreach. And I urge you to continue reading even if you feel that your church will never be open to change and the implementation of new technology tools, because in the last chapter I will provide you sound and practical advice on how to gracefully and tactfully introduce some of these new technologies into your church.

SO HOW DOES ONE UTILIZE COMPUTERS RUNNING WINDOWS FOR MINISTRY?

First, let's examine what a church considers ministry. If you were to do a random Internet search using Google or another search engine for the word "churches," most would generate links to a church's mission statement. After reviewing many of these individual sites, I discovered that most churches, regardless of their denomination, have a mission statement that contains the following items:

1. A call to train or disciple their members in the teachings of Christ;
2. A call to evangelize or reach their community with the message of salvation;
3. A call to grow and encourage the body of Christ through fellowship and commitment;
4. A call to gather together to worship God; and
5. A call to involve their congregation in service and missions.

If you look at the basic programs and services of the average church, you will see their structures centering on accomplishing these five ministries. I am a firm believer that today's church will find it easier to accomplish their mission if they make effective use of technology and computers. All it takes is a little imagination to see how many of the applications, programs, and services available through the Internet can be used to help enhance the ministry goals listed above. Let me list them again and we'll take a brief look at some of the many ways you can use your computer and Windows programs or online services to help accomplish each of them.

But first let me tell you another story. I recently met with a small group of church leaders at a conference and explored the mission statements of each of their churches. We started by taking a look at how churches sought to accomplish them before 1985, before the advent of computers. Now, this particular group represented churches of various sizes and denominational backgrounds, but the programs and methods used to accomplish the mission statements were the same. To achieve the first statement—a call to train or disciple their members in the teachings of Christ—everyone agreed that this was accomplished through providing a Sunday School program. To accomplish the mission of evangelism, the group shared stories of past revivals, which they usually held twice a year and usually consisted of week-long meetings held at the local high school's football stadium or a tent on a vacant lot. The mission of growing and encouraging the church in fellowship was accomplished most effectively through food gatherings like "carry-in" dinners or "pot-luck" dinners, as well as special "socials" held in what many churches called their "fellowship hall". When it came to the mission of gathering together for worship, the most obvious answers were the services held before lunch on Sundays, many of which included several hymns, an offertory, someone providing special music, and then a sermon. In regards to service and missions, most in the group concluded that their church accomplished missions through their connection to a specific denomination.

After taking a look at how they accomplished their missions in the mid 1980s, I asked if they knew of churches that were still doing "business as usual" today, and nearly everyone knew of some churches that had the same basic structure, programs and methods of accomplishing these missions as they did 20-plus years ago. I then asked them if they considered these churches as "growing," and the answer was no. Personally, I know of churches that still function exactly the same way they did more than 20 years ago, without incorporating any of the many technology tools made available over the last 20 years, and I can't think of one that would be considered growing in membership, or as having a significant impact on their community. In fact, the only churches I know of that are reaching their community with the message of Christ, expanding their ministry and effectively ministering to their congregations are those that are making use of today's many technology tools available to them and their ministries.

Let's take a look at a few of the ideas presented in this book on how churches can use technology to accomplish their mission statements.

A Call to Train or Disciple Their Members in the Teachings of Christ

Bible study software programs have become a vital tool for preachers and teachers over the last 20 years. You can use these software programs to do in-depth Bible study, including Greek and Hebrew word studies, take advantage of online concordances, lexicons, dictionaries, and much more. These capabilities allow your ministry to use desktop publishing to design and create handouts, including outlines, maps, definitions, references, etc. Using peripheral equipment to project these materials on a screen in front of the congregation or in a classroom setting opens the door to a wealth of opportunities for pastors, staff and laypeople to take advantage of technology. Various mapping programs and services are also available for purchase both on disk or online that are searchable and downloadable based on specific scripture passages (such as one of the journeys of Paul) or a historical period of the Bible. Additionally, there are now Bible-specific lesson programs like LessonMaker from WordSearch that can create lesson handouts complete with questions based on scriptures or subjects.

A Call to Evangelize or Reach Their Community with the Message of Salvation

When I was a young pastor in the late 70s, I pastored the only church in a small town in central Missouri. We were close enough to a larger town, however, to utilize that town's resources. That being the case, one of the ideas I had was to host a rolling skating party at that town's skating rink. I planned a two-hour affair, which afforded me the opportunity to share a word or two about Christ at around the one-hour mark and then invite visitors to come and talk with me during the second hour if they wanted to know more about being a Christian. We decided to hold these special skating parties once a month. And for the first couple of months we had a great crowd, but no one responded to our invitation to become a Christian. The third time, however, I asked two high school students, both of whom had recently become Christians, to share their testimony during our break in the middle of the skate party. I gave them a little coaching on how to do this, and they were very enthused about the opportunity. During our break I introduced them, and both shared their recent experiences in starting their walk with Christ. When they finished, I offered to speak to anyone wanting more information about becoming a Christian. To my surprise and joy, three people come over to talk with me, and all three eventually became Christians. I learned an important lesson that night: testimonies from real individuals that stand as peers have a much greater impact than those from "paid" messengers of Christ, like me.

The computer is all about communications, and the church has both the opportunity and obligation to share this message, the Good News, using every viable communications method available. This does not mean, however, that a church's Web site or broadcast emails are used best when they carry only the message of the church's staff. These same methods of communication can be used as evangelistic tools when you allow your church members to express their faith using these same tools.

I met up with some youth ministers in Olathe, KS, several years back who shared a great example of utilizing technology to help members share their faith. Each year in discipleship training they have a course on how to share faith. As they prepared the course for the church's young people, they also decided to revamp the youth portion of their church's Web site by publishing their testimonies on the Web site and encouraging them to invite their friends, teachers and family members to visit the site and read their testimonies. They instructed the young people to break up their testimonies into four parts:

1. Their life before they became a Christian;
2. How they realized their need to become a Christian;
3. How they actually became a Christian; and
4. Their life now as a Christian.

As the young people finished their assignments, the youth leaders set up the youth Web site's opening page with a link to each testimony, and included a photograph of the young person. They also printed business cards for each young person with a link to their specific page so that they could hand out the cards to teachers and friends, encouraging them to visit their personal site. The result was an increase in the number of young people attending church services and the number of young people seeking out youth ministers for information on how they too could become a Christian.

The funny thing is that all of this preceded the popularity of social networking sites like Facebook. Now that personal Web sites are even more popular I would think churches would be wise to encourage all members who use these sites to post a testimony for others to see, with links and contact information for those seeking more information.

Take Your Message Outside Your Walls

In the past, only very large churches were able to utilize mass media communication tools such as radio or television. The Internet, however, has changed all of that, and now any church can make minimal financial commitments to use similar tools via the Internet. For example, a church can now broadcast the audio recordings of their church's services, special classes and membership information on the Internet by streaming from their Web site, or using podcasting tools. Streaming allows your ministry's audio files to be found via popular search engines and makes them available to listeners around the world. And now, editing of audio files is both available and affordable, which allows your audio broadcasts to have professional sound quality without the use of expensive recording techniques.

The same is true for video. Although the cost can be a bit higher than distributing audio files, it is not cost prohibitive for even the average-sized church in America. And camera quality continues to improve as the price continues to drop. Additionally, many of the tools that used to be hardware specific, such as a video switcher (allows you to combine input from various cameras), are now software specific and include some fantastic video editing tools and services.

Of course, most churches also realize that to effectively spread the Word it takes more than just mass communication from the church staff, rather a commitment for "lifestyle" evangelism on the part of their membership. Many of today's larger churches are not only "seeker friendly," they also put an emphasis on their membership being willing to share its faith with other friends, neighbors and families. Now that computers have helped to bring about a great desire for personal communication tools like email, instant messaging, text messaging, etc., a smart church will help provide information about the Gospel in a form that can utilize these tools, thus enabling their membership the opportunity to forward their messages to potential prospects. In a way, many of these new formats have taken over the position of the Gospel tract, when print was king.

A Call to Grow and Encourage the Body of Christ Through Fellowship and Commitment

There's no doubt that social networking has had a major impact in our lives, proving to be a very successful platform for both meeting new people and restoring past relationships. For example, online dating services have been around for well over a decade. At first, many people frowned upon the idea that a lasting and meaningful relationship started through an online introduction could last. Yet statistics now show that after 10 years people who've met online and married have the same success and failure as married people who've met through other means. So if a relationship as intense as a marriage can be started online it should come as no surprise that friendships and other relationships can be started, maintained, and even restored through social networking services. And, while these social networking sites were first more popular with young people, it's now fairly obvious that people of all ages are utilizing social networking sites for the same reasons. Based on my experiences, Christian relationships can flourish in this environment, and one of the reasons may be that the more means that we have to communicate, the more opportunities we have to express our true selves. If fellowship is defined as the opportunity to get to know one another, then tools like online discussion boards, text messaging, instant messaging, posting FAQ (frequently asked questions) on your churches' site, and providing opportunities for your membership to become involved in ministry, are just a few of the ways computers can help accomplish this mission task.

When it comes to commitment, a church must help educate its members on the importance of stewardship. Once again, computers have changed the way this is accomplished. More and more every day traditional forms of money—coin, paper and checks—are giving way to digital electronic debit cards, which dominates today's commerce marketplace. Most of us purchase gas, clothes, food (both at the grocery store and at the fast food restaurant on the corner) and just about everything else using a debit card. Churches must embrace the new method of commerce if they hope to present a relevancy to stewardship. Online and electronic giving is catching on in many churches, although some have to overcome the objections of those who stubbornly hang on to the "way we used to do it".

A Call to Gather Together to Worship God

Computers have now entered our worship centers, and many churches have moved away from traditional services, including the use of projectors and multimedia presentation software to shoot the lyrics up on a screen. This has also opened the door for a variety of other computer applications, including video. Computers combined with the Internet now also provide the opportunity for online giving. Granted, taking an offering has always been part of the worship service. But now, computer technology is offering worshipers the opportunity to give during a worship service using their debit card. How great is that?

There's an unspoken truth among the computer literates of the world, and it goes something like, "Want to know how to use a computer? Ask a 14-year-old." As churches seek to incorporate technology into their ministries, one of the more common ways to successfully accomplish it is to utilize the talents of its own members to implement the changes. Need a better Web site? Want to post pictures of your events online? How about capturing video? While some churches do seek to outsource these tasks to professionals, others might be more advantageous by recognizing the value of using their own talented and qualified members in these areas of service.

CHAPTER 2

Computers and Worship

What is worship? It all depends on how you use the word. According to the Encarta Dictionary, as a verb it could mean to "take part in religious service." However, as a noun, it is defined as, "religious adoration, devotion and respect given to a deity." The church today seems to struggle with how to combine the verb and the noun definitions when it comes to worship in our churches. Some believe that worship should be traditional, in a sense, although it is actually very hard to define what would be truly traditional for the church.

The very first organ was brought to America and donated to the Brattle Street Church in Boston Massachusetts by Thomas Brattle in 1717, as part of the terms of his will after his death. However, the church refused the donation because they felt that the use of an organ during worship would not be true to the worship experience. Before the Great Awakening (which started around 1730), most worship services in American churches were very orthodox. During the Great Awakening, most of the hymns now considered traditional were new and exciting—a wonderful use of secular songs with added Christian lyrics to help make them more palatable. When this style of worship didn't seem appropriate inside of the church buildings of the day, evangelists moved them outside under the brush arbors and tents, thus creating a style of worship now considered extremely traditional and conservative in regards to today's church services.

SO WHAT DO COMPUTERS AND WINDOWS HAVE TO DO WITH WORSHIP?

The use of computers in worship is just one of many ways to use technology to enhance today's modern worship experience. The 1950s saw the widespread incorporation of the piano and organ into worship services, and the 1960s saw the advent of public address (PA) systems. In those early days, PA systems were installed in a locked closet and all of the sound settings were set the same whether it was being used for speaking, music or the choir. No one ever made adjustments. In contrast, if you check out the sound booths of today's larger church buildings you will find controls with hundreds of knobs, and one or more persons adjusting the sound throughout a worship service. The 1970s saw the use of pre-recorded background music on cassette tapes, mainly for soloists and even for the entire choir. But the '70s also saw something else: the Jesus movement. With the addition of what many referred to as "Jesus Freaks," a new type of worship began to emerge. And, just like the Great Awakening, it wasn't easily adapted into the modern church worship. However, once it was born into "coffee houses" across the nation, it wasn't long before it was invited into what had been traditional worship. Worship was surely enhanced by the inclusion of guitars and drums, which also led to the use of amplifiers, theatrical lighting and drama during the worship experience. Something else very important started soon after the Jesus movement: mega-churches. Bill Hybels started Willow Creek in 1975 and Rick Warren started Saddle Back in 1979. Both had a great advantage in adapting contemporary worship service styles, and the use of computers and technology into worship, yet both didn't assume a church with traditional services; they started their own churches from scratch with a new attitude regarding the use of computers and adapting to a contemporary worship style.

HOW DID COMPUTERS GET INTO OUR WORSHIP SERVICES?

As computers became ground zero for multi-media tools, they quickly became the most efficient way of enhancing the modern worship experience. As worship services progressed and became more contemporary, the use of Hymnals was pushed aside mainly because they don't include contemporary Christian choruses. Churches adapting to a contemporary worship experience began moving away from traditional print hymnals and started projecting song lyrics up on a screen. At first, many employed copy-machine generated song sheets handed out at the door as the congregation entered the building. Later on, overhead projectors were utilized to replace the song sheets, which required a person to print the information on a transparency and then be available at each service to change the transparency to coincide with the music. However, it was just a matter of time before churches discovered the video projector, Microsoft PowerPoint, and the ability to put the words to songs, sermon notes, announcements and much more, up on a screen.

WORSHIP PRESENTATION SOFTWARE

Once the door was opened to add computers to the worship service, specialized programs and services quickly followed that added additional features to enhance on-screen presentations. Microsoft's PowerPoint was designed to provide presentations for the corporate world, but leaves little flexibility to change the order of the service. During a service, the worship leader may decide to sing an additional verse of a chorus, or even change the order of what was originally planned. For this, specialized worship presentation software programs were developed, such as EasyWorship and MediaShout. Both programs accomplish the flexibility of worship presentation by allowing the program to run different aspects on multiple screens, and most Windows computers can accommodate them by simply adding an additional graphics card. Installing the programs on such a system allows for one screen to display what's actually on the main screen being viewed by the congregation, while the other displays a menu of items that can quickly be selected for projection on the main screen.

MediaShout

Here's how easy it is to set up a presentation using MediaShout. The program presents you with a window that is divided into three sections, allowing you to easily move content from your libraries to your program and onto your projections for your congregations to view.

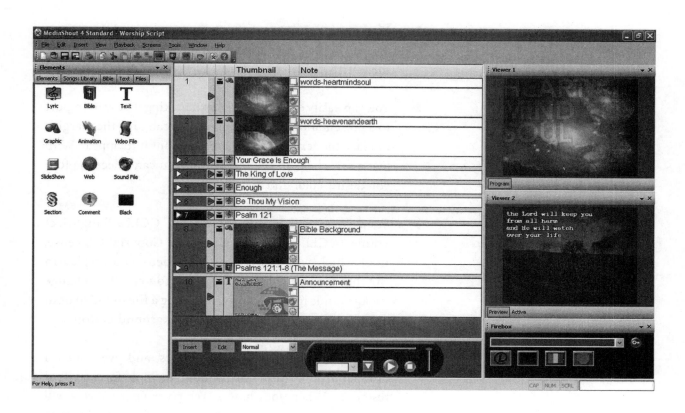

The first pane on the left displays what MediaShout calls "decks". The customizable elements deck—which include lyrics, Bible, text, graphics, video files, Web, sound files, slideshows, and more—gives you easy access to the elements you use most often.

As you prepare your presentation, you can click on any one of the decks in the first pane to open up your library of content. To create a presentation, you would click on an element and then browse through the decks to pick a song, Bible verse, or a text item you've already set up. Click on the element you would like to create and drag it to the script pane, drop it in place and click the cue to play it out to your congregation whenever you are ready.

In the example displayed, a user would click on the "graphic" deck to view all of the graphic files. By dragging the one called "words-heartmindsoul" into the middle pane, called the script pane, the graphic is ready to be used to start your worship service, since it is in the first position. If you look at the right side of the screen, you will see two different viewer windows. The top viewer is cued to show what the audience is watching, while the second one is set to show any of the other elements of the presentation as a preview. In the example in the screen shot above, you will notice that the user is checking out the preview of the seventh element of the presentation, the scripture of Psalm 121.

▶ You can also combine elements, making it simple to put text or a Bible verse along with a graphic or logo, or combine them with a video or picture.

▶ You can easily drag and drop text, making it easy to import to a presentation. Once dropped, you can drag the margins to place the text exactly where you want it to appear. With just a few clicks in the text editor, you can select the font you desire, color and text size.

▶ Song lyrics can be imported from CCLI's SongSelect online (CCLI stands for Christian Copyright License, Inc.) which will assure that the video's you display in worship are being done so legally). You can then change backgrounds for the song by dragging a file or video onto a song or stanza, or click on the background button.

▶ You can now display live Web pages, and even open a browser from within MediaShout to look for and find resources. When you show a Web page, your viewers will not see the menus or other information that would appear from the browser.

▶ MediaShout now features Stage Display as well, which is a text-only display that you can use that allows your worship team to see what your worshippers see, only without the graphics.

▶ You can use Section Cues to create loops for announcements or lengthy groups of photos.

▶ MediaShout can import and convert PowerPoint slides into a lyric, text or graphic cue with the added option of saving the existing backgrounds as separate graphic files.

▶ MediaShout has a VJ-ready feature (VJ stands for Video Jockey) allowing you to switch backgrounds on the fly between programmed text. You can simply turn on background mode to play media directly from the decks behind your text and then go back to your pre-programmed media by switching back to normal mode.

EasyWorship

EasyWorship allows you to present lyrics or Scripture with stunning video backgrounds, and comes with many exciting features.

Those on stage have access to helpful tools they can use as they carry out the progression of the worship service. EasyWorship calls this feature "Display Foldback," and it can project text and customizable backgrounds to a third output, position a clock, preview the beginning of the next text slide, and preview current and future PowerPoint slides. Included is a feature called "Video Jockey," which gives single-click control for live, on-the-fly background switching. You can now transition between backgrounds and feeds, independent of live text.

EasyWorship gives you access to their new online media store and, of course, their media works seamlessly with their presentation software. You can browse, download and organize your favorite media resources in EasyWorship without actually opening another browser.

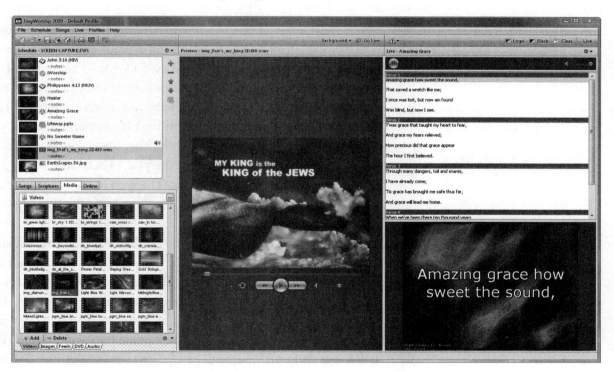

The 2009 version of EasyWorship is also a new step forward in design, with updated buttons and icons throughout, a more modernized look and feel, with general layout improvements and updated interface controls for video, DVD, and feeds. EasyWorship's design will automatically customize for Windows XP, Windows Vista or Windows 7.

If you already have a SongSelect Lyric Service subscription through CCLI, you can log into your account from EasyWorship, find the song you want, click the import button and EasyWorship will basically do the rest.

This program is designed to provide features for worship presentation that PowerPoint simply cannot provide. And if you have a lot of content already in PowerPoint, EasyWorship can import and convert your PowerPoint files, which can become very important whenever you have a guest speaker. For example, when I travel to speak at churches, I always prepare my presentation in PowerPoint. With EasyWorship, a church can easily incorporate my work into the rest of the service and run it all from EasyWorship.

THE RIGHT FONT IS CRUCIAL

When using projection in worship, everybody wants to achieve that "wow" effect, and both programs mentioned thus far allow us to combine fonts, graphics and even videos, to help present the lyrics of our songs or the outline for our sermons. But when it comes to fonts, you don't want to be *too* creative. Fonts need to make their point without being noticed. If you *notice* the font you are using, you should probably think about using another one. Because I travel a lot throughout the year, I get to attend many different worship services. It doesn't happen often, but I have been in a worship service where the use of fonts actually distracted from the worship experience.

You also don't want fonts to be hard to read. I know that some people try to use a font to make a statement, and this is great if you are creating a trademark. In fact, some decorative fonts work well for trademarks. One that comes immediately to mind is the Coca Cola trademark. Yet even they moved to a simple clear font many years ago and shortened their name to Coke, although the old font and trademark still gets posted on some bottles or cans. Today, such fonts go past our eyes too quickly. If Coca Cola was starting today, I doubt they would have chosen such a difficult to read font for their trademark.

This is an example of using a font that is difficult to read!

Imagine reading an entire paragraph written in the cursive text shown above. We would probably become too frustrated to finish the paragraph. It's OK to be creative when picking a font for your songs and sermons, just be careful to make sure the font is readable. This also means there needs to be clear spacing between both letters and words, and the spaces between lines needs to be clear. One good test is to print it out on a piece of paper first, have someone look at it for only a second or two and then ask them what they saw. If they come away with some of the key words then the font did its job in helping to get your message across.

As you try different fonts, backgrounds and even video loops, be sure to check readability from every part of your building. The view and effect can be different. You want to be sure it is a pleasant and readable experience for people in the back row, the front row and those on the far sides of the room.

ONE MORE WORD ABOUT HYMNS VERSUS CONTEMPORARY MUSIC

I love the old hymns. And when I'm driving alone, many times I'll use the time to talk with the Lord. In the course of spending time with my Savior I almost always become reminded of the hymns I used to sing so many years ago. Back in the 1970s and '80s when I pastored, we used to sing hymns from the hymnal every Sunday, and over the years you end up knowing them by heart.

I have many fantastic memories associated with those old-school hymns. But if I step back and look at many of the hymns that I love, I realize their message is lost on seekers and young people today. And I'm not talking about teenagers. I'm talking about people in their 20's and 30's. Think about some of the language in those fantastic hymns. Frankly, you would need someone to translate. Check out the following:

▶ I love the hymn, "It Is Well With My Soul," but the lyrics state, "When peace, like a river, attendeth my way . . . " and later mentions " . . . thought Satan should buffet . . . " I believe many people don't understand what these phrases mean!

▶ The hymn "At Calvary" was one of the first I ever learned to play on the piano. It contains a line that reads, " . . . the law I'd spurned . . . "

▶ In the hymn "I Need Thee Every Hour" there's a line that states, " . . . Temptations lose their power when Thou art nigh . . . "

▶ The first verse of "His Eye Is On The Sparrow" states, " . . . When Jesus is my portion . . . "

Again, I love these hymns. But if I want to share the message of Christ with the people of today I'm not so sure words like "attendeth", "buffet", or "spurned" would help, nor would phrases like "the law I'd spurned" or "When Jesus is my portion" be any better understood.

DISPLAYING SONGS REQUIRES A LICENSE

Once churches put away their hymnals and began projecting their songs on the screen, something important happened. Using song lyrics for a public meeting requires a copyright. When you purchased a hymn, you purchased the copyright for each book to be used by your congregation. However, when you simply took the words to a hymn and projected them up on a screen, you were using multimedia to make copies of one song to be used by many, thereby violating the copyright laws. In fact, I remember many years ago when I was invited to attend a Christian publishers' meeting and share my thoughts on the future of technology. At that time the Internet was new, and presentation software wasn't all that prevalent. But I remember that most of the people in attendance where leading officers from various Christian publishing houses responsible for hymnal and Christian music publishing. Frankly I wished I could have taken back the opening of my presentation because I had shared with them my belief that churches were beginning to make the move to a more contemporary style of worship, and had predicted that many churches were moving away from the use of hymnals. As the group offered more feedback and comments, I remember that several of those present were angry and wondered aloud where Christian music would end up if artists and songwriters were not paid when their music was first published in print. I even remember one who was visibly upset and a bit depressed. One person, however, seemed to save the day when he said optimistically, "Things are going to be fine. We just have to find a new way and change the business model!"

Well, the business model did change, and Christian artists do get paid as a result of the creation of the CCLI and their vision to provide local churches with a *practical* way to use worship music in their services while complying with copyright laws. Again, CCLI stands for Christian Copyright License, and CCLI provides the ability for churches to pay a small fee to purchase the right to display song lyrics up on a projection screen and do so legally.

"Our heart is to serve the local church," says Howard Rachinski, founder of CCLI. "We want to help churches enhance their corporate worship expression conveniently, affordably and legally."

Federal copyright law prohibits a church from copying a song in any form (lyric projection, song sheets, transparencies, bulletin inserts, etc.) without prior permission from the song owner. There are often fees required, and permission must be granted for each individual song copied.

The Christian Copyright License is a more convenient and cost-effective way to secure permission to copy songs for congregational singing. It is a contractual agreement involving songwriters, song owners and publishers from around the world. For an annual license fee, churches receive legal authorization to copy from a list of more than 200,000 songs suitable for congregational singing. CCLI's Christian Copyright License covers the song catalogs of over 3,000 song owners and publishers. It is by far the most comprehensive list of its kind.

Twice a year, CCLI conducts a license holder survey to track song usage. The survey results are a valuable resource for the Christian music industry, since they show which songs the churches are using most.

The License Agreement

Here's a simplified version of the terms of agreement under the Christian Copyright License:

What You *Can* Do . . .

▶ Print song lyrics in bulletins, programs, liturgies and songsheets for use in congregational singing.

▶ Create your own customized songbooks or hymnals for use in congregational singing.

▶ Create overhead transparencies, slides, computer graphics, or any other format whereby song lyrics are visually projected for use in congregational singing.

▶ Arrange, print and copy your own arrangements (vocal and instrumental) of songs used for congregational singing, where no published version is available.

▶ Record your worship services (audio or video) provided you only record live music. Accompaniment tracks cannot be reproduced. You may charge up to $4 each for CDs and tapes and $12 each for DVDs and video tapes.

What You *Cannot* Do . . .

▶ Photocopy or duplicate octavos, cantatas, musicals, handbell music, keyboard arrangements, vocal scores, orchestrations or other instrumental works.

▶ Translate songs into another language. This can only be done with the approval of the respective publisher.

▶ Rent, sell or lend copies made under the license to groups outside the church or to other churches. (It is OK to distribute tapes to shut-ins, missionaries or others outside the church.)

▶ Assign or transfer the license to another church or group without CCLI's approval.

Find Out More

The Christian Copyright License is an annual license, and terms are in effect only while the license is active. If the license is not renewed, all rights are terminated effective on the expiration date. The Christian Copyright License is very affordable and is based on a church's regular attendance. Annual fees begin at $50, and the cost for an average-sized church is just $175 per year. For complete information on all licenses, just log on to CCLI's Web site at www.ccli.com. Or call toll free 1-800-234-2446 (Mon.-Fri., 7 am to 4 pm PT)

A WORD ABOUT PROJECTORS AND SCREENS

There is one important step between your computer and the screen, and that is the video projector. It's hard to imagine a new church building being built today without consideration being given to video screen and projector placement. However, the older the building is, the harder it will be to implement the use of projection into your worship. In this case I would suggest that you seek the advice of older churches that have already updated their systems, as well as any professionals that might be available in your area (companies like Fowler and Shepherd Multimedia provide consulting services nationwide).

You must also realize that there are many different solutions designed to fit any number of different applications. Things that must be considered are the size of the room, the angle of the pews to the screen, the lighting, among many other. All of them will all play a part in your decision to get the right solution for your building. I can tell you that when it comes to buying projection equipment, you want the best your budget can afford. And remember, if you go with a projection system the quality of the screen is just as important as the projector.

Following are a few other points to consider when purchasing a video projector:

Resolution—Most all manufacturers are moving towards WXGA (which is a format that provides a wider screen size that has become accepted by TV's and computer monitors) units that project natively in the wide screen format.

Brightness—There is no such thing as a projector that is too bright. Always buy the brightest projector you can afford. HOWEVER, remember that the life of a projector is relatively short (you don't have a cell phone or even a computer that's more than five years old, do you?) so don't spend so much money that you are forced into a long-term relationship with your projector. Most churches seem to be happy with something in the 3500–6500 ansi lumen range. Ansi Lumen is a standard rating system used to compare how bright the projector displays.

Display device—Today you would consider LCD or DLP formats—and there are pros and cons to each. At this point in time DLP is successful in both the low end (i.e., home theater) applications and in the super high end (i.e., $25,000-plus) class of products, but LCD tends to dominate everything in between.

Durability and dependability—Check with other churches and ask what projectors they use and recommend. And consider your intended use. For example, will it be permanently mounted in the worship center, or will it be moved from room to room on an AV cart? What's the expected life of the projector bulb? Again, don't settle on the least expensive unit because in the end "You get what you pay for."

Where to buy—Most manufacturers will honor their warranties if the products are purchased through their authorized dealer networks. That said, super cheap units purchased for super cheap prices from various online retailers may not count, so beware. Buying online to save $75 on the projector isn't a "deal" if the unit comes without the bulb (read the fine print for "bulb sold separately"), or it's sold without the remote control (remotes are almost always included if you buy from a reputable dealer), or without a warranty.

THINK OUTSIDE THE BOX

Once you have the ability to project basic presentation software up on a screen, you've opened yourself up to a variety of exciting ways to enhance your worship service. And since the concept is new for many, those succeeding are definitely thinking "outside the box" and creating new and exciting ways to draw attention to a ministry or group. In my travels I've seen slideshow presentations that include pictures of recent church events, and even recent youth mission trips, all put to music. Here's an example:

This one came via email from Phyllis Tyner, Director of Christian Education and Preschool at Chapel Hill United

Methodist Church in Indianapolis, Ind. She created a special presentation for a Sunday morning worship service for Veteran's Day. She wrote:

"A few years ago, when Veteran's Day landed on a Sunday, I wanted to do something special. So, in September, I put out the word for pictures of those in our congregation or their families who had served. I was overwhelmed with the response! I made an album to sell (a nominal fee for printing cost relief) and made a slide show of all the pictures I received, in addition to displaying all the pictures on large bulletin boards in the narthex. The first album was over 150 pages and the second was almost 200! People were so proud to have the opportunity to honor their loved ones. I got photos going back to WWI, and even photos of those who had served for England and France. I also asked for items to display and again persons were very generous—a purple heart, an iron cross, a saber, uniforms, and samples of food ration stamps. I have done something different each year, such as adding posters of the WWI and WWII era to the display, and this year I am going to ask for stories from those at home who supported our war effort. I got the idea at a luncheon I attended, when I was sitting at a table with ladies who were talking about their younger days and what it was like during the war. I thought that their must be more great stories out there, so I'm going to find out. Scanning the pictures, setting up the album, etc, is quite a bit of work. This year, I am going to offer a free disk of the slide show instead of the album! So many people loved the display and look forward to it each year. The new personal connections that have been found among our membership were wonderful to watch! I think this is a ministry for those who often go unnoticed in our congregation, not to mention an education opportunity for our children and teens, and I will continue it at long as I am here."

Phyllis scanned the photos into a file, saved it, and then imported each picture into a PowerPoint slide presentation and added her own text. She set the slide show to show each picture for eight seconds. The concept was so well received that she created another set of pictures showcasing the events and ministries of the church. She used the same process, only had it display on a screen in the narthex so people visiting the church could get a feel for the fellowship and ministry. She simply used the loop feature in PowerPoint to set the presentation so it would play over and over again.

USING VIDEO IN WORSHIP

There is a chapter later in this book that covers more information about creating and using video. However, the point of this chapter is using technology to enhance worship, so let me give you an introduction on using videos in your worship service.

There are so many fantastic ways to use video in worship. It can be a great enhancement to every part of the worship service. We are a video generation, so video can be used to enhance messages, announcements, the song service, the atmosphere, and so much more.

I realize that some churches struggle with the idea of including video in worship, fearing they may be viewed as too worldly. However, I also believe that if Jesus was preaching today he would use video clips to help make his point, much the same way He used parables and stories in His time. You can imagine Jesus using visual props to help illustrate his point, such as taking a handful of seed and throwing it on the ground when telling the parable of the sower. In the same way, video is not intended to replace preaching or instruction, but to enhance and illustrate the message. One of my favorite places to find, purchase and download videos is from a service called SermonSpice. I mention this because I think their name makes the point. Video in a worship service shouldn't be used to replace the sermon, but rather to illustrate—to add spice—to the message.

There are a wide variety of ways to use video during a worship service, and it should be clear that I am not suggesting that a church use video for everything. In fact, I would suggest that you only use video maybe once a week, using one of the methods described below. I have a good relationship with Darren McDonald at Shepherd Multimedia, and I've heard him speak on the subject of using video in worship. And even though he is in the business of helping churches use multimedia and video in worship, he shared with me the following thought:

"If we have erred in the church, it is that we have elevated media usage beyond its proper place and balance," he said. "I believe that video use in the worship service should be like ketchup in the value meal. I like ketchup as long as it's used in the right quantity (who likes fries swimming in ketchup?) and in the right place (I like it on my burger, but not in my drink). Like ketchup, media—if used in the right quantity and in the right places—can be an amazing addition and compliment. If overused, or used at the wrong times, it can destroy the worship service."

So, with that in mind, here are a few ways I have seen video used in worship. Each has been very effective, but again, I wouldn't suggest using only a few in one service.

Countdown Video: These videos are designed to start five to ten minutes before a service starts, and you can find a variety of themes for them on the Internet. Some are designed for youth services, while others are very reflective and soothing and would work in semi-traditional settings. The purpose is obvious: If your congregation can glance at the screens and see how much time they have before the service starts, it helps with getting them into their seats—and quieting them down—in preparation for start of the service.

Call To Worship Video—There are many short videos that can be used to get a congregation into the right spirit for worship. The really good ones immediately cause me to reflect on the majesty of God, or the love of Christ, etc. If you have a particularly "friendly" church, and find it difficult to get everyone to go from visiting in the aisles to sitting in their seats, then using these types of videos might help them get into the "right" spirit of worship.

The Offering Video—I once saw a fantastic video used during the time of offering that was designed to help the congregation see all the many different places their offering was being used around the world, and in the ministry of the church. It was shown during the time of the offering, instead of the usual singing or special music that usually takes place during this time. It had a fantastic impact on me!

Announcements Video—Most active churches need to have some time to promote different events, ministries, programs, etc., and videos are the perfect way to help get your messages across effectively. And many of the programs available for churches actually provide videos for your use. However, many churches tend to create their own videos when it comes to their announcement times. The beauty of this is that you can use your lay people to really make these announcements come alive. For example, if you are seeking volunteers for your Vacation Bible School, interview some of the people that have served previously in this capacity and have each give a short one or two sentence testimony about how exciting or blessed it was to serve. Or maybe it's time to promote your Vacation Bible School. You can use video from last year's VBS, or shoot some new video of your regular Sunday School sessions showing the children around a table participating in a lesson, or doing some crafts, or playing a game. People love to see other members of the church sharing the joy of serving their church. This tends to have a much greater impact on your congregation than listening to a paid staff member announce events and dates. And what about the cost and quality of creating your own videos? Read on . . . I'll be covering that in the section about informal videos.

VIDEO LOOPS FOR YOUR SONG SERVICE

It's no secret that churches have moved from hymnals to displaying the words to songs on a screen. This gets their members looking up and singing together, instead of fumbling with a book and singing while looking down at the words. This has also grown popular because today's contemporary song service is constantly introducing new songs, so hymnals or songbooks quickly become outdated. Of course, you can put some cool graphics and pictures behind the text of your lyrics. But you can also do more! Many of the same Web sites that sell Christian videos also sell video loops. Using some of the multimedia programs we've already mentioned—like EasyWorship and MediaShout—you can have a looped video running behind the lyrics. This is a fantastic way to draw attention to the message. If you are singing a song that reflects the mighty creation of God, it helps to bring out the emotion and splendor of that song by displaying beautiful clouds slowly moving across the sky behind the lyrics. Video producers have created a host of fantastic Christian video loops that can be used to enhance the lyrics of songs that are being displayed.

SERMON ILLUSTRATIONS

For 15 years of my life I pastored and served a church that had a Sunday evening service. That means that during those 15 years I preached over 1,500 sermons. I knew the value of using illustrations to help make the message come alive and stay in the thoughts of my congregation. Back then, we didn't have the technology to use video in worship, but if we had I certainly would have used it at every opportunity.

Illustrations come in a variety of types. Sometimes a bit of historical information can be used to help make your point, or a humorous story could work depending on the particular subject. Of course, a dramatic story or personal testimony can also help to bring your message home to your audience.

With video, there are many ways to help make your message come alive. Many Internet sites that provide videos for download and use in your worship service have search capabilities that let you find videos by subject, or even the scripture passage you're looking to illustrate. For example, I've seen videos that explain the meaning of a specific Greek word or passage. Other videos are dramatic, humorous, and even historic. I remember one of the first videos I ever saw used as a sermon illustration involved "man-on-the-street" interviews. They asked people what they thought about Jesus. Of course as a preacher, I could tell my audience that some people believe Jesus to be a prophet, or a healer, a teacher or a fraud, while some hold that he is the Son of God. But to actually see people asked this question, and to hear the same responses I would give, helps to really drive home the point about the different views people hold about Christ. Those on the video that did not see him as the Son of God did not look evil or mean either, but rather like my neighbors or fellow co-workers. This did a lot to help understand that those around me needed my testimony on the truth regarding Christ.

Bottom line, consider making your own videos for sermon illustrations, because I've seen some simple, church staff-created videos that have made a dynamic impact.

I had the opportunity to hear Adam Hamilton preach at the Church of the Resurrection in Leawood, Kan., on the passage in John 10:27 where Jesus is stating that HIS sheep hear and know His voice. I could tell by looking around that the crowd that day there were probably few in the congregation that had any personal contact with sheep, or could actually relate to the fact that they are domestic and develop a relationship with their care taker (shepherd). So, Adam found a rancher that had a large herd of sheep, took some people and a few cameras down to his ranch and interviewed him in his living room. Adam asked the rancher about the nature of sheep and their faith in the shepherd, and the rancher was more than willing to share a few interesting facts about sheep as it related to the illustrations Jesus used in the scriptures. Adam then asked the rancher to explain his method of calling the sheep into the pens at night, and asked if he could give it a try. The rancher was more than happy to oblige, and the video then shifts to the two gentlemen walking outside to the gates of the sheep pen where Adam gives a shout out to the sheep in an effort to lure them into the pen. He uses the exact words, in the exact manner in which the rancher demonstrated, but to no avail. And the cameramen did a great job. They had close-ups of the sheep looking up from the fields in the direction of Adam, but not a single one made a move toward the pen. So, after a bit of a laugh Adam asks the rancher if he can show how it's really done. The rancher then proceeds to shout the same calls Adam had tried earlier, only this time the sheep come running from all directions, all heading to the rancher and the safety of the pen. When the video ended and the house lights came back up, the congregation broke out into applause. He'd succeeded in giving the congregation the opportunity to experience the very point Jesus was trying to make in the Scripture, instead of just saying it and expecting them to take it as fact. It was quite powerful, had the desired impact, and I doubt if anyone in attendance would ever read or hear that scripture again without replaying the scenes they'd just witnessed in their minds.

A WORD ABOUT "INFORMAL" VIDEOS

We really do live in exciting times. Just a decade ago, if a church was to use or create video they would have been considered building a studio, purchasing professional cameras, having either staff or volunteers serve as production engineers, and more. The obvious goal would have been to create something of "television" quality, because that would have been the only use for such technology. Today, however, the Internet has changed all of that. Now people are easily creating their own videos using the cameras that came with their computers, or the cameras on their cell phones, and they're posting them on the Internet with relative ease. There have been plenty of examples of amateur videographers that post their homemade videos on Web sites like YouTube, only to discover that their work has captured the public eye of millions of viewers when they only intended to satisfy a few friends and family members. I remember someone once sent me a link to a wedding reception video where the bride, groom and their invited guests performed a choreographed dance to Michael Jackson's "Thriller." Within a few weeks, the bride and groom had appeared on talk show, and millions of people had viewed the video, despite the fact that it was initially intended only for a few friends and wedding guests. This points out something important about the video medium: that it's not so much about quality as it is about content. If you have something to say, something important to share, use video. You'll want to make sure the lighting allows you to capture the moment, and the audio is good enough for the message to be heard clearly. Other than that, informal, unprofessional video works just fine. There is more information on how to create your own videos for worship, as well as for streaming on your Web site, in chapter 7.

USING VIDEO CLIPS FROM MOVIES

Another popular and successful video technique being used in churches is the use of short video clips from popular movies, and there are many great illustrations to be found in today's movies. In the past, a pastor might have used a segment from a popular book or story to make his point. Today, grabbing a short clip from a movie can have the same effect. And the more popular the movie, the better the reaction from the audience. People love to share a common experience or emotion, and if there's a scene from a movie that invokes a moment of grace, mercy, anger, love, or some other emotion, then it's perfect for use as an illustration—especially if it helps to connect that important point of the sermon to the clip and binds it to a common experience.

It's a fact that more and more churches are showing videos, and it's not just limited to worship services and classrooms. You're also seeing youth pastors engaging in things like movie nights at the church, and even child care departments that will show a rented movie as a special event while the parents attend some other event at the church. Most churches, however, do not realize that showing an entire movie or grabbing a short clip from a movie or television show, and displaying it during a meeting or worship service, can violate licensing agreements resulting in an illegal act. When you view DVD's at home, you always see that FBI warning that shows up before the movie starts. And if you are watching the DVD at home with your family, you can ignore it because it doesn't apply to you. But if you show that same video in a church setting, you're putting your church at risk for a major lawsuit.

Ever wonder what that FBI warning actually says, or means? Basically, it explains that the video is authorized for personal, home-viewing use only. Special permission must be granted for any public performance—and that includes use at a church. Violations can result in substantial fines, some as high as $30,000 per infringement.

THE CVLI SOLUTION

There is a simple, inexpensive solution to showing videos legally in a church setting. Christian Copyright Licensing, Inc. and Motion Picture Licensing Corp. (MPLC) have partnered together to create Christian Video Licensing International (CVLI), which provides legal coverage to allow churches to show thousands of pre-recorded DVDs.

Two options are available. The Family Values Producer Package contains titles that focus on religious and family-based themes. The Total Producer Package also includes titles from many of the major studios, including Universal, Warner Brothers, Disney, DreamWorks, New Line, Fox, MGM and Paramount. Annual license fees are reasonable and are based on church size. Group licenses are also available for daycare centers and church-based schools.

For more information about this new resource for churches, call 1-888-771-CVLI (2854) or visit www.cvli.com.

USING TEXT DURING WORSHIP

Most churches want you to turn off your cell phone when you walk into the building, and most will either post a note in their bulletin, or have a notice displayed on one of their screens prior to the start of the worship service. However, some churches are now starting to ask their members to use their cell phones as part of the worship experience, mostly by conducting live text polls. Pastors can ask their members to vote on a variety of subjects then project the results live up on the screen. The services allow you to do true/false polls, yes/no polls, or even multiple choice polls, with the results being displayed in colorful bar or pie charts that appear as a Web site and are simple to project for everyone to view. Some even have a "refresh" mode that can update the results every few seconds.

This type of polling is conducted through what is known as shortcode texting services. There are several different methods for doing text polling, and they're produced by different companies with various rates. In most cases, however, the cost is small and the results are exciting.

For example, imagine the following scenario . . .

A pastor asks his congregation if they've had to deal with fear during the last week, and he asks them to be specific:

- ▶ Have they dealt with fear concerning making ends meet with the bills?
- ▶ Have they dealt with fear concerning their jobs?
- ▶ Have they felt afraid about their retirement plans, and/or getting old?
- ▶ Have they feared for their physical safety?
- ▶ Have they been afraid of being alone?
- ▶ Have they felt fear concerning the future of a relationship?

Then, pose the question to the congregation again; "Have you been afraid at any time during the last week?" and have them text their "yes" or "no" answer to the predesignated number. I would venture that most of us deal with fear almost on a daily basis. And by giving the congregation the opportunity to reflect on the questions first, then provide the ability to reply anonymously, you'll find that many people will respond with a greater degree of honesty. Imagine the foundations you've just laid for a sermon on "fear not," as the results to your poll are displayed on a screen for everyone to see in real time.

WHAT ABOUT THE OFFERING . . . IS ELECTRONIC GIVING FEASIBLE?

For many people the offering is a very important part of the worship. But in America, how we use, handle and exchange our money has changed drastically in the last ten years. Every year now more and more people no longer carry cash or a checkbook. More and more people now do banking online, and pay their bills the same way. In today's real world people pay for almost everything using a check or debit card. Yet when they come to worship, many churches still insist they write a check or put cash in the offering plate.

Online giving is becoming more and more popular for churches, especially in allowing members to make donations and pay their tithe while visiting a church's Web site. For many, however, removing the opportunity to pay their tithe during the worship service seems to take away an important part of the weekly worship experience.

To help bring the electronic offering opportunity closer to the worship experience, some churches have begun to use donation kiosks now being offered by several companies. These can be located in the lobby or narthex of any worship center, allowing people to use their debit cards for donations. They can allocate direct amounts of money to into a variety of areas of contribution. For example, they might have the option to donate a percentage of their gift to the general fund, and another percentage to special funds such as missions or a building fund.

There are now, however, actual opportunities that allow congregations to give electronically right from the pew during the worship experience. Several companies are now marketing hand-held wireless devices that can be passed down the pew just like a basket, allowing members to swipe their debit card and make a donation during the offertory part of the worship service.

In giving electronically, some Christians have expressed their concern to me that using a plastic debit card to make a contribution is not really "giving." But look at it this way: I don't think anyone found fault with the first time someone threw a dollar bill into an offering plate instead of a silver or gold coin, right? And I would have loved to have been there the first time people started using checks to give a donation. After all, a check isn't money, but a promise that you will get money when you turn it into your bank. The point I am trying to make is: there's always going to be some resistant to change. Today, the growing standard for monitory exchange has become plastic, and if the church wishes to encourage people to be good stewards then they need to allow them to make their contribution in a manner that is acceptable by most of society.

CHAPTER 3

Computer Communication Tools and Options

As I have already stated, the computer has become the communication tool for our time. And, since we as Christians have a "story to tell to the nations," using a computer as a communication tool for ministry is a natural fit. The hardest part is determining which of the many opportunities available are we going to use.

LISTSERV

The concept of a LISTSERV has been around for a long time, and is still considered popular today. A LISTSERV is an email group that has been setup to allow people the opportunity to join or leave the email list at their convenience, without the aid of a human administrator. Eric Thomas was credited with creating the first LISTSERV back in 1986. The idea was simple: someone could use a LISTSERV software program to establish an email group centered on a specific subject. People could join the LISTSERV by sending an email to a specific address, and by joining the LISTSERV you can then see all of the emails sent to the group. If you have a question or comment for the group, everyone sees it when you post it. For many, the LISTSERV concept has been replaced by Yahoo or Google groups, which accomplish the same purpose. However, LISTSERV's are still around and working because they lack the advertisements and marketing that sometimes dominate the group email services at Yahoo and Google. I personally belong to several email groups and LISTSERVs. The service from www.WeLoveGod.org is a popular one as well.

With some LISTSERV groups, you can set up RSS feeds so that messages are sorted for easy reading, and/or some allow for a digest. With a digest, you don't have to have all incoming and outgoing messages from the group landing in your email box, rather access them as separate documents so you could read off of them sorted by subject in one location.

Years ago I was doing a radio show and asked listeners to call in and share how they were using technology for ministry. I received a phone call from a woman in the St. Louis, MO., area who had been teaching a senior high school Sunday School class at her church for several years. As some of her students prepared to graduate and move on to college she was asked to switch and teach the College and Career Class. She realized, however, that most of her students would be scattered around the country while attending their college of choice, so she started a LISTSERV and encouraged them all to join. Each Monday she would send out an email giving an overview of what had been happening at church, i.e., prayer requests from others in the class, and a few personal notes about the prior week's lesson. Before long, many of her former students began to respond and leave messages and prayer requests on the group's LISTSERV. During this special time in those students' lives when many of them would normally lose connections with their home church and possibly their high school friends, her former Sunday School students were keeping a connection as a result of regular communications with the church via the LISTSERV. As the school year progressed and many of her former students began to make new friends, some of those "new" friends became interested in the group and asked to join. Of course the teacher welcomed them with open arms, and before the school year was over the group had doubled in size. When spring break rolled around, many of her former students came home and found they were instantly connected to each other, and a large percentage came back to worship at the home church again. When I spoke to this woman during the radio show, she had been running the LISTSERV for three years, and she raved about the addition of new Christians to her class of students, most of whom had become connected from the LISTSERV.

YAHOO GROUPS

Yahoo Groups are similar to a LISTSERV. Just like a LISTSERV, members can come and go as they please by simply joining the group. They do that by sending a special email to the group's moderator, who then accepts the member and sends a response. Yahoo Groups, however, can provide much more than a LISTSERV, including a Web site where group members can access additional information such as past messages, group member information, group photos, the ability to have a group calendar (with items such as birthdays, upcoming events, etc.) and various polls.

There are many ways to use such email groups to help develop relationships, increase connection, and even promote discipleship within a ministry. Here are a few examples:

▶ Ask The Pastor Group! Join the group and ask the pastor a question. Even if you don't have a specific question, members will definitely enjoy seeing the questions being asked by others, along with the pastor's answers;

▶ Bible Study Email Group. Each week members will receive a Bible lesson via email, and then prior to next week's lesson, members are encouraged to ask questions and enjoy the group discussion concerning the lesson;

▶ Support Group For Young Married Christian Couples. Provide a resource to ask questions and raise discussions related to topics and problems facing young married couples. Additional support groups can include Christian Singles Group, Blended Family Group, Divorce Support Group, Widow and Widowers Support Group, etc. The list goes on . . .

BROADCAST EMAILS

Broadcast emails have become very popular with churches and ministries. A broadcast email is an email—or email newsletter—that goes out in mass emailing to a collected list of email addresses. Many churches who used to publish regular newsletters and send them out by postal mail have switched to sending out an email version. Many have done so because of the cost savings, but there are other advantages. For example, paper newsletters can get lost. Most of us can relate to forgetting the time of an upcoming special event at the church, which usually turns into frustration when you can't remember where you left the church newsletter. However, if your church sends newsletters via a broadcast email, you can always find it quickly using the search function of your email program.

There are many ways to help make your broadcast email a hit. If you are sending out broadcast emails yourself instead of using a service like Constant Contact (more on that in a later chapter), make sure you don't put all of the email addresses in the "To:" or "Cc:" space (in case you didn't know, "Cc" stands for "carbon copy"). Instead, be sure to learn how to use the Bcc. Bcc stands for "blind carbon copy," and by doing it this way each person receiving the email won't see the long list of names and email addresses of everyone you sent the email to—which can also violate the trust of those that gave you their email addresses in the first place.

It's also important to create a good subject line for your broadcast emails. You don't want to sound like an advertisement, but it needs to grab the attention of the recipients, as well as make clear the true subject of the email. SPAM laws define SPAM three ways. First is whether or not subject line is untrue, and we've all seen SPAM emails that do this. They claim the email is from a friend, or they use "RE:" to imply that someone is replying to something you've already sent to them, all in an attempt to get you to open the email. Be sure when you send out your broadcast emails that you are honest about its subject, and that the subject line really express the actual intent of the email. SPAM laws also state that legitimate emails must be honest about where they are coming from, so be sure you are using a real email address that people can use to respond to you. Finally, if you send out a broadcast email you must provide information on how someone receiving your email can unsubscribe from the email if they so desire. It is also important that they can trust a "safe" unsubscribe link. If you are sending this out from your own lists using Outlook, or sending from a Church Management Software program, be sure to follow and note all unsubscribe requests. Again, one of the advantages of using an email service is they maintain the unsubscribe process for you.

When you send broadcast emails, send them using HTML (hypertext markup language) format, which allows you to add color, graphics, and a little overall excitement to them. Generally, emails created in HTML format have a 35 percent greater chance of being read, and of generating a response. Realize that most people use preview panes (such as in Microsoft's Outlook or Outlook Express) so limit the size of your HTML to 600 pixels wide. If you are going to attempt to send out HTML emails without using an email service such as Constant Contact, be warned that you need to know how to handle those in your group that have turned off the ability to receive HTML email. If not, they'll be receiving an email with lots of garbled code and no message. Email services that provide HTML templates automatically create a text version of your email from the materials and text you provide, and their service has the ability to know which type of email to deliver based on the email settings of the recipients.

Consider the content of the email, the subject line and the text, to avoid having your email—and email address—from being blocked from a recipient's inbox. For example, if you're sending an email that discusses the dangers of online pornography, it's not a good idea to use the word "pornography" in the subject line, or even in the text of the email. This is especially true if you're sending emails to a Christian audience, because many of them have email filters that cannot differentiate between a warning against the viewing of pornography, or actual pornography itself. The way to get around this is by putting the article in a format that is not read by the filters, such as a PDF file or MS Word document, and sending it up to a server. This way you can provide a link in the email for readers to click on to view the article. You still would need to refrain from using the word pornography, and instead, maybe, refer to the dangers of "viewing inappropriate materials." I can tell you from experience, we never thought ahead about sending out an email about the dangers of online pornography, and had a bit of a mess on our hands when we had to deal with all of the SPAM and blocked email reports from our original list of more than 50,000 email addresses!

Since you want to ensure that your emails are delivered and not marked as SPAM, you might consider using several services available on the Internet that can check your email and give you a probability rating on the likelihood of your email being flagged as SPAM by ISPs (Internet Service Providers) and mail servers. Two good ones are www.Lyris.com and www.Sitesell.com, both of which are free. Remember, most email services provide a SPAM checker, so take advantage of such a service and don't assume your content will not get flagged. What you don't know can hurt you. If you send your email from a standard email account and it generates SPAM complaints, you won't know about them. You also run the risk of having your entire corporate email server blocked. I remember years ago we used the services of Gospelcom.net, which helped ministries get established on the Internet and provided free Web hosting. I remember there was a time when one ministry sent out a broadcast email that was marked as SPAM, and it was discovered that for a brief time all of the ministries hosted on Gospelcom. net had trouble getting their emails delivered to several important ISPs. Gospelcom.net quickly fixed the problem, but for some time broadcast emails from any ministry had to go through a screening process to help protect everyone else using their services.

So, when is the best time to send your broadcast emails? Emails are now averaging at least three days before the bulk of your readers will actually receive and read them. This is because for most people, emails are not unique and they receive many throughout the day. As a result, people do not check their email as frequently. And, many people receive emails at work and at home. Most have two different addresses. The speed at which they receive and read your email will depend on which addresses they've provided, and where it is being delivered. If it is going to a work address and you sent it on a Friday afternoon, there is a real good chance they won't see it until at least Monday morning. If they are using a home address, they may not be able to check it on a daily basis, especially if they have to deal with using a computer all day, every day, at work. This doesn't mean there won't be some that read emails almost immediately, but it does give you an idea about providing some lead time. Churches that send out an email noting a change in a meeting time or location the night before the meeting might discover that most did not receive the news. That's why three days is a good benchmark for providing a lead time for most emails.

What is the Best Way to Send Out a Broadcast Email?

Many have discovered that email programs such as Microsoft Outlook or Microsoft Outlook Express have a limit to the number of emails they can send out at one time. In addition, many Internet Service Providers (ISP) seek to limit the number of broadcast emails that are sent through their server. Their fear is that outgoing emails from their server or service will be blacklisted as SPAM, so they are very cautious in allowing large numbers of emails to go out with the same subject and content.

In addition, many email services like America Online (AOL) continuously watch for large numbers of emails that hit their service all at once from the same server, or with the same subject or content, and will simply drop it from delivery.

The good news is that there is a solution! For a reasonable fee you can use a broadcast email service like Constant Contact to send out your broadcast emails, which has many advantages. Constant Contact, for example, has a myriad of helpful features that will make your broadcast email newsletter very readable to your congregation. Its greatest feature, however, is its high delivery rate. They can guarantee that approximately 97 percent of your emails will make it to the intended address. They can do this because they spend an enormous amount of time working with ISPs around the world, assuring these providers and servers that emails coming from Constant Contact are not SPAM. They accomplish this by not allowing their services to be used by those that send SPAM emails out to harvested lists. Additionally, the independent email performance firm Return Path, Inc., audits their service and backs up their 97 percent delivery claim.

What is a harvested list? There are many ways to "grab" email addresses, including "spider" programs that search the Internet for email addresses by looking for any word followed by the "@" sign, such as anything@anywhere.com. There are many other ways to capture and harvest email addresses, and there are just as many people out there that like to gather large lists of email addresses in order to send out SPAM emails. They may not know if the email addresses are valid, nor do they know if the recipient really cares about the product or service they are promoting, but since the cost of sending out millions of SPAM emails is relatively inexpensive they don't really care who receives it or not because they're basically playing a numbers game. If you have an email address, I am sure you are aware of how annoying SPAM can be.

So, to assure ISP and email servers around the world that emails coming from Constant Contact are legitimate and not SPAM, Constant Contact has initiated procedures to ensure that their customers are sending out emails that are wanted by their intended recipients.

First, they ask customers to verify that their starting list is made up of email addresses of people wanting to receive their broadcast emails. They'll ask you to verify this when you set up the new account, and before you import a list. You will be asked to call in by phone to speak directly with a member of their customer support team in order to verify that your list only includes those people who've signed up to receive your emails.

If you are a new customer, Constant Contact also reserves the right to send out your first broadcast email in sections a few days apart from each other, which allows their customer support team to check for SPAM reports, unusually large numbers of bounced email addresses or undeliverable emails. If these numbers is too large then there's a good chance they would cease to send out the rest of your list.

They also monitor and stay up to date on the latest legislation and regulations—so that they make sure your email campaigns comply with all laws and regulations.

They also build and nurture relationships with major ISPs so that if an issue does arise they can get it resolved quickly.

As a co-founder of the "Email Sender and Provider Coalition" and a member of "Messaging Anti-Abuse Working Group", Constant Contact is an advocate for small businesses and associations in the fight against SPAM.

But besides increased deliverability of your emails, Constant Contact also provides many exciting features to help you present your message in a professional-looking way. And it's these features that greatly increase the chance that your emails will be read. Here are some of the features I value most:

▶ A step-by-step wizard to walk you through the creation of your emails;

▶ A preview function that allows you to see the finished email, as well as send a sample to yourself or others who need to approve it before it is sent to your email list;

▶ Drag-and-drop capability, which allows you to easily grab one section or story from your email and move it to a different spot in the email;

▶ Over 300 templates, many categorized by holidays or themes. You can modify or build each of these templates according to you individual or ministry specifications. While different templates provide a variety of colors, you further customize your email by easily changing the color scheme or the font. Their templates fall into the following types: Email newsletter templates, Email promotion templates, Email card templates, Email event invitations templates, Holiday and seasonal theme templates, Industry theme templates, Basic templates, and a custom template option which they provide for an extra fee;

▶ They can spell check your emails in 12 different languages;

▶ You can use their Anti-Spam check to get a rating on your email in order to see if it might be flagged by some Spam filters;

▶ You can schedule your email to go out immediately, or set up a date and time in the future when you want it to be delivered;

▶ It is easy to grab content from previous emails and use them to start a new email, which is fantastic if you are sending out a regular church newsletter, since the contact information, times of services, location, etc., would normally not have to be updated or re-entered each time you send a new newsletter;

▶ You can have multiple lists and select which ones you wish to send your email to. For example, if you had a choir list, a youth list, a single adult list, etc., specific emails might be sent to them separately, or a church-wide email newsletter could be selected to send to all of your lists;

▶ It's easy to insert images and pictures. You can upload as many as five images for free and store them on Constant Contact. This is great for images you might use over and over like your church's logo. You can also purchase the option to store additional images, if needed;

▶ It is easy to resize images you insert into your email;

▶ Constant Contact provides a stock image library with more than 3,400 images for an additional cost of only $5 a month;

▶ It is easy to add links to other Web sites, or content such as PDF files. While you cannot add an attachment to a Constant Contact email, it is relative easy to post the file you would want to attach, such as a Word document or

PDF file, and then provide the link in your email. User would then have to click and have the file downloaded to their computer to view;

▶ Constant Contact can provide some great reporting on how many of your emails were opened, how many links were clicked, and can even give you a report on which emails were bounced and why (address unknown, mailbox full, etc.);

▶ Using their templates, you can present your members with some fantastic graphic HTML newsletters. If you want only text, Constant Contact creates text-only options for you automatically. When your members sign up, they can select the "text only" option and Constant Contact will keep track of that for you, too;

▶ They have the ability to insert a special coupon option, which can be formatted and included anywhere in your email;

▶ They have the ability to create and send out surveys;

▶ They have the option for you to use a PayPal click-to-buy feature, which is a great tool for churches selling tickets, or any other items, or need online registration to a paid event;

▶ They can provide a "Forward to a Friend" link within your email. Just select which part of the email you wish to forward and then encourage your members to use it to send it to a friend, which ultimately helps spread your message;

▶ Constant Contact also does a fantastic job in helping you maintain your email lists. They provide HTML code that can be added to your Web site to present your lists to visitors in order to encourage them to sign up. They provide various looks for the opt-in signup box, one of which will most likely fit nicely into your Web site's look and feel. When a person clicks to sign up for your emails they will be presented with your customized welcome information. Upon signing up, a special customized welcome email is then sent. You can capture just email addresses, or create your signup form with a list of questions and required or optional ID information (create up to 15 custom fields). You will receive a weekly report from Constant Contact with details on how many people signed up for your email lists. As discussed earlier, one of the items that make a broadcast email legal is the ability to safely unsubscribe, and Constant Contact provides a safe unsubscribe option at the bottom of every email that you send. You can also add an unsubscribe comment box, which can help you obtain vital information on why the recipient opted out of your email list.

▶ Constant Contact also provides free phone, email and chat support. And, they provide a free trial as long as your list is less than 100 people. Finally, Constant Contact works well with many of today's Church Management Software (CMS) products.

Since a service like Constant Contact allows you to set up many different lists on one account, I strongly encourage you to segment the information you send out via broadcast emails. In days past, churches mailed a single newsletter, some once a month. In that one newsletter they would include different segments of information covering every aspect of their ministries.

Today, we live in an age of information overload, although many people only read the information they are personally interested in. Therefore, I encourage you *not* to send just one email newsletter with information about every segment of your ministry. Instead, design and set up several different information emails and give your people the option of signing up only for those specific ministries they're interested in. Because of the way Constant Contact has structured their customer accounts, this works perfectly with their service. Your costs each month are based upon the total number of people who have signed up to receive your emails, not the number of times you send out emails to one or more of your lists (I think there is a limit, but I have never hit it). Also, when you use the HTML code that Constant Contact provides for your Web site, there only needs to be the one place to sign up. After a person visits your church's Web site and enters their email to sign up, they will then see a list of all the different emails to select from. They can pick as many email groups as they want. This way, whenever there is some specific news for the youth group and their parents, you can pick a template, create a spiffy newsletter with your desired information then select the email list of the people that requested youth information. If there is an important church-wide promotion, or announcement, you would simply select all of the lists. And don't worry . . . if a person signed up for information on more than one list, Constant Contact will only send them one copy of your email.

TEXTING

While email is still a viable method of getting information out to your congregation, it has become less popular as a communication tool for young people and young adults up to the age of 40. For many members of this group, texting has replaced email as the communication tool of choice. Instant Messaging (IM) was very popular with young people, especially before texting became a standard feature of most cell phones. With IMs, two people could send short messages back and forth in real time, and it was a popular communication tool for young people sitting in front of their computers at night working on homework (or doing whatever else).

But when the wireless phone companies began to offer texting services on phones, the switch to texting was on. In fourth quarter of 2007, more text messages were sent from cell phones than actual voice phone calls, and many cell phone companies moved away from charging by the text message and added bulk texting plans to their cell phone services. Some have even added unlimited texting for a small fee.

Texting and Ministry

Text message are typically only 140 characters long, and would not, on the surface, seem like a logical choice as a mass broadcasting tool. However, group texting is catching on. Shortcode texting, or SMS, was put to great use in the 2008 presidential election by many of the candidates. Shortcode texting services basically have paid an aggregator to register a specific shortcode (called a shortcode because it is one or two numbers shorter than a normal phone number) with the wireless phone companies, which allows their customers the ability to register a group name with the number. In the case of a church, they might pick ChurchPrayer as their group name. Once the name is registered, they simply inform their congregation to text the word ChurchPrayer to a specific number, such as 123456, and the user would be set up to receive prayer requests from the group.

Realize, however, that you're not collecting cell phone numbers. You're simply encouraging members to opt-in to one of your groups by texting the name of your group to a specific number. The opportunities for this type of use are many. I have been using a texting service for one of the groups my wife and I lead for over six months with great success. In fact, I would say group texting is probably responsible for our group doubling in size during the last six months. Let me explain.

My wife and I lead a singles group at our church. The age range is posted as 40's–50's, but many in our group are in their 50's, with a few in their 40's and 60's. When we introduced to the group the idea of using group texting, almost everyone immediately said they didn't text. I could understand their apprehension. After all, I knew that this was not the demographic age for those that would text on a regular basis. However, we discovered that everyone in our group had cell phones that could receive text messages. And, we had at least one or two in our group that did text, normally to communicate with their children. We asked our group to allow us to sign them up and give group texting a chance. At the time we introduced the concept to our group, we had about 15 members. After just a couple of weeks the number of members had risen to 17, and we attributed that to our group texts.

Because texts are limited in the amount of information they can convey, we still used emails to announce events or inform our group about ministry opportunities. However, each Friday night, about two hours before our meeting, I began to send out a text with a simple meeting reminders, including information on what we were planning for dinner, and what chapter we might be studying that night. Our group loved it! They quickly began to tell other members of our group who were sporadic in attendance and encouraged them to sign up. I remember specifically one gentleman who had attended our meetings a half dozen times in the previous year, but had now started to attend almost every Friday night. I asked him what happened to move him from being an occasional visitor to a regular attendee, and he told me it was because of the group texting. He told me that he had always wanted to be more active with the group, but because the meetings were on Friday night, and he didn't always have contact with any of the group's members during the week, he would simply forget about the meeting. "Now, I get a text every Friday reminding me about the meeting, with just enough time for me to get cleaned up and head to church," he told me.

Over the next six months we saw our Friday night attendance go from an average of 15 to an average of 29, with 42 people signed up for our group texting announcements.

One more advantage of group texting is the speed in which your message is sent, received and read. Because our audience consists of middle-aged singles, most of whom are divorced, my wife and I decided to invite all of them to join us each Sunday at a restaurant for lunch (they were to pay for their own meal). However, before the group texting service, it was difficult to decide where we might meet for dinner. We also had several members that attended other churches on Sunday, or that attended earlier services at our church and weren't there at the end of the last Sunday service to find out where we were meeting for lunch. The group texting service solved this problem. I could easily send a text to the group right from my cell phone (you can also send them directly from the texting service's site), and within a few minutes everyone in our group knew where to meet us for lunch. We've had as many as 18 people meet up with us as a result of being able to quickly and easily get our lunch plans out to the group via group texting.

Our church's youth minister also uses the texting service with even greater results, mainly because of the fact that texting is an obvious fit for the younger crowd who love to text.

The cost to set up this type of service runs about $25 a month for one to three different groups. So, for example, you could set up a text group for your youth group, your prayer group, and then one for your entire church. And another advantage of group texting is that it does not require individuals to give personal information in order to join. Some see this as a failing, since they want to capture data on everyone attending, involved or even interested in their church. However, many in our society are becoming increasingly concerned about their personal information and crave more privacy. If you set up a church-wide group for texting announcements, it would probably be well received within your community. By setting up a text group for your church and then promoting it in your community, you would be allowing people the opportunity to join and receive information about upcoming events, sermon series, concerts, new ministries, etc., all without anyone having to give you their name, phone number, address, etc.

Text BELIEVE to 44636

A good example of using short code or SMS texting in this manner can be found at the United Methodist Church in Western Pennsylvania. During the 2008 Christmas season, they set up an account with a SMS or short code service and put the message "Text BELIEVE to 44636" on billboards. When people took up the offer and texted "BELIEVE" to the number they received a text that said, "Hope is reason 2 believe. It lives in each of us. Share this xmas w/people of PGH United Methodist Church. Reply ZIP for church or later visit UnitedMethodist. org". When people replied with their zip code, they received another text with the names, addresses and phone numbers of the closest UMCs to the referenced zip code. Bishop Thomas J. Bickerton told ABC News that the United Methodist Church was very pleased with the response they received from the SMS marketing campaign. They received about 100 responses a day, and churches all over the area reported an increase in the number of people dropping in during their services during the holidays.

Many Options

There are many different ways to use SMS texting, and in chapter two I shared how to use this service to do live text polls during a worship service or Bible class. Here are some of the other features that SMS services can offer:

▶   You can set up multiple group managers. Once you set up an account and then a group, the service allows you to enter the email addresses of additional people who can serve as managers of the group. Managers can then send messages to the group. Once a person receives their email invitation to be a group manager, they can click the link which will take them back to the service so they can register. They will be required to enter their cell phone number, which they will then use as a manager to send text messages directly from the site, or from their personal cell phone or texting device.

▶   You can set a group to be "announce" only. Promote this group (for example, text "your church" to 564646) and people will receive your important announcements with your church's phone number, Web site, address, service times, etc. You can even use this to help people receive specific information about events or upcoming ministry opportunities. For example, set up a group and call it "newmember." Then put a notice in your bulletin or newsletter that lets potential members know that if they text "newmember" to your short code, they will receive a reply text with information on "new member" classes and functions. You can also include contact information for those that wish to register or need more information. You can make this evangelistic as well. Imagine creating a group called "moreaboutjesus" and encouraging people to text to it, with a reply announcement about where to go or who to contact for more information about Christ. One of the biggest advantages of sending information to people via texts is that the information is constantly with them on their cell phone, and ready whenever they are to respond to the information. And since most of us are hardly ever without our cell phones, the information remains until someone decides to delete it. So, providing important contact information to people via a text announcement can be a fantastic ministry and service.

▶   You can turn on "reply" and use the service for text registrations to your upcoming event. Normally the option to reply is turned off in SMS group texts. But you can simply turn it on and use it like the aforementioned UMC program in Pennsylvania. By turning on the reply option you can use your text message to ask for information that can be used in a variety of ways. For example, you might want to actually use text messaging as a way to register for an event. Simply set up a group that can represent the event, encourage people to text the group name to your number and they will receive an email asking them to register by replying with the information you require, such as name, phone number, email address, etc.

▶   You can also set up a closed group, which is perfect for special groups like church Elders or Deacons. Once the group is set, if someone else was to text to join they would receive a message stating that the group is closed, with additional contact information if there are additional questions.

▶ You can also set up texts to a specific group to go to a micro blog on your Web site, which is perfect for prayer groups. In this case, texts not only go to everyone that signed up to receive text prayer requests but also to a special window on your Web site for others to see the last few text messages that were sent as prayer requests.

Text Messages Get High Open and Read Ratings

Information is only valuable if it gets into the right hands, and is read. Since we live in an age of information overload, it is becoming harder and harder to get your message heard. Now that many churches are moving to email newsletters instead of mailing print versions, they might be assuming they have a higher open and read rate. The statistics, however, don't make that case. These days it takes about three days before broadcast emails will reach their intended targets, mainly because people read their emails both at home or work, and they are normally not at both places at once. Most people now read emails once a day, and filter through the many promotional and corporate emails they receive, concentrating their attention on those of a personal nature.

A large ministry once shared with me that they had utilized some tracking capabilities in a few broadcast emails they had recently sent out. Even though their lists of email addresses were legitimate and didn't bounce, their open and read rate was hardly ever higher than 40 percent even though the subject line made it clear that the email contained requested information on a certain ministry. Text messages, on the other hand, are superior when it comes to open and read rates. In fact, texts are seen and read between 98 and 99 percent of the time, mainly because they go directly to our cell phones, which are either on our belts, in our pockets, or in our purses. Even if you didn't notice a tone or signal when you received a text message, you'll know you have one because your phone usually tells you the next time you pick up your phone.

Texting Prayer Requests

Texting prayer requests for your congregation just might be one of the greatest ministry opportunities for group texting, and the reason is simple: it fast, accurate, and easy. Did I mention fast? It's great to share ongoing prayer requests with a church in the Sunday bulletin, but it doesn't help the person that needed prayer the Tuesday before when they suffered a heart attack, or were involved in a car accident.

My first introduction to group texting came from Bob Hunt, executive pastor at the WildWood First Church of God in Eastern Kentucky. He told me that he had set up a couple of texting groups in his church, and one of them was to text out important prayer requests. I didn't consider Eastern Kentucky to a hub for technological innovations, yet I was surprised to learn that in early 2008 his church had enthusiastically adopted group texting, and especially for prayer requests. On an average Sunday, Hunt told me his average attendance was somewhere in the neighborhood of 500 (from nursery school to senior adults). And so, one Sunday he announced from the pulpit that the church had set up a new texting service for prayer requests. He instructed them to text the group name PRAY to 313131 if they were interested in signing up. He told me an astonishing 187 people signed up just that one Sunday!

Imagine if someone in that church needs immediate prayer, whether it was for a heart attack, a death in the family, or even an automobile accident. Pastor Bob could simply send a text, either by visiting the Web site and typing in the appropriate text box, or by texting directly from his phone, and within seconds people would have received the prayer request message at work, school, home, or wherever else they were at the time.

I can relate to this on a personal level. Earlier I shared about my wife's recent car wreck. She was able to call me quickly and tell me she was hurting and that someone had already called an ambulance. When I arrived, I only had the opportunity to talk to her briefly as emergency personnel were working on her and trying to get the ambulance underway. As I followed behind the ambulance on the way to the hospital I did something that I would never otherwise recommend: I sent a text message out to our Bible study group. It stated simply that my wife had been in an accident and I didn't know how bad she had been hurt. I explained that I was following the ambulance to the hospital and asked them to pray. I can't tell you the impact it had on me and my wife that night, just knowing that our group was praying for us right then and there. In fact, by the time we got to the hospital I was receiving personal text messages assuring me that prayers were being sent on our behalf. While waiting at the hospital I also received dozens of additional phone calls and text messages from other brothers and sisters expressing their support and prayers. It was fantastic to be on the receiving end of such ministry, all made available by modern technology.

TWITTER

Unless you've been cut off from civilization for the last year, you've probably heard a thing or two about Twitter. Twitter is many things to many people, and I talk about Twitter in the next chapter when I write about social networking services. But here's a quick introduction.

Twitter was started as a social networking service where people can invite others to "follow" them by visiting the Twitter site (www.twitter.com) and reading the 140-character text messages sent out at any given time. Twitter is also happens to be a free texting service. At present they can't do everything a shortcode texting service can do, such as allow for multiple managers, or live text polling, but they have adapted their services to allow it to work like many basic texting services. You no longer have to visit their Web site and establish an account to follow someone. You can simply set up your name for anyone to follow, and then encourage people to join right from their cell phone by entering your username. For example, just like shortcode texting services, you can set up a username like "ChurchPrayer" and then encourage people to text "Follow ChurchPrayer" to 40404 to access your most recent posts.

The advantage of using Twitter, or any other shortcode texting service, is that it is managed by the user. The user opts in to specific lists, or in the case of Twitter specifically picks who or what they wish to follow. In the e-book *The Reason Your Church Must Twitter*, author Anthony Coppedge says, "The point is that most churches (the vast majority?) struggle to keep up with an accurate database to contact their congregations. As a result, churches can often over communicate or simply send the wrong information to the wrong person. With Twitter, the biggest hurdle will be in explaining how your church is leveraging a new, faster and easier method for keeping your people informed. Best of all, they'll not receive nearly as many SPAM emails from the church." Later on in the book he adds, "I recommend that every church set up multiple Twitter accounts for the purpose of reaching the right people with the appropriate demographic-specific information."

Since texting with Twitter is specific, quick, direct and—most importantly—free, churches can set up a large number of accounts, allowing users to be very specific about the information that will be heading their way. You can set up specific Twitter accounts for every group in your church, every choir, every worship band, your staff, your elder or deacon board, and even your custodial staff, and have each group follow their own account to contact them with quick, concise tweets (tweets is what they call text messages sent out via Twitter).

You can get lots more information about Twitter in the section on social networking services found later in this book.

CHAPTER 4

Personal Communication Age

Something important has happened in the last 15 years, and it has changed everything about the way we communicate. And since communication is central to a society's ability to grow, govern and educate its members, it is vital that the church grasp what has happened too. Communication is imperative when it comes to ministry. Today, we refer to our prospects for Christianity as seekers. They have questions, and we have the answer. However, the only way to get seekers the answers to their questions is to meet their needs for communication. I know that sounds like the most obviously redundant statement I could ever make, but I want you to take a minute to examine its simplicity. Because while there are hundreds of millions of seekers in our nation, and the church has THE answer, for some reason we are not getting the them the answers to their questions. Something is definitely wrong in this area of communication. And, it relates to what has happened in just the last 15 years.

COMMUNICATION HAS CHANGED, DRASTICALLY

It is interesting how historians have attached a name to certain periods of time in our history. And I wonder if those living during these periods of time realized what age they were living in? For example, did a wife ever turn to her husband and lament that they were living in the Dark Ages? Or did a husband ever turn to his wife at the dinner table and express joy that he had a job down at the factory because they were living in the Industrial Age? Interestingly enough, if you were to try to figure out what age we are in now you would find many different opinions. In fact, the last "age" everyone seems to agree on that proceeded this age, whatever it might be, was the "Information Age." When you think about it, the very nature of such an age might endanger the ability of historians to ever agree on the name for our present or future ages, since the increase in information came as a result of an increase in knowledge, opinion and individuality. So, what does this all have to do with the change in communications? I believe the Information Age has evolved, and we have moved into what I call the "Personal Communication Age."

The Information Age gave us the printing press, telegraph, radio, television and other methods of mass communication. However, few people had control over what was communicated to the masses. This occurred because of the costs associated with using mass communication devices during that time. It took large and expensive presses to produce a city-wide newspaper or national magazine. It took expensive equipment, highly trained individuals and the ownership of satellites in space in order to broadcast news on televisions that could be viewed by the masses across the nation and around the world. However, as technology advanced so did the availability of affordable communication tools. Cell phones began to keep us in constant contact with our friends and families. The Internet provided a World Wide Web where anyone could post their thoughts and opinions and have the same readership as would those that owned the massive print presses and barrels of ink. But this didn't simply provide additional methods for mass communication. It was also fostering something else that was brewing quietly in the background: the growing distrust in the messages of mass communication.

Walt Wilson explains it this way; "Americans no longer view truth as objective reality. Modern society and certainly our political leadership support the language of ambiguity. The line between right and wrong is no longer as clear as it once was or should be. Political leaders in the United States think 'spin' is [a] morally acceptable manipulation of truth. The absence of truth breeds skepticism." (*The Internet Church*, page 59)

At the same time that the skepticism of mass communication by national leaders began growing, technology began providing individuals the opportunity to make connections with different networks of individuals. These networks had a "personal" connection or relationship, and therefore had the appearance of a greater trust. This does not make information sent through personal communication methods truth. It just means that people are more likely to believe such information, and they are more likely to react, accept and act upon information they receive from someone or something connected to them by a personal communication tool or method.

It should also be noted that America has a general mistrust for national news services, as well as their political leadership. However, I agree with Walt's conclusion that the practice of adding "spin" to news is acceptable. It seems that most of the people in positions that inform the public feel compelled to add their personal commentary, and as a result our newspapers, radio shows and television network and cable news shows all carry labels of conservative or liberal that most have become comfortable with. Biases are certainly present in personal communications with friends and family members, but here it's acceptable and, because of the relationship, normally trusted.

Let me give you an example that has become a historical example of the move away from mass communication methods, and also serves as an example of the "appearance" of personal communication. The *Wall Street Journal* ran a story of a 15-year-old ninth grader at Central Academy in Macon, Miss., who, for a science project, decided to find out how far she could get a personal appeal to go using email and the Internet. She set up an email address on America Online (AOL) and called her project "howfastorfar2003@aol.com." She planned to run her experiment for six weeks, and sent out her email to 23 different addresses that she's gathered from her parents and friends. Here is the message she sent out:

Hi:

I am Shannon Syfrett a 9th grade student at Central Academy (Macon, Mississippi). I am working on a project for my 2003 Science Fair to be held February 25th, 2003. I am trying to see where and how fast e-mail can travel in a period of six weeks. I am keeping track of how many e-mails I get back, and what cities, states, and countries they are coming from. I am hoping that you will be willing to help me with my project! There are only 2 simple steps that will help me to track this email:

1. Please send an e-mail to the following address: (address deleted for the purposes of this book). In the subject of the e-mail please include your city, state, and country. You do not need to include your name. Please respond only one time.

2. *Please forward this e-mail to everyone on your mailing list. I will be keeping track of the number of responses, as well as the locations. Therefore, send them even to people in the same town. In my science project, I am trying to demonstrate how fast and how far information can travel on the Internet in a six week period. If you receive this e-mail after February 23, 2003 please disregard it, since the project will be over.*

Thank you VERY much for your help!

Shannon Syfrett

As a part of her science project, she was required to forecast the results, and she projected she might receive somewhere between 2,000–3,000 return emails. In hindsight, there was really no way she ever could have anticipated, nor prepared herself, for the actual number of responses her simple experiment would eventually garner.

The day after she sent the email she received 200 responses, an average of one email every 7.2 minutes. In just a few more days she had received emails from 47 states and 25 different countries, including Australia and Zimbabwe. In less than two weeks she had received 8,768 emails, and within just three more days she received an additional 12,013. She was now averaging an email every 7.2 seconds.

Within a few more days she received a whopping 37,854 emails in one day!, and that's when AOL pulled the plug on the experiment. Final tally: in just three-and-a-half weeks, Syfrett received 160,478 emails from 189 countries!

There are many lessons to be learned from the experience of Shannon Syfrett. And let's not forget that the story first appeared in the Wall Street Journal, which I imagine doesn't spend a lot of time reporting on the science fair projects of 15-year-olds. They obviously recognized the importance of this story, and that what Shannon had discovered by accident would have an impact on marketing and communication for many years to come.

You have to wonder why Shannon received so many responses from so many strangers. Try to imagine getting that kind of a response using traditional mass media. For example, I doubt that when this book rolls off the presses it will be in the hands of 160,478 different people in 189 countries within three-and-a-half weeks (I can hope, but I am realistic). And let's not forget another important part of this story: the number of people she received a response from—160,478 different people—in a relatively short time. It wouldn't be a bad assumption to predict that she would have reached millions with her message if it would have been allowed to run its full course. If you are a pastor, you have spend years preparing and training to present your message. You have spend thousands of dollars on getting your degrees, and probably have a decent library of books behind your desk on the wall. You receive a paid salary to share your thoughts and message with your congregation. With all that training, money and knowledge, you will probably never say something so profound that it would be shared word of mouth by millions in such a short time as Shannon's email.

TAPPING INTO PC

So, what happened? Shannon tapped into what I call the "Personal Communication Age." Even though she only started with 23 email addresses, as the numbers grew people were still receiving the message from someone they knew personally, as opposed to getting an email from a total stranger. If Shannon had one million email addresses and sent her message out through the Internet to such an immense list, I doubt she would have received 1,000 responses. The secret to what happened here is that each person heard of Shannon's science project from someone they trusted, and therefore took the time to read the message and felt a compelling need to respond and help, albeit not because they knew Shannon, or would ever meet her, but because her message was handed off to them from someone they knew personally.

An article from *South Coast Today* (http://archive.southcoasttoday.com/daily/02-03/02-16-03/d06bu147.htm) examined how the email spread as a result of the "personal" communication trail":

> *John Krueger, a Lutheran minister in Tempe, Ariz., who says he doesn't know Shannon, answered her e-mail and sent it along to Chad Montabon. He is teaching English in Vietnam but picked the message up while he was in Thailand*

and forwarded it to a friend nicknamed Muskratking in Antarctica. Anita Morley, who runs an orphanage in Ulan Bator, Mongolia, says she answered the note after she received it from Linda Paulus, a missionary in Papua New Guinea, who says she got it from her niece in Ohio.

John Carr, who is helping build a containment structure around the Chernobyl nuclear reactor in the Ukraine, answered Shannon after he says he got the message from Richard Hopp, a retired engineer in Florida, who says he also forwarded it to a pal in Venezuela after it was forwarded to him from his daughter at Mississippi State University. A Marine somewhere near Iraq ("no city, no state"); an Air Force sergeant on the Indian Ocean island of Diego Garcia, a staging area for any Middle East war; and sailors on 17 U.S. Navy ships sent e-mails. One, aboard the USS Harry S. Truman, added poignantly: "If it's not too much to ask, please pray for (me)."

Many churches have recognized the fact that they can now broadcast mass media tools digitally via the Internet. Instead of printing and mailing a newsletter, they can use broadcast emails and send out the same information via the Internet. Instead of purchasing television or radio time, they can now podcast or stream video via the Internet. These are certainly important accomplishments in taking advantage of computers and technology tools to help expand your ministry. But using personal communication tools takes it one step further. Let me illustrate:

A couple of years ago a friend of mine at a leading Christian publishing house shared how they began to explore new business strategies based on trends in personal communications and viral marketing. Here is how viral marketing is defined by Wikipedia:

"The buzzwords viral marketing and viral advertising refer to marketing techniques that use pre-existing social networks to produce increases in brand awareness or to achieve other marketing objectives (such as product sales) through self-replicating viral processes, analogous to the spread of pathological and computer viruses. It can be word-of-mouth delivered or enhanced by the network effects of the Internet. Viral promotions may take the form of video clips, interactive Flash games, advergames,

ebooks, brandable software, images, or even text messages. It will spread, person-to-person, like a virus, helping to get your message out to the masses."

In the case of my friend's example, they wanted to promote an online Bible study led by one of their more popular authors. They had sought to promote such online events in the past, but had achieve only limited success. They discovered that even when people had requested information about specific online Bible studies by this particular author, tracking software revealed that only about 40 percent of those actually opened the response email. In addition, emailing this interest group did not provide any guarantee that they would forward the information to other potential attendees—even if they asked them to do so. So they hired programmers and a consulting firm, and created a viral marketing tool to help promote their next online Bible study. Basically they created an e-greeting card that carried a message of prayer and support. The e-card basically stated that the person sending it was thinking about those receiving it. It expressed their appreciation for their relationship, and wanted the recipient to know that they would be praying for them on that date. They then sent these to the list of those that had sought information about the particular author. Additionally, they included several other elements. First, they encouraged each recipient to think of five others that had impacted their lives in a positive way. They also encouraged them to visit their Web site where they would find a template allowing them to enter the names of their five friends, and an expression of prayer and support similar to the original message. Second, they created a map of the world that showed the location of each person visiting. It would then trace the ISP of those they had sent the e-greeting to. Each e-greeting that went out encouraged the recipient to do the same actions: think of five people that had influenced them, and visit the publisher's site to send out five e-greeting cards to their friends. By coming back to the site, they could view the map and see their original dot on the map, as well as the dots of the five friends they had sent the e-greeting to. Subsequently, as their friends sent additional greetings and prayers to more people, the dots on the map would increase. Over time, as the dots continued to increase in number, you became aware of the power of encouragement to your small group of friends as the support and prayer message spread from person to person. Third, whenever you closed the e-greeting or the publisher's Web site an additional browser window would open telling you about the upcoming online Bible study. The results were fantastic.

The first thing they discovered was that while only 40 percent opened the original email from the author, the open rate jumped to 90 percent among those that had been forwarded the email from the original batch of emails. And while they had started with a relatively small list of email addresses—maybe 2,000—within weeks their e-greeting card had been sent to millions, helping to promote the upcoming online Bible study and giving the publishers the best attended event of its kind ever.

Here's another passage from the definition of Viral Marketing in Wikipedia:

> *"The goal of marketers interested in creating successful viral marketing programs is to identify individuals with high* Social Networking Potential (SNP) *and create* Viral Messages *that appeal to this segment of the population and have a high probability of being passed along."*

In the case of Shannon Syfrett, it is obvious that there was no specific Social Network Potential defined. Her message was simply shared, person-to-person, friend-to-friend because of the relationship that existed between the sender and receiver of the email. However, by targeting the message to those of Christian support, appreciation and prayer, the email and accompanying information went out to a Christian Social Networking Potential, and thus a targeted market.

While the application of viral marketing might seem out of reach for the average church, I believe that with imagination and a little nudge from our Lord some churches that catch on to the concept will also find a way to apply it to their situation. As a local church, your goal might be to help get information out just to those within your community. I would think that if you started with information, or a video that would be unique to your community, it would help to spread your message to your targeted audience, such as the prospects within your community This could happen, for example, by sending out a humorous video of something or someone that would have only specific appeal to those that live within the community. If it could catch the attention of the people, and spark a desire to share it with friends, your accompanying message could easily—and quickly—saturate your community.

The application of personal communication methods are best used when combined with many of the other computer tools and services shared within this book. Here are a few examples I can think of that would work.

Watch videos on YouTube or GodTube and pick one that is pretty current and entertaining. If you are using something from YouTube, be sure it is appropriate to present to your church. I recently watched a hilarious video on YouTube that focused on the reaction of babies that tasted something they didn't like. The faces they made were very funny, and the way it was put together made it very entertaining. You could send something like this to your membership with a message. For example, you could encourage them to watch the video and make the following remark:.

"Sometimes religion can leave a bad taste in your mouth, sort of like that experienced by the babies in this video! Aren't we glad Christianity is a relationship with a living God, and not a religion which consists of nothing more than a list of rules? Take some time today to remember that 'The Joy of the Lord is My Strength!'"

If you were to send out such an email, I would be consistent about it, and I would inform your membership that these serve as an opportunity for outreach and evangelism. Encourage them to send it to their friends, families and neighbors within the community, and to those they work with. By doing this you'll be taking advantage of viral marketing, and giving your membership the opportunity to help share their faith. By just sending this video to their friends they are helping to convey several important items of information:

▶ They're letting those they send the email to know that they are Christian and attend church;

▶ They're letting people know that their pastor has a sense of humor, because people tend to think church staff are consumed only by religious thoughts;

▶ This will open the door for the person receiving the email to have a contact with the church and pastor, so that during a time of need they will be one step closer to making that first contact; and

▶ Hopefully the initial recipients of the email will also forward it on to their friends with the intent of sharing video.

This is viral marketing, and it makes use of basic "personal communication" tools. In addition, you will always want to include some basic contact information at the end of each email. Don't use these emails, however, to promote a special event, sermon series, or push for funds. Keep them simple, fun and to the point. And by consistently repeating the contact information and time of service you will again be taking advantage of viral marketing skills. HotMail was one of the first that offered free email. And in the beginning they didn't have a lot of money for advertising, so instead they put a fixed footer at the bottom of each email that was sent by their customers stating that the email was sent via their free email service. As you can imagine, word about Hotmail's free service spread quickly because the majority of all those initial emails were sent between people that knew each other, with the consistent advertisement reminder at the bottom of each one.

Of course there are other personal communication tools other than email. If you want to see them in action just hang out with a teenager. A recent friend of mine, a single mom, had a family crisis come up that required her to leave town and spend the night away from home with other family members. She had a 16-year-old son at home, and she figured that he couldn't get into too much trouble staying by himself for one night, especially with such short notice. She informed her son at 5 p.m. that she would be leaving and traveling 100 miles to a relative's house to spend the night. Because of the crisis she felt that taking her son would be detrimental to the situation and that he'd be better off staying at home. After all, it could also serve as an opportunity for the son to show some responsibility, right? At 10 p.m. that same evening she received a call from one of her neighbors with the news that they had been forced to call the police department because there were more than 100 teenagers at her house having a wild party. The mother was quite emotional as she was telling me this story, and venting her frustration at how irresponsible her son had been, Personally, I was amazed at the prowess of his communication skills! In just a few short hours, her son had managed to send out invitations and gather over 100 of his closest friends and acquaintances for the party. And I'm willing to bet that even more were invited but unable to attend on such short notice. How did he do it? Most probably by simply sending out a text message to a few friends, who in turn sent it to a few more friends, etc., etc., etc. He probably didn't intend for so many people to show up, rather he had hoped to have a small party with minimal damage in order to get by without getting caught.

Most people over the age of 50 that decide to have a party with 100 guests would spend weeks, if not months, planning the event. We could safely assume that it would take weeks just to send out the proper invitations and get replies!

It's a new day. New tools are in play, and we need to learn how to use them if we want to get our message out to the masses, in a personal one-to-one way!

DON'T "CHURCH" IT UP

If you decide to try personal communication methods and viral marketing, let me give you a warning: do not "church" it up. The purpose of such a ministry is outreach, and the goal is to simply open a door for future opportunities for ministry. Do not try to send out videos that are preachy. Do not include rotating crosses in the HTML emails, or have hymns playing in the background. When Jesus did outreach, what made him so unique was that he met the people where they were—in the streets. He spoke their language. He could have donned the religious garb of the day as the priests were instructed to do. Instead, he came to seek and save those that were lost. He hit the highways and hedges and left all the religious trappings behind.

SOCIAL NETWORKS

Social networking has established a strong foothold in our society, and one that will undoubtedly continue to grow. Reports have shown that people (not children, not teenagers, but ALL people) that are on the Internet are now spending more time on social networking sites then they are using basic email.

Social networking sites do what their name implies: they help people connect and network. They do this by allowing people to have their own site, or page, where they can display information about themselves and invite others to connect. They can post their thoughts, pictures, videos, favorite movies, favorite songs, etc. They also offer a large number of applications that people can use to enhance their site, or to increase connections with others. People can also start, join and participate in groups centered around a specific topic, subject, belief, organization, school, etc.

Problems, Concerns and Warnings

One of the first popular social networking sites to grab the attention of the media was MySpace. Young people were especially attracted to MySpace because it was free, and because it allowed them to have their own site. Most people cannot afford, or do not have the ability, to create and maintain their own Web site. MySpace provided people their own "space" on the Internet, with plenty of tools to both connect with others, and easily upgrade their own information. And, because it as free young people quickly encouraged others to join and make a connection.

But along with popularity came a few problems, and MySpace began to make the news amid rumors that sexual predators were using the site to connect with young girls and boys. MySpace did require users to be at least 14, but there was no real way to enforce such a requirement and soon the press was issuing warnings that MySpace was not a safe place for young people. Unfortunately, the bad publicity made many Christians jump to criticize the potentially bad aspects of social networking without regard to the possible positive results.

Ever since, social networking has been somewhat of a divisive subject among many Christians. Of course, those with children still at home have a vested interest in seeing that their children are protected from predators and inappropriate materials. And I don't suggest in any way that anyone other than a parent has the right to decide on what procedures they instill in their home to protect their children. It is their right, and their call, to protect their children from harm. That said, I would also suggest that the danger is not as great as some have perceived it to be, and that there are many methods and tools that can be used to protect young people from any potential danger (more on this topic later in this chapter).

I would suggest that social networking sites like MySpace and Facebook offer us a fantastic opportunity to reach out to friends, families, schools, workplaces, and communities to share our faith, as well as make ourselves available to minister to others who are in need. Many churches are setting up groups for their memberships, and many church management software companies are creating applications that allow church groups the ability to network with their databases through Facebook, so there is no valid reason for churches not to encourage their members to use social networking sites as a way to share their faith.

I have been asked many times about my view on social networking. And like I said in the previous paragraph, I uphold the rights of any parent to make the decisions they feel are necessary to protect their children, but my personal opinion is that there are safety methods and tools that any parent can use to keep their children safe while using social networking sites. Therefore, I think the advantages far outweigh the negatives.

Social Networking and Evangelistic and Ministry Opportunities

I remember the story of a wedding Jesus told us about in Luke 14:16-23. First, the man in the story sent an invitation to all of his friends and family, inviting them to honor him and his family by attending an upcoming wedding. He sent the invitations traditionally through his servants, and some of those invited gave the servants excuses as to why they would not come. When his servants came back and told him this, it made him very angry. He instructed his servants to go into the streets and invite the poor, the crippled, lame and blind. His servants did so, and still there was room. So the man told the servants to go outside the walls of the city and invite those out on the highway and the hedges (the country side). He told his servants to "compel" them to come in, that his house may be filled. God wants His house filled!

Did you ever wonder why God didn't seek to compel those within the city, his family and friends, to come to the wedding after they made such poor excuses? I believe it was because they knew better. They had tasted of the man's friendship, they knew his blessings and the way to his house, yet they neglected such a wonderful friendship and an opportunity to attend the upcoming wedding. When he sent his servants out of the city, it was reflective of God opening the door for those of us out in the world, the Gentiles. And, with that there is an extra effort, a "compelling" that he offers in order to get us to come out of the dark, to come in from the highway and hedges, to partake of the joy of the marriage at his house.

Our society has adopted personal communication tools. They have adopted the Internet and all of the new methods of communication that go with it. Communication is taking place. Relationships are being developed, with old ones being restored and new ones being birthed. People are sharing the joy of their lives with others. And, there are those that are hurting, seeking help and comfort. Both groups also have questions, seeking a relationship that is lasting. A "living water" that will end their thirst. The question for us today is, "Will we go into the highways and hedges where they are and try to reach them?"

Social networks have become a new communication tools in themselves. Sites like Facebook and MySpace are an open mission field. Some Christians have stepped forward and begun to use such services as a place to connect with their friends, brothers and sisters in Christ, and as a place to tell their story about their redeemer. They've also given us a sign as to how personal communication tools and services will shape the way we will be able to minister to our members, as well as to our communities.

Walt Wilson said, "It occurs to me that George Orwell, in his classic *1984*, could not have been more wrong as he viewed the future. He saw a world of grey sameness in which people would be reduced to numbers and controlled conformity by worldly authorities. Just the opposite has taken place. The Internet has not only created the market of one, it has developed without central control, and yet has become a very personal way to touch other people and deepen relationships among friends." (page 72, *The Internet Church*)

Yet, while some Christians have openly adapted to emails and Web sites, they find objection to going into the arena of social networking sites, partially because it is a representation of the world. You cannot control all of the advertisements and marketing on your social networking site. In addition, these sites allow for organized groups that are objectionable to many Christians. Of course, this means they also allow for Christian groups to organize and flourish. On the contrary, however, there will also be organized groups that are openly anti-Christian or at least objectionable for many Christians.

Andrew Careaga, in his book, Connecting with the Net Generation—eMinistry, says:

"To reach these online seekers of God and to draw the cyber-church into the fold, the traditional church must do the following three things:

1. *We must enter the world of these cyber-seekers. We must learn about them and from them to understand how they respond to the workings of this new medium;*

2. *We must strive to understand the medium itself and its place and influence in our culture; and*

3. *We must consider how we as the church should respond to the Net's growing influence in society. (pages 23–24)*

There is little doubt—at least at the time of this writing—that Facebook is the social networking site of choice for most people. That doesn't mean, however, that it's the social networking site for most young people, since statistics now show that the demographics of social networking are shifting from youths to more adults. There is also little doubt that social networking has had a major impact and influence on our society. I completely agree with Andrew that if this is where the world is communicating, and that this is where we need to be with our message of hope, peace and love.

MySpace

Let's start by looking at MySpace—the service that made social networking famous. Since they were the first to really grab the attention of many, and grew at a fantastic rate, an examination of their features will be helpful in understanding everything a social networking site can offer.

Social networking sites are all about, well, social networking. Therefore, MySpace has a lot of different ways to help you connect and develop your friends list. If you discover a friend who has a MySpace site, you can send them a friend request. If they accept, you can post information on their site. The same is true of your site; you have control of who gets to be on your friends list, and contribute to your site. Your friends are able to post comments about their day or their mood, and all of it will show up on your site so you can keep track of your friends.

Of course, the easiest way to build your MySpace friends list is to just tell your friends to join it. But there are many other ways to find and add friends to your list.

MySpace works with most of the Instant Messenger programs on the market, such as Windows Live Messenger, Hotmail, AOL, Yahoo!, Gmail and AIM. When you use these programs, your MySpace friends will be able to note it and exchange instant messages with you.

MySpace provides a search feature that allows you to enter a person's name, which then generates a list of MySpace sites that were set up by people with the same name. Unfortunately, if it's a popular name, you'll have a fairly big list of people to go through to find your friend. It may also be a bit harder because some people think it's clever to post a picture of an item or scene rather than an actual picture of themselves (for some reason people love to post a close-up photo of just one of their eyes). As you can imagine, it can be difficult to figure out which site is the one that represents the friend you are seeking!

MySpace gives you the ability to find new friends based on similar interests and associations. It also compares the friends you have with your friends' friends then suggests common connections.

Using several different applications or group searches, you can also connect with old friends from high school or college, and many churches have set up groups that allow you to find friends—old or new—who are in the same congregation as you are.

MySpace also provides an application that allows you to search through your email box and compare the addresses with those that also have a MySpace account. Use this application to find your contacts on MySpace and make a friend request.

Users can post a notice about their status or mood, which is then sent to those that have been approved to be on their friends list. This is part of the social trend that has made sites like MySpace so popular. In the "real world" you may not see or talk to many of your friends on a regular basis. But using a social networking site like MySpace gives you little bits and pieces of information about what is happening in the lives of your friends. Sometimes people share a prayer request, sometimes a praise, sometimes a joke, or sometimes they can end up sharing very trivial information. For some this can be annoying, but it obviously works for most people because social networking is pretty popular! It should be noted that these postings are usually short in size, with a limit to the number of characters that can be sent. This coincides to the applications that are available on many cell phones, which allow users to receive short messages, just like texting (which is normally set at 140 characters), from their friends and family members.

Users can also make posts to their bulletin boards for everyone on their friends list to see, which is more similar to sending all of your friends an email. The major advantage to posting on the bulletin board is that the length of the message can be longer. Each bulletin, however, will disappear in 10 days.

MySpace offers a blog feature, which allows you to post longer articles, thoughts, editorials, etc. You can create blog text in MySpace, or use MS Word and then cut and paste directly into the blog. The blogs also allows visitors to leave comments. If your site is private, only your friends can leave a response. One of the cool features of the MySpace blogs is that it gives you the ability to translate your blog into another language, including:

English	Italian
Albanian	Japanese
Arabic	Korean
Bulgarian	Latvian
Catalan	Lithuanian
Chinese	Maltese
Croatian	Norwegian
Czech	Polish
Danish	Portuguese
Dutch	Romanian
Estonian	Russian
Filipino	Serbian
Finnish	Slovak
French	Slovenian
Galician	Spanish
German	Swedish
Greek	Thai
Hebrew	Turkish
Hindi	Ukrainian
Hungarian	Vietnamese
Indonesian	

Isn't God good? Imagine the ministry opportunities alone that this blog feature offers to ministries and Christian brothers and sisters seeking to communicate to those around the world. And it's FREE! Anyone can come to your blog site and be able to read your message in any of these different languages. This feature is so cool that—I'll be honest with you—I've used the blog translation tool to translate emails I've received in languages I couldn't read. I post them, translate them to English, read them and then delete them. How cool is that?

If you share something in common with others outside of just being friends, you can also set up a group and invite others to join that have the same interest. The group moderator can determine who can join, and can approve or deny requests to join. Each social networking site may have its own distinct advantages—and MySpace may be losing membership to Facebook—it appears to this writer that MySpace still has more groups. I will be discussing some of the Christian groups as well as the frustration of finding Christian groups on MySpace later in this chapter.

In the meantime, MySpace has continued to add more features for their users. They include:

▶ MySpaceIM, which is a stand-alone software for Microsoft Windows that allows users to get instant notifications of new MySpace messages, friend requests, and comments;

▶ MySpacetelevision which is a just-released video sharing Web site similar to YouTube;

▶ Following in the footsteps of Facebook, MySpace has introduced an API which allow users the ability to create applications for other users to post on their profiles;

▶ MySpace offers a variety of mobile applications that work with many of today's cell phones, allowing it to send friend notifications, emails and other information directly to your phone;

▶ MySpace allows users to set their own privacy settings, which controls who can and can't see your information, pictures, comments, etc.; and

▶ MySpace has just launched a host of additional features, including a news service, a place for members to post classified ads, polls, and forums.

MySpace Applications

MySpace has a lot of cool applications, and one of the things I liked best about them is the ability to search for applications based on subject. Many applications add content to your site, such as a quote or scripture, and other apps provide something to do for those visiting your site. Of course, I entered the word "Christian", and here are few of the applications I found of interest:

Are You A Good Christian? WWJD by Quizzes
Ask yourself WWJD? See how good of a Christian you are. YOU HAVE TO ANSWER EVERY QUESTION HONESTLY! (5449 users)

Christian Images by PolarBear
Add Christian image to your profile: Jesus Christ, Blessed Virgin Mary, the Pope, Christianity. (5362 Users)

Famous Christian Quotes by MyChurch.org
Famous Christian Quotes (2428 Users)

Spread Gods Word by Nukem Games
Are you a Christian determined to bring people to the lord. Install and invite all your friends. (3983 Users)

MySpace Groups

As stated earlier, I have found some fantastic groups on MySpace. One evening I became completely engrossed reading posts in Christian discussion groups devoted to young people. It reminded me of my youth and my participation in what has come to be known as the Jesus movement. I found strong Christians helping their weaker brother and sisters, and discovered most of the content to be very sound.

However, the way MySpace is structured it is difficult to find the good groups without being confronted by those with offensive content. I recently wrote an editorial about MySpace and the many different Christian groups that can be found on the site. I encouraged the readers to check them out, and the first feedback response I received via email is below:

> *Say Steve, when did a Christian network sponsor bi-sexuals? You need to study your Bible, and then consider running a "Christian" website. Till then, go somewhere else with this kind of junk! "And many shall come in my name" wow!!!*
>
> PATRICIA (Last name withheld)

Of course, the problem with emails like this is that it left me with a lot of questions. Did they visit our Web site at Christian Computing Magazine and find some content they thought promoted bi-sexual relationships? How did Patricia come to the conclusion that we were "sponsoring" bi-sexuals? It took a couple of follow-up emails, but we finally figured out what happened: Patricia was on our site, read the editorial I'd written about MySpace and followed the links to a couple of the Christian groups that I included in the story. In the process, however, she inadvertently clicked on "groups" within the MySpace menu and was offended by some of the groups listed, including some that supported the homosexual experience.

Even if you went to "groups" on MySpace and got past the long list of possibilities—which does, in fact, include groups under the category of Gay, Lesbian and Bi (with 47,079 different groups)—the category where you find many great Christian groups is called Religion and Beliefs (125,751 groups). When you click on this category you will discover there are many different groups within it that would probably offend most Christians, including groups like:

Universal Masters (Public Group)
Founded Feb 25, 2006 with 40.933 members

Atheist and Agnostic Group, III (Private Group)
Founded June 13, 2004 with 36,899 members

The Pagan Circle (Private Group)
Founded Aug 1, 2004 with 30,277 members

Occult Studies (Private Group)
Founded May 13, 2006 with 30,032 members

For some, I realize that I just validated your belief that Christians shouldn't be on MySpace. The four groups I listed above appeared on the FIRST page of the 125,751 groups under the category of Religion and Beliefs. And if you are uncomfortable or offended by even knowing that such groups exist then maybe you should avoid MySpace all together. However, I feel that MySpace is a true reflection of our society. When I go into a bookstore there are books I would read and recommend even to my children. Yet most bookstores also have books that I would not recommend, and many that I would find rather offensive. The same would be true when visiting a local mall to shop. I have some stores that are my favorites, while there are also some that I find embarrassing when I have to walk past them.

The good news is that there is a GREAT Christian presence on MySpace, and here are a few of the groups that I found—and applaud:

Daily Bible Verse for MySpace (Public Group) 172,976 members
Christianity (Public Group) 107,204 members
Christian Singles (Public Group) 20,011 members

Fellowship of Christian MySpacers (Private Group) 3,620 members
Hume Lake Christian Camp (Public Group) 1,794 members
Christian Latinos (Public Group) 1,208 members
God's Girls (Public Group) 863 members
Pentecostal Christian Youth (Public Group) 809 members
Hawaiian Island Christians (Public Group) 791 members

There are at least 5,000 such Christian groups on MySpace when you do a search using the keyword "Christian". The list goes on and on.

While many of these groups are designed to provide opportunities for Christians to connect, some are designed to share the message of Christ. One of my favorite is a great example of providing a vital ministry, both to Christian members of MySpace as well as to the unchurched. It is called "The Prayer Board", and here is what they post as their introduction to visitors"

"It doesn't matter what you did, what you do or even what you are planning to do. This group is for you. In this group we are all sinners living under the grace of God. So, whether you are a preacher or on the other hand you think you are the greatest sinner, then I'm here to let you know that you are the one Jesus Christ is looking for. The purpose of this group is plain and simple: like the name suggests, it is a prayer board . . . All you need to do is post your prayer request and leave the rest to God . . . Yes . . .!! Its that simple!! . . . When you post or list a prayer request on here it shows that you are giving it up to God. So from the moment you start typing on that computer, God has already heard you and so when you post your request here I want you to leave with a burden lifted OFF your shoulder. Also if you find it hard to find something to pray for . . . just be visiting here regularly to pray for the requests that are posted on here . . . . . Also, if u have anything at all that you wanna share with the group . . . go ahead!! It's your group, so use it to minister the word of God and to encourage others . . .

PHILIPPIANS 4:6 -> Do not be anxious about anything, but in everything, by prayer and petition, with thanksgiving, present your requests to God."

You can find their group by doing a search on MySpace, or by using the link http://groups.myspace.com/prayerboard1

Comments from Christians on MySpace
Here are a few comments that I have received from Christian pastors and laypersons about using MySpace:

Steve ,

I thought you might like to hear from someone who, at 56, is even older than you! The central matter is not MySpace; it is how believers relate to this world. The point might be expressed like this: do we cocoon ourselves and our children in a safe, alternative Christian culture, replacing the worldly rock music, books and television programs that we used to watch before we became Christians, with their "Christian" equivalents; or do we equip ourselves and our children to live in this world as believers? To do that is harder, requiring us to depend on God's grace and the guidance of the Holy Spirit.

Our tendency is to create an alternative world in which we isolate ourselves from the world in which most people live. That is not what I see in scripture; nor is it what I see in the lives of the great saints whose reputation has survived. It is a form of legalism that makes it difficult for us and for our children to relate to those around us. As my own MySpace site (www.myspace.com/cyclingmartin) will I hope suggest, we should never be afraid of being regarded as "fools for Christ". What we should learn to do is what Jesus did—the One who was accused by the most seriously religious people of His day as consorting with sinners, with wine-bibbers and the dregs of society. He was also the one who, because "He Himself has suffered, having been tempted . . .is able to rescue those who have been tempted." (Hebrews 2:18)

I am not advocating that Christians should behave as unbelievers. God forbid it! But I am saying that one should not legislate as to how any individual believer might engage in a discourse with this world so as to reach others for Christ. How we do that is a matter for individual conscience . . .

Martin Adams

Steve,

God bless you, Steve. I am first of all a follower of my Lord Jesus Christ, and then I am a wife, a mother, a grandmother. I am involved with the youth group at my home church and it was through these young people that I was introduced to MySpace. The kids challenged me to get involved and help change the environment there by offering the Word to those who wanted to hear it. I have to say, at first, I was shocked to see some of what is posted there on these young people's pages, but then why should I be? The world is a dark and perverse place and these pages mirror what they are living. So, I, like many concerned parents and youth workers, began to get involved with touching those around me with the love of Christ. I have been blessed to receive many positive responses to these outreaches. I truly believe that we, as caring and concerned Christians, should be out here on the frontlines, giving our youth the support and encouragement they need, for THEY are the ones who will lead this generation to Christ. May God touch your heart and life and bless you abundantly as you go about your daily work.

Pam Balog

Steve,

Oy! How in the world are we supposed to shine Christ's light in a fallen world if we just lock ourselves into our Christian ghettos and refuse to interact with pop culture? I've never understood the "Christians should stay completely apart from the world" mindset, and how that's supposed to work with the Great Commission.

Besides which, MySpace provides an opportunity for Christian fellowship for those of us who like hanging with other Christians seven days a week, rather than simply on the days the church doors happen to be open. And it's a great forum for friendship evangelism. And the music pages belonging to Christian bands probably draw non-Christians as well, at least if the music is any good, because good music will have crossover appeal. I first found MySpace because I heard a Christian song on the radio that I really liked, and did a Google search for the band, and found a link to their MySpace page.

Now, given how many non-Christians listen to CDs by artists with crossover appeal, such as Switchfoot, or Jars of Clay, or Plumb, do we really want to stifle this ministry by ridiculous, legalistic notions like "Christians shouldn't participate in MySpace?" And this doesn't even cover the influence Christian bloggers may be having, or simply individual Christians sharing their viewpoints in the non-Christian groups and forums. How are non-Christians supposed to understand a Christian world view, much less come to value it enough to investigate and seek out the truth of Jesus Christ, if we remain hidden in our safe little Christian coffee-klatches and refuse to mingle with the unsaved?

My take on things is that Christ didn't free us from bondage to sin just for us to put on the legalistic, self-righteous shackles of modern-day Pharisees!

I wouldn't be a Christian today if it weren't for a wonderful woman who believed in reaching out with hands of love to those who didn't share her beliefs. It's called loving your neighbor as yourself. But first, you have to get to KNOW your neighbor!

Evie Delacourt

Steve,

In my opinion, MySpace is a great place for Christian teens. It's a great place to make friends, there are tons of Christians on here, and there are hundreds of Christian blog groups. Being on a Christian blog group has helped me grow in my walk with Christ. If you are a new believer and you are relatively introverted, then MySpace is a great place to meet Christian friends . . .

Kevin Wright

Steve,

I am a 44-year-old pastor and I have a MySpace account. My teen-aged sons put me onto it a couple of months ago. I blog about twice a week, and regularly interact with youth in my congregation and others through this site. I also have a personal Web site through Yahoo. But the MySpace site requires a greater willingness to be vulnerable and personable. MySpacers seems to be much more interested in authenticity than in a slick site. So that's what I strive to do. I probably share more of my struggles and challenges than many in my congregation would prefer (of course I already do that through my preaching ;), but there is an accountability and a freedom in that. MySpace helps us connect with people, not just look like a good little Christian with them, but truly connect with them. MySpace has a lot of critics, and rightly so. But it also it a great tool for sharing authentic Christianity with those who use it.

Brian Hawes

Facebook

While MySpace was certainly one of the first names in social networking to catch the public's eye, Facebook is fast becoming the social networking site of choice. It offers many of the same features as MySpace, but goes about things a bit differently. Let's begin our exploration of Facebook by taking a look at some of its features.

Like MySpace, in order to encourage communication and help keep your friends up to date on your life, Facebook offers the ability to post a short note about yourself, which can then be seen by friends. You can also post links, photos, videos, other attachments, or use a host of various applications to post additional information about yourself.

To make it easy to view all this information, Facebook created what they call "The Wall," which is basically "information central." This is where friends can post comments to your site, and where your comments or other posts first appear. Basically, any action you take on Facebook appears on this "Wall," and much of the information appears in the form of short posts. You can respond to a post on your wall, as can other friends, and create a short discussion list under each post. If you need to send a more in-depth message you can use the inbox mail service to send a message, which is much like standard email.

As I mentioned previously, you can also post attachments to the "Wall." Attachments can certainly improve communication, and allows your or your friends to suggest links to view a picture, read a PDF article, or view a video. Of course, it's good to remember that attachments present some degree of security issues, just as they would when receiving attached files in an email.

You can add photos to your Facebook site and easily tag them and add comments. Tagging a photo allows you or your friends to identify a person in any photo by name. Multiple people can be tagged in one photo, and if someone posts a photo of you on their site and it is tagged, Facebook will send you a message to tell you you've been "tagged." According to Facebook, posting photos is quite popular, with over 1.7 billion user photos and 2.2 billion friends tagged in user photos. On any given week, there are more than 60 million photos added to Facebook.

Facebook also has basic blogging services called Notes, which allows you to post an article, and users to post comments to articles. You can include photos with your blogs, and you can import blogs from services such as Xanga, LiveJournal, Blogger and others.

Facebook allows users to use different features to make a connection, some of which can be used to contact connections you haven't heard from in a while. For example, you can send a "Poke" as a way of getting someone's attention. When first introduced, the Facebook Poke was a feature without any specific purpose. However, users now use it to send a virtual "nudge" to someone they are awaiting an answer or comment from, or just to say a quick hello.

Facebook also offers users a Marketplace to post free classified ads. At present, the Marketplace is free and ads can be posted under the headings "Housing," "Jobs," "For Sale" and "Other."

Facebook now allows the ability to add events, and users can set it up to include the event name, network, host name, event type, start and end times, location and a guest list of friends invited. You can also make the event open, closed or secret.

Naturally, Facebook has "Groups," and much like groups anywhere else users can start special Facebook sites that people with similar interests can join. Group sites allow users to post questions, comments, blog, post photos and promote events. I personally belong to several groups and have noticed an increased number of ministries and para-church organizations setting up groups on Facebook. Additionally, Facebook has realized the marketing potential of their site and are adding new features to enable companies to set up various marketing groups. To help this out, they recently eliminated the 5,000-friends limit that existed since day one of operation.

With video being one of the most important and popular mediums of our day, Facebook has added some great features to allow their members to create and post videos. If you have a camera and microphone on your computer, you can simply click the video icon at the bottom of your Facebook site and record and post videos. Just like photos, you can tag your videos with information about friends, too. Facebook also has plenty of applications ready to help you upload and post videos created from your cell phones, and you can record and post videos up to 20 minutes in length. Needless to say, this is a GREAT connection video tool, and there will be more about using video later in the book.

Sometimes you might want to text someone directly while in Facebook. As you can imagine, Facebook makes this a very easy task by using their live Chat feature. You'll find the chat icon at the bottom right of your screen. Clicking on it will open a new window with a list of your Facebook friends who are currently online (obviously you can't chat with people who are not currently online!). Click on your desired person to contact and a pop-up window will appear on their screen with a place to view your message, as well as type replies. Posted profile pictures also show up, so that users don't forget who they're chatting with, right next to the last status comment posted by that particular user.

Facebook Applications

Facebook provides an excellent list of applications for users to try, all sorted under the following categories:

- ▶ Business
- ▶ Education
- ▶ Entertainment
- ▶ Friends & Family
- ▶ Games
- ▶ Just for Fun
- ▶ Lifestyle
- ▶ Sports
- ▶ Utilities

As you peruse the list of Facebook applications, you'll notice that each one provides you with a rating. This is not based upon usage, but rather a vote by those that have used the application. They use a five-star rating system, with five stars being the best. They also provide you with the number of Facebook users currently using the application. Something else they also that I find informative is they list the number of your friends that are using the application, if any.

You can also search for applications, and doing a search for "Christian" applications typically brings up the following results:

Christian Greetings—3-star rating
Send Christian greetings to encourage and uplift your friends
and family. Spread the word of God through Facebook! 42,858
monthly active users—9 friends

Old Fashioned Christian Sunday School Songs—3.5-star rating
See how many of your favorite childhood Sunday School songs
you can remember. 30,825 monthly active users—4 friends

Christian Photos—5-star rating
Send a collection of wonderful Christian photos to all your family,
church members and friends. Christian photos make us connect
with each other in heavenly way, give to you hope and make your
page shine with holiness. 10,942 monthly active users—1 friend

Which Bible Character are You?—2.5-star rating
Take this fun quiz and find out which Old Testament Bible
character your personality most likely matches.127,002 monthly
active users—17 friends

Christian Connections—2.5-star rating
Give gifts from the heart of Christianity. Whether they are for
a special holiday or a special friend. Help the world to be more
Christian through the gifts they give and receive. 6,098 monthly
active users—1 friend

Daily Bible Verse by MuChurch.org—4-star rating
Display a new Bible verse on your profile every day. Save your
favorite verses and send encouraging verses to your friends. 115,842
monthly active users—19 friends

Christian Icons—3-star rating
Send icons to your friends of God, Heavenly Angels and Saints!
1,508 monthly active users

Sweet Christian Gifts—3.5-star rating
Send Christian gifts to your friends.11,542 monthly active
users—1 friend

Famous Christian Quotes by Mychurch.org—4.5-star rating
Get quotes from famous Christian leaders on your profile. Be
inspired by great preachers and thinkers like Billy Graham,

St. Francis of Assisi, Mother Teresa, Rick Warren, Martin Luther, and others. 1,539 monthly active users—1 friend

Which Mighty Woman of the Bible are You Most Like? —4-star rating
Find out which mighty woman of God you are most like in the Bible by taking a short quiz. 130,967 monthly active users—15 friends

EBible by Greek Bible Study—4.5-star rating
With Bible you can read with your friends, share notes, accelerate your spiritual growth; KJV, NASB, ESV, Greek, Notes. 6,411 monthly active users—3 friends

Daily Bible Scripture
Daily Scripture and verses displayed on your Facebook profile. You can choose from many different translations to suit your beliefs. Add your verse today! 41,444 monthly active users—9 friends

My Church by MyChurch.org—3-star rating
Connect with your church on Facebook, between Sundays. 35,165 monthly active users—28 friends

The Bible—4.5-star rating
Complete Text of the Bible (ESV, NIV, WEB, KJV, MKJ, GRK, RST). Best full text search by word stems. Send list of select verses to your friends. 1,918 monthly active users—3 friends

Send Bible Blessings—5-star rating
Send gifts to your friends that are related to Jesus Christ and the Bible. Encourage them and share your faith at the same time! Some are serious, some are silly—because Christians have fun too! 237 monthly active users

One Year Bible Online by Thunder Software—5-star rating
Welcome to OneYearBibleOnline.com, an online guild for those desiring to read through the Bible in one year. Each day's 15-minute reading takes you thru passages from the Old Testament, New Testament, Psalms and Proverbs. 1,155 monthly active users—3 friends

Church by LifeChurch.tv—3.5-star rating
Church is an app that allows you to be part of an online church community inside of Facebook. It was created by and is connected to LifeChurch.tv104 monthly active users—4 friends

These are just a few of the more interesting applications I found on Facebook. If you read through the list, you can certainly see the fantastic opportunities for ministry. There were several churches that had applications that I didn't list, and I know that more are coming. I recently had the privilege to view a Facebook application that will soon become available that works in conjunction with a Church Management Software's (CMS) membership directory (ACS's Facebook application is mentioned later in the book). While many CMS companies provide a way to allow members online access to membership directories, they also realize that more and more churches are wanting to be where they know their members are already located—places like Facebook, and other social networking sites. With this new application, members can request access after installing the software, and the moderator for the application can approve them to allow the ability to see a list of all current church members, which may include photos, contact information, and a note on whether or not they belong to Facebook. As you go through the list and see people you know that are on Facebook but not currently on your friends list, it will be a simple matter to send an invite so you can then share all of the connection tools Facebook provides.

Also, you'll notice in the applications above the ability to have a group Bible study, and encourage your fellow Christians with a specific verse of the day, as well as the option to offer visitors to your site the ability to search the entire Bible.

Facebook Groups

When I searched the word "Christian" on Facebook groups, it returned a list of around 500. Here are some that I found that were either very popular, or very interesting. You'll see that some of the member numbers are actually pretty impressive:

I'm a Christian . . . And I'm Proud To Say It!!! 531,507 members
This site is set up by the Campus Crusade for Christ International. When you join the group you will be presented with a short message about why you need Christ and how to accept him. You are then given a link to one of their sites that provides more detailed information on how to accept Christ, as well as links to other articles that are seeker friendly.

Obviously this is a great evangelism tool. You could simply send an invite to anyone of your friends that may not be a Christian. The title of group should hopefully be a brief testimony in itself, and if they decide to accept the invite from you to join they will be presented with the information on how to become a Christian. If you were using Facebook to cultivate a relationship in order to share your testimony and your faith, then including an invite to this group would be a fantastic follow up!

100,000,000 Christians Worship God! 985,252 members
This is probably one of the biggest Christian groups on Facebook. As a result they give disclaimers to warn that when you visit their discussion groups, there will be some non-Christians that have joined the group. Some have come because they are seekers, while others have joined to fight and cause conflict.

This group was featured on CBN News (http://www.cbn.com/CBNnews/364791.aspx)

6 Degrees of Fellowship—The Christian Experiment
276,755 members
This group is one of several that are simply looking to show that there are many Christians using Facebook. Its purpose seems to be the encouragement of Christians to join in order to achieve a high number.

While it doesn't appear that this site has discussion boards, you can scroll through its membership list and click on any one of the many Christians' profiles. Group members have also made some 4,000 posts to the group's "wall" with various links to Christian sites, words of encouragement, etc.

Christian 6,034 members
This group provides discussion boards and posted articles, and includes topics like:

Commentary on the Sermon on the Mount
The Modern Day Christian Standing
Beware of the new world order
How to treat others
The Power of prayer

Largest Christian Facebook Group Ever 39,266 members
This is obviously not the largest Christian Facebook ever, but I liked the participation from its members. They have some interesting discussion topics, and I noticed that they seem to generate

more responses to discussion questions and comments than other sites. Some of the topics include:

Creation "Science" really?
Biblical Contradictions?
A Cry for Help . . . I need a Christian influence to help me
When the dead rise . . .
Deceptive teachings

Christian Girls are More Beautiful Because . . . 36,061 members
Who can argue with this? (not me!!)

This group also has some fantastic discussions going on in their group, including:

The Battle for your Generation
Atheism and Theology
7 Reasons for Singles to Wait for Sex
Tattoos
Baptism
Which denomination has the most beautiful girls?

This last one had some interesting posts!

And the list goes on. It is very encouraging to go through the list of Christian groups on Facebook. Among the many more groups are the Christian Aggies, comprised of Christians who went to Texas A&M (7,933 members), and the Christian Syrians (1,689 members). There's also a group for people interested in Christian games (1,972 members) and a site group for those interested in Christian Filmmakers (1,363 members). In doing research for this book I discovered an old friend, Bill Rayborn, who had a group set up for Christian Music with 1,572 members. I was also very surprised to discover that someone had set up a group for *Christian Computing Magazine* readers! They only had 25 members, and the most common post was "how do we find Steve Hewitt's profile among all of the other Steve Hewitt's on Facebook!" But I was pleasantly surprised to learn about the group and have since joined it and introduced myself to its members.

I must say, though, that there are things I like about the way Facebook manages their groups, like the fact that when I click on the group icon I am presented with a list of the other groups I have joined, as well a list of other groups that my friends have joined. Additionally, when you visit a group's site you are presented with a list of other groups that Facebook thinks you might be interested in based on the subject of the group you are visiting.

What I don't like about Facebook's group feature is that its difficult to sort the lists of groups. An upgrade would be the ability to search the groups based on group size, or to see which groups are the newest to Facebook.

It should be obvious from the applications and the groups, as well as the basic features that Facebook provides, that Christians can easily expand their ministry. I expect more and more churches will use Facebook for their pictorial directory and online membership directory, or set themselves up as a private group, and connect it to their Church Management Software database. I hope that over time more churches will become involved in using Facebook as an evangelistic tool, and encourage their members to share their testimony and faith on their Facebook site.

Privacy Concerns with Facebook

Facebook raised a few eyebrows recently regarding privacy issues due to a change in its user license agreement. The old user license agreement stated that Facebook would remove all of your personal information from its servers upon the closing of your account. Unfortunately, Facebook itself realized that this wasn't entirely true. For example, if you had posted a reply to a discussion on a friends' site and then removed your site from Facebook, your post would still remain. The same was true with every tagged photo, or every comment made in a discussion. Facebook realized that if all of these were removed when people deleted their sites then it would leave a lot of holes in a lot of places. For example, what if someone had responded to your comment on someone else's site? If Facebook removed your comments then it would make the response seem out-of-place or inappropriate. To remedy this, Facebook changed its user license agreement and removed the part about completely deleting a user's data when they closed their site. This upset many people as many feared that in some way their content was being stored and retained by Facebook. However, Facebook has since reworded its user license agreement to explain what happens when you delete your data and leave Facebook. Hopefully, this has quelled the fears of privacy experts.

HOW CAN I PROTECT MY CHILDREN ON SOCIAL NETWORKING SITES?

There are several ways to protect your children from the dangers they might encounter while using social networking sites. You will want to protect them from things like inappropriate content, cyberbullying, communication with strangers that might be predators, and you will want to prevent them from communicating or posting personal contact information or other confidential information that might hurt them if it fell into the wrong hands.

First and foremost, have your own account and insist that your child accept you as a friend on their site. This will allow you to see their posts, as well -as allow you to visit their site and view the comments posted by their friends. I would also spend time with them on the computer and on the social networking sites. Discuss with your children the importance of what they post, and show them that some colleges are now checking out prospective students by doing a search of social networking sites to see what is posted. In such cases, if a prospective student's site is full of complaints about parents and school, and hints of living on the wild side, this will affect their admissions into college. Of course, this advice is for children (teenagers) that are still living at home with you. You will have little impact in what your children post once they have moved out on their own.

Covenant Eyes

Covenant Eyes is a Christian company that provides both an accountability and filtering service. Their software has the ability to view a page and give it a rating based on the content and level of offensive materials. Covenant Eyes' dynamic scoring system provides context-based analysis of every URL, giving a parent a virtual "over-the-shoulder" look at a person's use of the Internet, and the optional filter provides an extra level of protection with Covenant Eyes' unique age-based sensitivity level filter setting. So, Covenant Eyes has a scoring system for both MySpace and Facebook. If a new person asks to be a friend with your child, and your child then goes to the new friend's page, Covenant Eyes will see it and judge it before your child gets there, and if the content is rated as offensive it will be blocked.

Parental Monitoring Software Program

While insisting on being your child's "friend" and being active on the same social networking sites is wise, as well as using programs like Covenant Eyes to screen and filter content, there is one more line of defense I encourage parents to use if their children are still living at home and accessing a computer. Being a friend on your child's site does not allow you to read email correspondence between your child and others, which means that a predator or other unwanted party could make connections with your child through email without your knowledge. You're also not able to monitor conversations in chats. Remember, predators are more apt to use such forms of communication because their comments are not posted and permanent.

In addition—although it is rare—parents sometimes wish to direct their children to break contact with an unhealthy friend. This is especially true for younger teens seeking to create boyfriend/girlfriend relationships before their time.

Don't despair, there are some great solutions. There are many parenting monitoring software programs on the market that can provide some real peace of mind. And while there are many products on the market that might accomplish this goal, there is one in particular from a trusted name with many exceptional features. McAfee Family Protection sells for around $40, and provides an incredible list of features that will allow any parent to retain control of their family's computer and provide monitoring and accountability for young people living in the house and using the computer. WebWatcher is another popular and highly-rated program, but the cost is a bit higher at around $97. Other products on the market include eBlaster for around $100, Spector Pro for around $100, Spy Agent for around $70, ContentProtect for $40, Guardian Monitor for $40, IamBigBrother for $30, NetNanny for $30 and CyberSitter for about $35.

If you're a parent, I would suggest you use one of these products on every computer in your house, whether it's your personal computer or one you have gifted to an older teenager. If they live under your roof, you are still charged with keeping them safe and providing accountability.

Programs like these vary a little in function and features, but most provide complete protection for your children from all inappropriate content, social networking risks, and more, and they do this by monitoring and reporting everything that happens on your computers.

Below is a list of features common to these programs for you to become familiar with. It's best pay attention to the specific features of each program. In picking a product that works for you, you should also consider the age of your children. As for the features, note that some of these programs do not provide a "white list" of Web sites that you are allowed to visit, while others allow you to visit any site except those that would be "black listed" as inappropriate. Some of them provide great monitoring but do not block any specific Web site. Some are designed with tools that are appropriate for younger children, but are probably not needed for teenagers, such as specific "white lists" of approved email addresses that only allow emails to go to and from those on this list—a good idea for young children but probably too much protection for teenagers.

Here are a list and description of many of the features these programs have to offer. Become aware of what features you desire, and then look at the programs featured above to find the right product for your needs. Don't assume the cheapest product is the best. Remember, sometimes you get what you pay for!

Website Blocking—Programs that block Web sites normally have different settings that let you determine the level of filtering. By providing different levels of filtering you can better customize the program to meet the needs of your family, and/or the age of your children.

Program Blocking—If you allow your children or teenagers to access the family computer, look for the ability to block specific programs or applications from running on your computer if your children are online. Once set up, each family member will be required to log into the computer using their own username and password. For example, you may want to use a banking program on your computer but don't want your children to have access to the data, or the opportunity to accidently corrupt its files. You can now set the access availability for each program based on who is using the computer. You can also set the time-out feature, which determines how long your computer can stay inactive before it resets itself and requires a new log in to verify the user.

Email Blocking—This feature is probably more important for children than teenagers, but all of these features can be adjusted or turned off based on the age of the children or teenagers you are seeking to protect. For children, you can set up a list of approved email addresses they can communicate with, eliminating the fear that someone unknown will be sending your child unwanted emails.

Keystroke Logging—This is where you get into the power of really providing protection for your children in the areas of social networking sites like MySpace or Facebook. Basically when the program is running—and if you have set it up to require a username and password as each person logs in—keystroke logging will record every keystroke that is typed as your young person is using the computer. It then makes the captured text available to you whenever you want, giving you the ability to check if your young person is keeping the boundaries you have set regarding what they are allowed to share, or who they are allowed to talk to. Some of these programs will save the information to a private file for you to check when you are able. Others can send the private file each day to your email address, allowing you the ability to do off-site monitoring of what is being typed on your computer while you are at work or on another computer in the same house.

Screen Shot Capturing—So, you're now monitoring your young person's keystrokes, but what about what they are reading, or what's being sent to them from others using a chat window or IM? Most programs allow for screen shot captures, which are like snapshots that are taken and stored that allow you to see exactly what your young person is looking at. Obviously, it would be easy to fill up a hard drive with these screen captures if they are being taken constantly, but some of these programs allow you to set a timer to take screen shots at specific intervals. Others like WebWatcher, for example, watches for inappropriate words or content to appear and takes screen shots accordingly. This means less unnecessary pictures, and less time for parents to spend monitoring the activity.

Online Storage and Reporting—Some of the programs store keystroke logging and screen shots in private files for parents to access at a later date. Others can send you the information to your personal email address at a specific time each day. Still others allow you to set up an account online which lets you view and monitor the information from any computer—at home, at work, or some other place. The additional advantage of online storage and reporting is that the data cannot be tampered with or destroyed. For example, if a child is aware that they are being monitored (I address this later) they may be tempted to erase your hard drive or crash your computer in order to destroy the evidence. With online storage and reporting the evidence is no longer on your computer and cannot be destroyed.

Time Limits—Most parent monitoring software programs allow for time limits. Once again, these work because each family member must log in with their own username and password before they can use the computer. These programs can set up limits two ways: first, you can set specific times that your children or teenagers can access the computer. If you set the deadline at 9 p.m. on a school night the program simply doesn't allow access past that time. The programs I have seen that offer this feature provide a warning in advance, usually some a sort of countdown, so that they can finish what they are doing and have time to save their work. Second, these programs can be set up to limit the amount of time each person is allowed to use the computer. This will stop your child from being obsessed with being online and spending too much time in front of the computer. If you allow them one or two hours a day, they can use the time either after school, or some other time. But after the allotted time is used, they simply won't be allowed back onto the computer until the next day.

Instant Alerts—Some programs have the ability to note if inappropriate materials have been viewed, or restricted information has been typed, and they will send an instant alert to the parents, normally via email or text message. This allows you to react quickly to resolve a problem.

But I Trust My Children

Some parents react to my suggestion to use monitoring software with the statement, "But I trust my children." or "I don't want my children to think I don't trust them!" This has nothing to do with trust, and everything to do with accountability and protecting your children from the bad apples of the world. I respond to parents by asking the questions, "Does your child know everything you know? Does he/she have your wisdom and experience?" Of course the answer is no. That is why you need to install and use monitoring software. Children, especially teenagers, THINK they know everything they need to know about making important decisions for themselves. The reality, however, is that they are still living under your roof, and they don't know everything that they need to know. As parents, it is our right and duty to protect them.

Most of these programs are designed to be installed and run in the background, allowing parents the ability to monitor their young people without their knowledge. They don't want to deal with their young person's rants about "why don't you trust me?" I, on the other hand, have always held that in a good parent/child relationship it should be clear that subjects like monitoring have nothing to do with trust, but rather with parental responsibility. My boys are now grown and out of the house. But when my youngest was living with me, many of these parental monitoring programs were just hitting the market. I used them, and I informed my son that they were on our computers. I trusted that he would not misuse the computer, but I also helped ease his temptations by making it clear that God wasn't the only one watching his online activities—his earthly father was too!

I'M STILL NOT CONVINCED ABOUT SOCIAL NETWORKING

If you are still cautious about using social networking sites like MySpace and Facebook, it is certainly your choice. It should ease your mind that there are several Christian alternatives—sites that have many of the same features as both MySpace and Facebook but are designed for the Christian user. I will list several below and provide a brief overview of each. Please note, however, that after evaluating these sites, in most cases they can pose a greater danger to your child that the non-Christian social networking sites simply because they lack basic security features.

SOCIAL NETWORKING ON MYCHURCH (WWW.MYCHURCH.ORG)

Before I begin to share information about social networking sites designed for Christian individuals, let me first share about an exciting unique social networking site designed for churches!

MyChurch.org was created by Joe Suh as a ministry for his own church. He wanted to combine many of the tools his church was using, such as blogging, Yahoo groups, iTunes for podcasts, Evite for their events, and social networking tools to help their congregation stay connected. The result was the launch of MyChurch.org.

At present, over 30,000 churches have set up a MyChurch site, which allows church members the opportunity to network, read blogs and post comments, etc. One of the most exciting applications on MyChurch, however, has got to be its great, searchable directory of active churches, that allows those seeking a new church to opportunity to browse and search the entire list. Just moved to a new town? No problem … do a search for your town's zip code and you will be presented with a fairly accurate listing of all of the churches in your area. Some of those listed may not have a site set up on MyChurch, but if they do you will have access to a wealth of information about those particular churches, and may even decide one of them fits your criteria for a first visit.

If you're already using Facebook, you have noticed that MyChurch now has an application that can connect your church members using Facebook with the information posted on the church's MyChurch site. To take advantage of this connection, users must first find and join their church on MyChurch (you can do this from the application on Facebook and entering your church's information). Once you have the application working, you can post prayer requests, announcements, offer something on the classifieds boards, or discuss church content. Anything you post or comment on gets published back to your Facebook wall, and from Facebook you will also be able to see a window displaying the names and faces of the members of your church that are on Facebook and also connected to MyChurch.org.

CHRISTIAN ALTERNATIVES FOR SOCIAL NETWORKING

There are many Christians, especially those with children or teenagers in their home, that are not comfortable using secular social networks. As a result, many social networks have entered the marketplace that seek to provide many of the same services as Facebook and other social networking sites, but without the connection to advertisements that might be offensive, and with a content theme centered around Christianity. Many of these sites are also devoid of the groups and associations that they might find offensive on other secular sites.

As the list of social networking sites continues to grow, so does the list of Christian alternative sites. Currently, there are many to choose from, but here are a few that would be worth checking out:

Christian.com—This site offers individual profiles with connections to friends that you can add to your community.

Some of its features include Instant Messaging between members, and a prayer board that is set up similar to many Internet message boards. When I checked it out, there were 5,545 different requests up on the board, each one with a message listed under a person's name. If you click one of the name, you are taken to the person's profile that helps you get to know the person you are praying for. You can also request a reply, as well as view answered prayers, which is always exciting. You can also blog, find people, join groups, post questions or comments in forums, and post and view videos and podcasts. They also have section devoted exclusively for singles.

FaithFreaks.com—I think it's obvious from the title that this site is seeking to reach young people. While social networking certainly started with our youth, there are more adults using sites like Facebook than teenagers. Nonetheless, I found the "Take a tour" video to be especially loud and geared toward the younger audiences.

One of the things I found unique on FaithFreaks is the different categories presented when you set up an account. You can set one up as a person, a musician, a ministry, a church or a college. They offer most of the same features that you would expect on any other social networking site, like setting up a profile, composing email, sending friend requests, view all of your friends or only those online at the same time you are, check out their status, note birthdays, etc. They seem to encourage churches and youth groups to set up a page as well, and their search engine for groups has the ability to find groups based on a geographical distance from where you are located. For example, if you wanted to find a youth group, you could enter an email and find those within a certain distance from your zip code. This is certainly different from the "group" concept in most other social networking sites, where groups are made up of members using the social networking service and do not represent a physical gathering, per se.

The site also offers forums for discussions, a place to post prayers and the opportunity to post videos and music.

JCFaith.com—This site also offers many of the same features as most other social networking sites do, including blogs, comment posting, forums and discussion boards, and various tools and groups. Their video section, however, is different in that you don't actually post videos on their service. You actually post them on

YouTube and then provide the link that makes them available on the JCFaith site. Something else a bit unique about this site are the forms they set up to allow you to search their membership. You can select from a list of jobs, religious denominations, and dating status (dating, divorced, engaged, in love, looking, married and single). I wondered what you would do if you wanted to find someone who was married but also in love, since they were separate items and you could only select one. They also offered a gallery of pictures that I am assuming were uploaded by users. They were pictures of people without a lot of tags, and the day I checked the gallery it featured pictures that included two dogs tagged as "bo and duke my dogs" and a picture of two young teen girls simply tagged as "me and Emily". You could click on the picture and leave a comment. Most of the pictures were of young girls, and some of the tags simply stated "me".

The reason I mention this feature is because I believe it unfortunately opened the site up to prowlers. Basically at any time a person on the site could take a photo and have it posted to this open picture forum. It was easy to click on any of the pictures and follow the links back to their profile site. The day I checked their site, most of the pictures took me directly to the users profile page (only a few were set on "private", preventing me from accessing their profile page). This meant that I could click on public pictures of young people and then check out their profiles without ever being a registered user. If I was a sexual predator, this provided me greater access to the profiles sites of young girls and boys that I have ever seen on social networking sites such as Facebook or Myspace!

myPraize.com—This is another Christian social networking site that seems geared toward younger users, although they did have discussion forums, including one titled, "I'm no spring chicken," that apparently was for older adults. However, forums such are "music" seem popular and geared a bit more toward the younger crowd. Even though I was not a member I was able to read messages and replies on the discussion boards, view videos (again, actually streamed from YouTube), and I found it easy to follow links to view profiles. In the area of groups, they had many topics such as "Hobbies" where I found groups in support of specific Christian bands, those that love skating, girls that love shopping, etc. Their "Christian Church" groups included a "Jesus Roks" group that had more than 200 members and was one of the largest groups I found. At the bottom of the page I found a link to a blog feature, but frankly found it to be very similar to a discussion board.

YourChristianSpace.com—This site offered a clean interface with some good marketing on the home page, telling me right up front what they offer. They have detailed searchable profiles with photos, private messaging, online journals, personal message boards and blogs, birthday reminders, music videos, groups, events and listings. They had the ability to do a "browse" of their membership for people that fit certain criteria. I found their lists to be very similar to those I have seen on some dating sites. For example, if you were searching for someone to be a new friend, you could set the search criteria to look at how often they go to church (sometimes, on holidays, every Sunday, or never), if they smoked (trying to quit, yes, rarely), or if their drinking habits (no, socially, sometimes, or yes). Religious denomination was also a searchable criteria, and one that you would expect to find on this site. Something new to me was the ability to search for someone based on the year they were born again, which I'm guessing was added as a way to determine spiritual maturity.

I found it interesting that while they had some good use of ads, and most were Christian in nature, they also had signed up for GoogleAds and were promoting MySpace.com on the site.

ShoutLife.com—This site, like all of the others, offers the ability for users to set up a profile and communicate with friends through posts, IM and chat. With this site there seemed to be a unique connection to Christian comedy persons and groups. Viewing the profile pages had a fresh look, allowing a "shoutlife music player" application which gives visitors the opportunity to pick songs from a persons' list of favorites. The option to search for people was similar to Facebook in that you weren't searching for a "type" of person, but rather a specific friend, using their name, email address, etc. The site's groups are also a collection of people who meet within the service, not a promotion of physical groups located geographically. They seemed to have a good selection of groups, including many church and Christian related groups.

Xianz.com—This site seems to be pretty mature. First of all, I noticed that the video features contained videos that were actually uploaded to the site from users, and not steaming from YouTube.

And, I must say, this site seemed to have better protection than most of the Christian sites I visited. Because I was not a member I couldn't access their group list, events, forums, do a search for members, send a message, or most of anything else. But they seemed to be pretty feature heavy. Every time I clicked on any of the features I was redirected to a window that let me know the feature was restricted to registered users. I commend them for setting up the site this way. They *should* require people to register before allowing access to member groups, forums, profiles, etc., as a first line of defense to protect users from predators. However, the site did post something they called the latest "shout outs" in Xianz land (a reference to the name of their service.). The visible posts included pictures that I could click on, one of which belonged to a young lady with the nick-name of "flirty." I was taken immediately to her page, but I couldn't send her a message unless I was willing to open an account and log into the site. They have left a very serious security hole in their system. An unregistered visitor should NEVER be able to view the profile pages of young people!

www.faithout.com—In banner ads, Faithout.com claims to be a Facebook alternative for Christians. They help connect users with other members of your church, ministry, region, school or workplace, and feature the basic social networking tools. You can upload photos, publish notes and comments, allow people to join your site as a friend and then have their information post to your site, post videos, tag your friends, etc. They also have privacy settings that can limit the who sees your information, and how much if of it they can see, and they also encourage the creation of groups they label as fellowships. If someone sets up a fellowship for your region, school, church, etc., by joining specific fellow-ships, it will connect you with people with the same interest.

There are many other Christian sites popping up all the time, and I am sure by the time you read this book there will be many more. Here is a short list of additional Christian social network-ing sites I have found recently:

http://jesuscrowd.com
http://christianster.com
http://www.livekite.com
http://dittytalk.com
http://www.holypal.com

http://www.lifespace.cc/
http://www.faithlight.com
http://circlebuilder.com
http://www.voolos.com
http://www.whatusow.com

http://www.meetfish.com
http://www.gloryLane.com
http://www.JCPeople.com
http://www.mychristiannation.com

As you can see, social networking sites for Christians has taken off, and I am sure there are many other sites either already on the market, or ready to be released. I applaud the work each has done and I believe their intent is honorable. However, I am a bit worried as I browse through some of the Christian social networking sites because many of them seem to have less security than either Facebook or MySpace. If parents are assuming that their children are safe because they are not using Facebook, but instead are on a Christian social networking site, I think they need to take a closer look.

Warning to Parents

If the purpose of allowing your children to use a Christian social networking site instead of Facebook is for security, you need to give this some thought. On many of the sites I visited, I found less security than on Facebook. For example, in Facebook you can do a search for friends, but you are not able to view anyone's profile unless you log in and register. I found that I was able to find links and view profiles of members on many of the Christian social networking sites.

As I stated earlier, if you have young people still at home using social networking sites—Christian or otherwise—you need to insist that they set their site to private. This means that only their friends can see their information, posts, pictures, etc. If it is set to public then anyone can browse and find their site and all its posted information.

I was actually a bit shocked to find a couple of the Christian social networking sites encouraging their members to post pictures that appear in a gallery open for anyone to view—including unregistered guests! On one site I was amazed at page after page of pictures of young teenager girls, ranging in age from 12 to 15. I could click on any of the pictures and see who posted it (in most cases it was the girls in the pictures). I could also click on their name and go to their profile. In two out of four cases, these profiles were public and I could view their names, cities and states where they lived, along with any other posted information on their profile.

On one site you didn't even have to select the "gallery" to see pictures, as they were posted out in the open in one section of the home page. This same site also included the URL for the posting of the picture, so I could easily put that link within any other home page and pull the picture from their server.

After clicking on the picture in the public gallery of one young girl, I was taken to her profile. I found out she is 14 and lives in Los Angeles, California. She posted, "I've been living life for 14 years . . . and I love going to the beach and having fun with my friends. I've got brown eyes and I love to laugh, be crazy and have fun dancing at parties." She also posted some comments that I am unwilling to use in this book because the language is questionable for a Christian publication.

Honestly, if I was a predator I would find access to the innocent much easier on some of these Christian sites than on Facebook. Because Facebook and MySpace have been criticized in the public media they have instituted quick response services to take action if someone complains about harassment or cyberbullying. On one of the Christian sites, I read a blog (once again as a non-member) of a young 13-year-old girl that was very vulnerable. She had felt she had been bullied on the site and was crying out in anger. There were no replies or comments to her post and, once again, I could click on her link and go straight to her profile and find out the city and state where she lived, what she liked to do, and where she like to hang out.

Again, I think there are advantages to Christian social networking sites, but if parents are feeling safer about their children using such sites instead of Facebook, I want to issue this warning: make sure you have an account on the same service and have friend access to your child's account. I would then feel just as compelled to use one of the parent monitoring software programs I suggested earlier, as they are just as needed if your child is on a Christian social networking site as they are if they are using Facebook or MySpace. And please, if they are under your roof, insist that their profile be private.

One Christian Social Networking Site Gets Two Thumbs Up

After expressing my concerns about security for young people using social networking sites, even Christian social networking sites, I can recommend one site for those that want a site centered on security and safety for their family.

Hschooler.net (http://hschooler.net)—Hschooler.net is an online social network for Christian homeschooling families. The mission of Hschooler.net is to "connect families with the people, resources, and tools to train up young men and women to the

Glory of God." The service is intended to meet the unique needs of Christian parents, while also providing a fun, engaging, and edifying social atmosphere for Christian students. Basically, the same goals of most social networking sites.

Hschooler.net is guided by four core values:

▶   Honor the God of the Bible
▶   Put parents in control of their family's online experience
▶   Protect the privacy and security of all members
▶   Enjoy God's creation—have fun!

The service is distinctive from other social networking services because it recognizes the authority of parents, giving parents visibility and control over their children's activities (such as controlling what features they can and cannot use), and providing a level of privacy control not central to popular secular sites and services.

In order to join Hschooler.net, a person is required to agree with a Christian statement of faith and agree to abide by appropriate rules of conduct. Members of Hschooler.net will have access to tools and resources to help in their homeschooling experience, including general resources provided by Hschooler.net (e.g. Bible study and journaling tools), and resources being developed by the community (e.g. reviews of educational materials).

Since Hschooler.net is based on the authority of God, and under that umbrella the authority of parents over their family, an individual will be very limited in what they can do until they become part of a family account. After upgrading to a family account, parents can authorize other members of their family to participate in some or all of the social aspects of Hschooler.net. A family account costs $5 per year (new members receive a 90-day free trial period). This cost covers all members of a family. One reason for charging for family membership is to ensure that it is an adult who is establishing the family structure, since only adults should have access to a debit or credit card.

Hschooler.net makes it easy for family members to share their Hschooler.net activities with each other. All the while, the parents have complete control over what their students can and cannot do, and also how visible their activities are. Parents can also enable or disable individual tools and widgets for each member of their family. Widgets are bits of code that can be added to a Web site that will run an application—such as Java script—or an application that is actually hosted on another site. In addition, parents can set how broadly a family member can choose to share visibility about what they are doing in Hschooler.net. Using these controls, a parent may choose to significantly constrain what a young student can do, while providing complete freedom to a more mature member of her family. Within the constraints defined by parents, students still have a lot of flexibility in how they use Hschooler.net.

More specifically, there are generally seven levels that a member can use to set visibility for any piece of content created in Hschooler.net (e.g. an uploaded photo or a journal entry):

▶ Private (only the member)
▶ Parents
▶ Family
▶ Trusted friends (friends identified as trusted by parents)
▶ All friends
▶ All Hschooler.net members
▶ Public

For each child, parents can constrain the broadest visibility possible for each type of content. For example, for one child, the parents may allow the child to set visibility for uploaded photos to anything up to Trusted Friends (i.e. the child can set visibility to Private, Parents, Family, or Trusted Friends) and may allow the child to set visibility for journal entries to anything up to All Friends. For another, more mature child, the parents may allow the child to set visibility for all types of content to be as broad as All Hschooler.net Members.

The service has only been up and running for a short time, so watch for new features to be added as the service is refined.

CHURCH MANAGEMENT SOFTWARE AND SOCIAL NETWORKING

Currently, there are several Church Management Software companies that have connected with social networking services, or are in the process of doing so. Church Management Software companies made the connection to church Web sites years ago (see the next chapter for more information on that connection), and some are realizing that social networking represents more than just a connection into a site, rather a connection that can provide programs, events and communication tools.

Logos360

Logos360 is a social networking service, and an example of a church management software company (logosCMS) that has not only connected into Web site features, but actually offers churches their own social networking service. This means that a church's Web site can have traditional Web site offerings in addition to individual membership profiles. Each member can maintain their own profile, post pictures, videos, blogs and use communication tools to connect with their friends. At the same time, each members profile page will have information about upcoming events, prayer requests, and special announcements pushed from their church so it can get the information in front of its membership. Moreover, the members' information, including online contributions and registrations for events, can link to the main Logos database, which can save hours of data entry for the church's office personnel.

Logos360 also allows for sub-sites to be developed, which could emphasize specific small groups and allow them their own privacy so that members can share personal prayer requests or express personal needs. A sub-site might also serve as a welcome center designed to provide information for new visitors.

To get more detailed information on Logos go to their Web site at www.logoscms.com

ACSTechnologies also has introduced a Facebook application that will work with their database church management software solution. It is mentioned in more detail in the chapter on Web sites.

TWITTER—A NEW WAY TO SOCIAL NETWORK
. . . .

A very new way to connect and communicate with a group of your friends has hit both the Internet and your cell phone or mobile devices, and it's called Twitter. Wikipedia defines Twitter in this way, "Twitter is a free social networking and micro-blogging service that enables its users to send and read messages known as tweets. Tweets are text-based posts of up to 140 characters displayed on the author's profile page and delivered to the author's subscribers who are known as followers. Senders can restrict delivery to those in their circle of friends or, by default, allow open access. Users can send and receive tweets via the Twitter website, Short Message Service (SMS) or external applications. While the service costs nothing to use, accessing it through SMS may incur phone service provider fees."

So, with Twitter you set up an account and then invite people to follow you. When they do, they can read your comments by visiting their account on the Twitter Web site (www.twitter.com) or they can have your texts (called Tweets) sent to their cell phone, smart phone or mobile device. It is a bit different from having a Facebook account, but has quickly grown in acceptance and has begun to be used by many individuals as well as news services, merchants and commercial businesses.

Twitter, like Facebook and most social networking sites and services does not charge for their services. Once you let your friends know you are on Twitter they can find you and start following your tweets. You can also search for people and follow them as well. A tweet is basically like any other text message; you can insert hyperlinks to Web sites, post photos, videos, pictures, etc. Besides being a texting social network service, Twitter provides a profile page for each of its users. If you don't like to receive tweets you can simply visit your profile site to view what Twitter calls a micro-blog that allows you to see the most recent tweets from the people you are following. You can also view the tweets sent out by your friends with a time stamp showing you when they were sent.

While it is free to use Twitter, remember that depending on your cell phone service contract, there is normally a fee to receive text messages. Most people either pay by the text or have signed up for plans that allow a certain number of text messages each month. Of course, some plans provide unlimited text messaging as well.

When Twitter started, it was designed as a texting social networking site. The idea was for users to send out texts, or tweets, in answer to the question "What are you doing?" This was sort of like Facebook status updates; short messages that could be sent to your friends to help you stay connected. However, as happens with most forms of communication, many people wanted more and sought ways to utilize the free service for commercial use. For example, you will now hear many other mediums encourage you to follow them on Twitter. CNN news, for example, has set up an account and sends out short news bites throughout the day (I've been getting their "CNN Breaking News" emails for years.)

Churches have discovered Twitter as well, and have used it to communicate to their groups using the broadcast text service. And it's now easier to do than when Twitter first started. You actually no longer have to go to their Web site and open an account to follow someone else using Twitter. Just like short code

SMS texting services, you can enter their account name and send it to a short code number 40404.

By setting up such an account, youth ministers can then send a "What are you doing?" message, but instead of stating what they are doing they can send an announcement, such as "Don't forget the Bible study and fellowship tonight at 7p.m.!"

People have found all sorts of uses for Twitter, but at its most basic it is a social networking tool to keep connected with friends. It is a bit fascinating to receive tweets from your close circle of friends that let you know how their day is going. I also began following some of the Twitter accounts of IT leaders in the church and ministry field. Sometimes their tweets are about a new software program or service they were using, and I found the information both interesting and valuable. Other times they might be tweeting about what they had for lunch, which, for the most part, I found to be a waste of time (sorry friends).

A new study by Nielsen shows that approximately 60 percent of the people that start using Twitter cancel after just one month. This may be due to the fact that they are limited in the amount of information they can share at one time, or maybe because it's much harder to send links to videos, pictures, etc., than if you use a site like Facebook.

Twitter, however, continues to be used in creative ways. I recently heard that some street vendors with lunch carts are encouraging their customers to follow them on Twitter. As they prepare to move to their next location, the vendors send out a quick tweet that lets their customers know where they're going next. In January 2009, when a US Airways jet lost power after striking a flock of birds and landed in the Hudson River, a person on one of the ferry boats that helped evacuate stranded passengers took a picture of the plane in the water and the rescue effort around it and sent it to his friends via Twitter. It turned out to be the first picture to be broadcast of the near tragedy— well before traditional media arrived to cover the event. Several surgeries have also been covered by people in operating rooms sending regular tweet messages with reports of the progress of the surgery. And, in May 2009 astronaut Michael Massimino sent tweets from space while on a mission to fix the Hubble Telescope. Additionally, most of the information about the recent riots and unrest over the elections in Iran were sent via Twitter and cell phones, and allowed the world to observe events that the Iranian government didn't want anyone to see.

There are also many utilities coming on the market to help manage your Twitter account. One such utility is called Tweetdeck, which allows you to set up windows with different search criteria. For example, after this book is finished, I can use Tweetdeck to search for its title and see all the tweets from any and all accounts in Twitter that mention the book. Now that's pretty cool!

But while this may be a fantastic utility to monitor different subjects, it does have its drawbacks. That means that companies can—and actually do—monitor all tweets sent from Twitter watching for their company's name, or even other related subjects. When you see a tweet in Tweetdeck, you can actually hit reply and send them a text through Twitter even though you have not chosen to follow them, and do not show up on their list of friends.

The potential drawback is this: some companies are starting to use such services to send out marketing text messages in response to related subjects they are seeing in public tweets that come up in their searches. For example, you might tweet to your friends that you really need to get around to painting your house. That might trigger you to receive a text from someone, or some company, that thought you might like to know that a local home improvement center is having a sale on paint later that week. This has the potential to be a real problem, because SPAM and marketing emails have essentially ruined the effective use of email for many, and the last thing we need is texting advertisements being sent to our cell phones!

In essence, tweets sent via Twitter can be read by anyone, so a bit of caution must be used. A friend of mine recently lost his job and needed to relocate and sell his house. He put the house up for sale with a realtor and began to ask his church to pray that it would sell quickly since he was in need of a quick sale. He also sent out a few tweets to those following him on Twitter asking for prayer, and expressing his concerns about the house selling quickly to meet his needs. After a few days, his realtor called him and strongly suggested he stop sending out tweets about his house because doing so could end up costing him a substantial amount of money. He explained that some buyers were using search programs like Tweetdeck and searching for tweets from the owners of properties they were interested in buying. They then use the information—in this case, an owner desperate to sell—to make lowball offers on properties. And how did the realtor know my friend had sent out tweets about his house? Because he had searched for my friend's outgoing tweets and found his requests for prayer, just as a prospective buyer might do!

CHAPTER 5

Websites

So, how important is a church or ministry's Web site? Obviously the answer varies. If you look at a lot of church Web sites, most lack content and style. They either don't place a high value on the site or they really don't know where to turn to for help and resources. On the other hand, some churches have fantastic Web sites, and are actually accomplishing many areas of ministry through their sites.

Yet most churches could do so much more with their Web sites. In a recent survey conducted by Christian Computing Magazine (www.ccmag.com), only half of those readers surveyed were happy with their church's Web site. And understand, this was a survey not using the normal demographic for churches in America. This survey was conducted using the readership of Christian Computing Magazine, which means the survey was conducted using people who are considered pretty savvy when it comes to technology and the use of the Internet.

Some even questioned the value of their church's Web site. Many of them have had a Web site for more than a decade, and yet have not seen any notable results. I believe it should be obvious that this is a direct reflection on the site's ability to convey and conduct ministry, and that speak for itself. Another survey, this one from 2006, found that of American's with Internet access, almost 50 percent turned to the Internet when seeking help with big decisions in their lives. With the reported incredible increase in use of Internet services each year, it should be clear that most American's would turn to the Internet when they want to sell or buy a house, seek a new job, or seek a new spouse. If they are seeking solutions to their spiritual needs, they would obviously turn to the Internet to seek answers to their spiritual needs, and it appears that most are doing just that. Yet, most church Web sites do not contain answers, solutions or content that can help with spiritual needs. Instead we provide directions to our buildings, and the times of our services. People want solutions quickly, and they want answers that are direct and personal.

I believe a church or ministry's Web site is very important, and in this chapter we will cover tips about basic design, and discuss how to make it a "live" site that people will want to visit over and over. I will also share how you can use your Web site to help accomplish many of your church's mission goals, and we will look at some of the companies and services that are available to help you accomplish this purpose.

GIVE ME THE BASICS

On the plus side, most churches know they need a Web site, and it seems that churches everywhere have put up something on the Web. Unfortunately, there are more bad examples than good. While I believe it is best to have something rather than nothing, there are many books, Web sites, and articles available (many on the Internet) that can give you some guidelines. Here are a few of the ones I think are most important. In some cases, your Web person (if you have one) might have used some of these techniques. However, there are many professional companies that have the ability to track the user experience when they are visiting a Web site, and we have learned from them that some of the ideas we thought were "cool" have actually turned off visitors. You want people to come to your site and stay, read the information, and enjoy the overall experience.

What to Avoid

Do not use animated gifs. These were cool only when they first came out because it was exciting to see something move on your site. However, they quickly became annoying, and it is actually sad when you visit a site and find them still in use.

Don't use tiled or patterned backgrounds that can distract the visitor. I have been to some sites where it has actually hurt my eyes to stay for any length of time. Backgrounds that are understated can work, but they need to help make your site attractive without the visitor actually noticing them.

Don't present your information using centered text. This is great for a headline that might appear at the top of an article, but not for the text of the article itself. You are making your visitors have to work to read what you have to say, and they will probably leave if they have to work too hard.

Do not use bold and capital letters in an attempt to get your text noticed. I have been to church sites that had sentence after sentence of information in bold, or all capitals, or in bright red, believing that I would read what they had to say. This is SHOUTING, and people don't want to come to your site and get yelled at!

Keep the same look, feel and functionality throughout your site. There are different ways to navigate through a site, and once you've decided how to set it up be consistent throughout the entire site. You don't want to have submenu buttons running across the top of your homepage, and then down the left-hand side of other pages within your site. Be consistent.

And stay away from using Christian expressions or terminology that only your members will understand. For example, my wife and I lead a singles ministry called Mosaics for adults between the ages of 30-50. On our church's Web site, this ministry is labeled "Singles Ministry 30-50," not "Click here for information about the Mosaics."

Do not add music that starts up when people first land on your homepage. While you might think it's helpful, or helps set the mood, most will think it's annoying. I can't tell you how many times I've clicked on sites only to end up going somewhere else because of the music that started blaring from my speakers.

Don't clutter your home page. Too much information is not a good thing. Too many conflicting colors, fonts, graphics, different types of buttons or menus, etc., will distract and drive people from your site. When you are finished, ask someone to click and open the site for just two seconds and then close it quickly. Ask them what they come away with? Their answer—or lack of one—can tell you a lot about the effectiveness of your site.

Avoid Flash welcome screens or introductory splash pages. Also avoid the use of frames or fancy buttons for your menus. These all were briefly popular for, but successful sites have moved away from them as unnecessary distractions.

Use readable fonts. I know people like to be creative, and there are many fonts to choose from—many of which are available for free. But your font has to be readable or it is worthless. This is obvious when it comes to the text of your articles. You would think that all fonts are readable. After all, that's what they're supposed to be, right? While I would have to conclude that all fonts can be read, some make me have to work at it and I usually end up moving on instead of trudging along to read something that's proving difficult to do. Recently I sat in a session where designers reviewed church Web sites. There was one that had a revolving carrousel on the home page that promoted different ministries and events (something I encourage you to do). However, one of the promotions used a crazy loud font to promote one of the events or ministries. It was only up on the screen for about three seconds each time, but I had to look at it several time to try and figure out what it was saying. I finally had to look away and get back to the discussion—still not knowing what the event was about. Maybe someone thought that was cool, but the message was completely lost on me.

Do not make your home page about information from the pastor. Do not include a "welcome" from the pastor either. People want to connect with other people. They want to know that they will be making friends at the church, and not just following the pastor.

What Should I Do?

Now, let's discuss what you *should* do. And again, these are just basic elements. There are many more very specific things you can do with your Web site once you define your purpose. But even with the most basic of sites, there are things that definitely need to be included.

First, make your home page short. Use a clear and easy-to-understand menu list to help navigate your visitors to the information they desire, but do not expect them to scroll down through pages of information. Remember, the best page will have everything a visitor needs to see visible without ever having to scroll down at all (this is referred to as "above the fold").

One of the most obvious things people should see when visiting your site is your basic information. This includes an address (a link to a Google map or MapQuest is a good idea), times of services, and contact information. This information should be obvious. Don't make visitors have to search for it.

Use pictures of your people, but don't post posed pictures of your members (like you might see in a pictorial directory). Instead show pictures of your members while at worship, gathering and meeting in your narthex or lobby, and at Bible studies or small groups. Pictures like this will send an important message to those seeking information about your church. It will tell them more about the "look and feel" of your church than any other method. For example, pictures give them an idea of the age of your membership. Some churches have older memberships, and while there is certainly nothing wrong with this, if I was young adult with school age children looking for a new church, I'd be looking for a church that posted pictures of their membership with young adults with their children in tow.

Another example, most people want to know how to dress before they go meet new people. Should they dress in a coat and tie, or a dress? Is business casual appropriate? Should you wear jeans? If a person comes to your church for the first time in a coat and tie, and they are the only one dressed in a coat and tie, this will undoubtedly impact their visit, believe me. One good picture is worth a thousand words, and can let prospective new members know how to dress before coming to one the services for the first time. I also encourage you to use pictures throughout your site. If you are talking about small groups, have a picture of your members meeting in a home, sitting in a circle in someone's living room having a study. If you have a page about children's ministry, have at least one picture of the children while doing some activity. Even if you have a page for people to submit prayer requests, post a picture of some of your people while at prayer. The overall connection will be made that your church is about "people", not programs.

Some churches that want to include pictures of their members worshiping have expressed concerns regarding privacy issues. They wonder if they should obtain permission from their membership before they post any pictures on the Internet.

Here are some examples of ways churches have handled this:

Some have announced that pictures were going to be taken during the worship service. They inform those attending that they should contact the church office if they object to their photos appearing on the church's Web site. Another church provided an "opt-out" card in the bulletin that people could fill out and drop in the offering plate as it was passed during the service.

I know of another church that simply opted to shoot pictures after the regular services were over. They invited those that didn't mind the exposure to stay after the service for a few pictures. The worship team simply led those that remained in another song while the cameras took a few pictures for the Web site.

Your site should also provide additional information for first time visitors, both those that have church experience and those that might be seekers. Be open about this portion of your site, and make sure it's clearly labeled so people can find it with ease. You might even include it in the menu list with something like, "Here is what to expect when visiting our church." Include information about the type of music you use, childcare information, parking (if you have a special place for visitors to park, tell them before they come so they visit so they will know), what to wear, and if you have anything set up to help visitors such as an information center or coffee shop.

If you have multiple ministers, provide contact information for each. This should include each person's email address as well. I know of a minister who recently told me they didn't post their email address on their site because they were concerned about the addresses being harvested for SPAM emails. A good filter handles SPAM, so make yourself available and give people your email addresses. If you are really concerned about it, create a contact form instead. These allow the visitor to select the person they wish to contact, enter their question or comment in a text box and hit the submit button. The information is then sent via email to the appropriate person.

Make sure your church or ministry's Web site says "Welcome." And I don't mean to just put the word at the top of the page. Make sure it's looking over your site, and that it is inviting. Ask yourself the questions, "If you were an unchurched person, is it clear that you are welcome?" "If I have doubts, is this the place to come for answers?" If you answered no to either question, then you need to do something to make sure your visitors feel clearly, and completely, welcomed.

People expect to hear from the pastor and paid staff members when they come to a Web site. After all, that is the pastor's job, right? But also include a place for visitors to meet your members. You might want to do this on a separate page, and include pictures with captions, and even a host of little testimonies from members stating why they personally love to attend your church.

And make good use of color. Here is where you can involve the talents of some of your totally non-computer technology people. Ask those that are good at home decorating or design to check out your site. There needs to be a consistent color scheme running throughout your site. Don't just assume you can go with "blue." Some blue graphics in the home page banner can actually conflict with other shades of blue used in menu bars.

Check your Web site to see how it looks in various browsers. This should included Microsoft's Internet Explorer, Mozilla's Firefox, and Safari. And, don't assume that if you checked it using the latest version that it will pass the test. It's a hassle to keep multiple versions available, but you need to check to see if the site looks good in the latest version of Windows IE as well as previous versions—at least two versions back. This is a great way to utilize an old computer that you don't really have any use for anymore. Have it on the network and install it with outdated browsers for testing purposes.

Use black text on a white background for articles and text blocks larger than a title. This makes them more readable and easier to print. Nothing is more frustrating than wanting to print out an article from the Internet and having to deal with all of the wasted ink when you have to print pages with colored backgrounds.

Have people critique your site. First, be sure to have non-technical people go through your site. Watch them as they navigate around your site and ask them if they can find specific information. If they were coming to your site seeking information about a singles ministry, would they be able to find it easily? You might also ask an unchurched friend to check out your site. Ask him what terminology they might see but not understand. This will have immense value to the effectiveness of your site.

Assume that each page on your site could be the starting page for a visitor. People will occasionally send individual links to a page to their friends, or a search engine might take someone directly to a page that contained information the viewer was seeking. You need to be sure that each page contains a link back to the home page. In fact, protocol today dictates that the logo in the header should always take you back to the home page whenever it is clicked.

These are a few good starting points. If your page is missing some of the features I have just presented, or you know that you're doing some of the things I listed in the "don't do" list, one solution might be to start using one of the many Web site hosting services that were created to help churches create and maintain a good Web site. Later, I will be reviewing some of these and providing an expanded list of their features. But remember, just as it is important to have a site that follows all of the best Web design tricks of the trade, it is equally important to have a Web site that knows its purpose and can accomplish ministry!

I recommend you visit http://www.Internetevangelismday .com/churchtool.php and use their self-assessment tool to give your site a free evaluation report that can help you begin to see what areas of your site you are doing fine, and which areas need work.

Is Your Site Live or Static? Web 1.0 or Web 2.0?

There are two types of Web sites. Those that are static and those that are alive. What's the difference? A static Web site is basically equal to a billboard, a brochure or an advertisement you might run in a newspaper. Some refer to a site with these characteristics as a Web 1.0 site. If you don't have the tools, ability or commitment to keep new content on your site then I encourage you to do the best job with a brochure site. After all, it is better than nothing and some good can always be accomplished. However, I encourage you as a reader of this book to consider the ministry potentials that are available by providing a "live" site for your visitors. The term Web 2.0 refers to a "live" site, where communication is enabled between the visitor and the host of the site, or between different visitors. A Web 2.0 site is a Web site that is designed for a visitor to have the opportunity to interact with other visitors or information. It normally means that the site is constantly evolving with new content, and the content is always "live" and consistently changing with the input from the host, as well as comments and other content from visitors.

A church Web site should be designed with three types of visitors in mind. First there should be content for your members. Second, there should be a place for new residents who are Christians and have recently moved into your area and are seeking a new church home. And third, it needs to be designed for those who are seekers—people that have turned to the Internet to find solutions to a present crisis in their lives. People whose lives had been going along just fine, and who really hadn't felt a need for God in their lives, yet suddenly they are faced with a crisis that can include any of the following:

► They just discovered they have cancer
► They have just lost their job
► They have just had a loved one die
► Their marriage is breaking up
► Their children are in rebellion
► They are losing their home
► They are depressed
► They realize they are lacking peace or joy
► They are suddenly feeling unloved

People who are going through any one of these crisis will turn to the Internet for possible solutions. If they were to stumble upon your church's Web site, would they find hope? Or words of encouragement?

In the past, putting up a building with a steeple might have been enough. The purpose of the steeple was to inform those in the city that this was a place designed to help them connect with God. Today, we need to do much more.

The first thing you have to ask yourself is, "Are those that are seekers easily finding your site?" If the content is there and you are presenting solutions and information about the needs I have just suggested, and if you're doing a good job of making sure the search engines are aware of your site, then there is good chance seekers will find your site. Once there, will they see that you really care, and that you really have solutions? Of course you do, because God is the answer for all seekers. But is that really clear on your site?

Know Your Purpose

This is a good time to decide the purpose of your site. If your purpose is to simply reach those that are already Christians and have moved into your city and are shopping for a new church, then a static site will probably serve that purpose. The design tips I have shared, however, are still vital for making your site a success.

I remember meeting a man who shared with me his experience finding a new church via the Internet. He was originally from England and was relocating to New York. Since he knew the general neighborhood where he would be working, he sought churches within a close distance. One church seemed to really stand out, and he opened communication with the church through contact information he found on the site. He had submitted a few questions about theology and his beliefs and was confident in the answers received that they were a good match. They also seemed to have other ministries that he desired, such as a choir that had made contact and encouraged him to join.

After the man had made the move and settled in to his new home, he decided it was time to visit his new church. Upon his arrival at the doors of the church, though, both he and the people he'd made initial contact with were a bit surprised. The man, you see, was Caucasian, and the congregation of the new church he decided to attend was made up entirely of African Americans. On the Web site, there had been no pictures of any of the staff or church members, and while he had been in communication via email with several from the church there had been no indication that the membership was made up completely of just one race.

The good news is that everyone had a good laugh about it, and the man was warmly welcomed with open arms. He ended up finding a home at the church, and at the time he shared his story with me was still very much an active member. But the events caused the church to reevaluate their Web site. If something so predominant about their membership was not being communicated then where else had they failed in presenting the true nature and feel of their church to potential visitors?

Your Web site needs to be a reflection of your church. And your purpose needs to be established in order to determine what you will offer on your site. Many churches now seek to accomplish ministry from their site and recognize that their Web site is an extension of their outreach, discipleship, worship and other areas of their mission statement. Therefore a static site will not accomplish their main purpose, and a live site is the direction they must take.

What Do People Want When They Visit Your Site?

It is obvious that most people do not want a static or brochure site. Most want to accomplish something with their visit. They want to interact with opportunities and express themselves, such as in the posting of prayer requests.

Web sites have the ability to interconnect data. Let's imagine a church having an upcoming event. A brochure site (or static site) might simply announce an upcoming event, but a live site might be able to:

▶ Provide event information
▶ Allow for online registration, including online payment of any fees required
▶ Provide the ability to make reservations for childcare, if needed
▶ Listen or view media from those involved, or who attended the event in the past
▶ Provide the opportunity to volunteer (childcare, parking, ushers, cooks, etc.)
▶ Post comments and/or questions about the event

A Live Site Has Five Unique Qualities

1. Content
2. Community
3. Contribution (missions)
4. Connectivity (to ministry)
5. Construction

Content is information, materials, PDF files, audio and video files, online forms, surveys, discussion boards, blogs and more. Developing a community happens when you give people visiting your site the opportunity to connect with each other. Contribution is the method designed for your membership that will enable them to participate in providing content, especially for the purpose of evangelism or other involvement in service and/or missions. Connectivity enables members to move beyond just community, and have a direct connection to ministries carried out through the church. And finally, the method you use to help construct your Web site, and the potential to expand features to meet your needs, is vital and serves as the foundation for the success of your site's future.

Think back to chapter two in this book and remember the five basic areas of mission and ministry that most churches are centered around. Here they are again:

▶ A call to train or disciple their members in the teachings of Christ
▶ A call to evangelize or reach their community with the message of salvation
▶ A call to grow and encourage the body of Christ through fellowship and commitment
▶ A call to gather together to worship God
▶ A call to involve their congregation in service and missions

What content can you provide on your church's Web site that could help accomplish these ministries? How can you develop community on your site? Can you create programs that can be administered from your site to help your members contribute content and allow them to be a part of your mission? And how can you help them connect to your present ministries and, in particular, the various areas of your basic mission statement?

Combining the sections of a successful "live" Web site with a direct connection to your mission statement will help you develop your Web site's goals and mission. Take a look at the chart on the following page. This is one example of a church's Web site goals. I made the connections between the various qualities of a live Web site, with specific mission goals of the church, and actually gave examples of how to implement each of these into the rest of this chapter. I am not suggesting that each and every church apply all of these ideas to their sites. Some will do much more, while others will envision applications that I haven't even thought of (and if you do, I hope you will send me a note so I can share your insight with others).

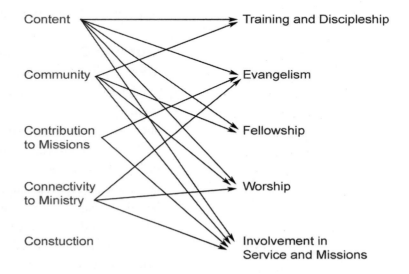

The Connection between website method and ministry!
(Mapping Out Your Purpose)

Let's look at examples of how providing content, connection, contributions, and a connection to ministry, you can help accomplish your mission statement.

USING YOUR WEB SITE FOR TRAINING AND DISCIPLESHIP

Most churches generate a ton of training and discipleship materials in the form of paper. The fact is that almost anything created for distribution on paper can easily be added to the Web site. Of course you can do it by just adding straight text onto a page for readers to find and use. However, many discipleship materials contain graphics, maps, charts and illustrations that help make the information in the materials clear to the reader. These don't have to get lost in the transition. Take materials like this and convert them to PDF format and simply provide a link to them on your site for people to download.

Think video! I know when most people think about putting videos up on their church Web sites they worry about the cost of cameras, lighting, editing, etc. Yet, here's some advice I keep repeating over and over again: informal video is now very acceptable, and doable! So, what exactly is informal video? Easy. It's video that is "real." It can be as easy as someone using the camera and microphone built into their computer to record a lesson. Or, because video cameras now do such a great job of recording using a room's available lighting that you can easily record a discipleship session, or even your new-member orientation classes, and put it all online.

Outside Christian Learning Services

There are several ministries that are starting to provide online discipleship classes. If you find that the materials fit with your doctrine and discipleship program, you might want to recommend such services to your members and visitors through your site. One such service that I like is offered by RBC Ministries, the publishers of "Our Daily Bread." It can be found at www.ChristianCourses.com, along with their catalog that includes over 120 courses at learning levels from introductory through graduate level. The faculty includes such recognized names as John Stott, Garth Rosell, Darrell Block, Walter Kaiser, Bruce Waltke, Haddon Robinson, Philip Yancey, Alice Mathews, and Larry Crabb.

Many of their classes are free, while some are accredited and require a fee. They utilize print (in PDF format), audio and video to present their classes. For example, their free class on "Why Study the Bible?" is available in video format (16.29 minutes in length), in audio format (15.50 minutes in length) and in a print version (transcript in PDF format). One of the unique features of the Old Testament and New Testament Survey courses is the interactive content offered. Examples include interactive timelines of the entire Bible, animated maps and photo tours, and many interactive review exercises.

They do require that you register, which takes only a few minutes.

Here are the sub-categories, along with a list of their current courses that are free:

Old Testament Survey
Genesis-Leviticus: God Builds a People for Himself
Numbers-Joshua: The Tragedy of Fear and the Glory of Faith
Judges-1 Samuel: Israel's Choice from God-rule to Human-rule

2 Samuel-2 Kings: The Difference Leaders Make

1 Chronicles-Nehemiah: Up From the Ashes

Lamentations-Job: God's Path Through Pain

Proverbs-Psalms: Singing the Sounds of Real Life

Daniel-Micah: Studies of Integrity—Good Men in Bad Times

Ecclesiastes-Isaiah: God Guides His People Through Poets and
   Prophets

Jeremiah-Ezekiel: Human Failure and Divine Success—
   A Study in Contrast

Jonah-Habakkuk: The God of Israel and the God of the Nations

Haggai-Malachi: No Substitute for Obedience

New Testament Survey

New Testament Basics: Things We Thought We Knew

Matthew-Mark: Two Presentations of Jesus

Luke–John: Two Interpretations of Jesus

Jesus in Galilee: Popularity and Misunderstanding

Luke–John: Jesus in Judea—Opposition and Rejection

Acts: Crucifixion, Resurrection and Proclamation

Galatians-1 Corinthians: Paul's Earliest Letters

1 and 2 Corinthians: Two Letters to a Tough Church

Romans-Ephesians: The Letter to the Roman Church and Letters
   from a Roman Prison

1 Timothy-Hebrews: Letters to Pastors & to a Church Struggling
   to Believe

James-Jude: Letters to Everyone—General and Johannine Epistles

Revelation: The Book of Revelation—The End and the Beginning

Know Why You Believe—Introduction to Christian Apologetics

10 Reasons to Believe in the Christian Faith

10 Reasons to Believe God Became a Man

10 Reasons to Believe in the Existence of God

10 Reasons to Believe in Life After Death

10 Reasons to Believe Real Christians Can Look Like They're Not

10 Reasons to Believe in the Resurrection

10 Reasons to Believe in Christ Rather Than Religion

10 Reasons to Believe in the Bible

The Da Vinci Code: Separating Fact from Fiction

The Miracles of Jesus

10 Reasons To Believe in a God Who Allows Suffering

History of the Christian Church
Foundations of the Christian Church: From the Early Church to the Great Schism

First Steps in Christian Counseling
SoulCare Foundations 101: The Basic Model
SoulCare Foundations 201: Understanding People and Problems
SoulCare Foundations 301: Provisions and Practices
SoulCare Foundations 401: Community Where SoulCare
    Happens
Ministering to People in Pain

Bible Basics
Old Testament Basics
New Testament Basics

First Steps in Effective Ministry
Introduction to Public Speaking
Leading from Your Strengths

Foundations of Effective Leadership
The Four A's of Leadership for Women
Group Dynamics

First Steps in the Christian Faith
Theology Basics
How to Study the Bible

World Religions Basics: A Comparison of Major World Religions

Getting to Know the Bible

Worldview Basics: A Comparison of Major Worldviews

Most of the courses have a quiz for each lesson, and students will be able to grade themselves after taking the quiz.

How Can You Utilize These Courses and Personalize Them for Your Church?
There are two different ways you could use the courses provided by this service. In either option, it's best if the instructor takes the class first to make sure they're familiar with the materials. You

could then encourage a group to take a specific courses at the same time, allowing them to log in from various locations, including their homes. You could also review the lesson objectives with the group and then open a discussion based with Online Forum questions and Personal Reflection and Evaluation questions that are offered online by ChurchCourses for each course.

Another option would be to meet as a small group at the church or someone's home, and using a computer with an Internet connection play select portions of the course and then open the discussion around the Online Forum questions for each lesson. Time permitting, the course instructor may also use the Personal Reflection and Evaluation questions in group discussion. If an Internet connection is not accessible, some courses are also available for download or on disc. You can also contact ChristianCourse.com and ask them about a partnership that would allow you to have a customized site that incorporates their classes into your ministry. Two good examples of this can be found here:

▶   Faith Baptist Church—Greenville, http://fbc.christiancourses.com

▶   Mothers of Preschoolers Ministry—http://mops.christiancourses .com

As you can see, you have a great start for Christian education and training just a click away. However, if you look at the actual structure of what they have done, you'll see that it's not too difficult to create your own unique content, convert it to PDF format and post it on your site. Of course, there is nothing wrong with posting your articles on the site in HTML format. Doing it this way means your articles are more likely to get picked up by search engines, which makes it easier for visitors to find materials specific to your site.

Doing it Your Way

After you can see from what RBC has done, it's not that hard to start a Christian education training program on your Web site, and it can be as easy as mimicking the RBC program. Create discipleship and training materials either in print, audio files, or a video, and post them on a site and allow visitors to click on a link and take the course. If you want some control over who can view specific materials you can establish a log-in system. In fact, most commercial Web site services designed for churches have the ability to allow its members to see content that is restricted for non-members or first time visitors. It would be a simple matter to set up an account level for your members that would allow them access to certain pages of course materials.

Of course, with training and discipleship courses you also must include the option for course takers to ask questions, make comments, and provide feedback. This can be accomplished in many different ways, including any one of the many blogging software programs or services available today. You can post a short article, or a larger one, with links to PDF files and other resources, and then allow for comments from those that used the materials. You could also set up a discussion board, or a chat room, and restrict its access to only those that are taking your training courses.

RefTagger will Bring the Bible Alive on Your Site

If you want to provide Bible study materials then RefTagger—an exciting free Web tool from Logos Bible Software—is something you definitely want to incorporate into your site.

With RefTagger installed on your site, visitors will be able to see pop-up window every time they move their mouse over a Bible reference. This pop-up window, which they call a ToolTip, contains the full text of the passage.

All you have to do to install RefTagger on your site is copy the customizable code that Logos provides and paste it into your Web site's template files. It will then be instantly applied to your entire Web site, allowing the references to work anywhere you have posted a scripture. You don't have to do anything special to make each reference work. And, although there are different ways of posting a reference (different abbreviations for different books in the Bible), RefTagger takes it all into account and finds finds every reference regardless. You also have the option of adding a special icon that is hyperlinked to the specific passage in Libronix.

But what if you install it and decide you don't like it? No problem . . . simply remove the code from your template and everything reverts back to the way it was before you installed it for your site.

Give it a try. Visit http://www.logos.com/reftagger to learn more about it, and see just how seamless RefTagger can work with your site. It really is pretty cool!

USING YOUR WEB SITE FOR EVANGELISM

There are many ways to use a Web site to promote evangelism. Of course, you can present the Gospel. You can also create a video, post directions on how to confess your sins, or even post suggested prayers for people to use. However, as posted on the "Internet Evangelism Day" Web site (www.Internetevangelismday.com), there is a difference between presenting the Gospel on your site, and having an evangelistic Web site. Here is how they explain it:

▶ Most non-Christians are not seeking for God.
▶ Most online non-Christians have no wish to search for Christian Web sites.
▶ All online non-Christians are searching for Web sites on needs they have, and topics that interest them.
▶ Therefore to reach non-Christians, we must create Web sites around the topics and felt needs that they have. This is the bridge strategy.

Using the Bridge Strategy

A bridge site must be truly about the topic or need that is its starting point. There must be no sense of "bait and switch"—this is not a "decoy trick." But we can then transition across, with integrity, to:

1. Life StoryPages—of the Webmaster, or other people associated with the site topic. (Church sites might be tempted to call these Testimony Pages, because that is the term we are used to using, but try to avoid church jargon.)

2. Parallel Pages—Almost all secular topics contain embedded within them a spiritual parallel which can be drawn out.

3. "Meaning of Life" questions—Pages which ask leading questions.

4. A Gospel Presentation—The three previous categories of page can gently lead to an explanation of the way of salvation (within the site, or as an off-site link).

As I mentioned earlier, I believe one of the best evangelistic tools out there are the real life testimonies of your membership. At least once a year, most churches have a specific time when they emphasize evangelism and encourage their members to learn how to share their testimony with others. Using the Internet and a church Web site now gives you many opportunities to use those testimonies.

At a conference where I spoke about church Web sites and their opportunities for ministry, Aaron Stone, network administrator for the First Assembly of God Church in North Little Rock, Ark., shared with me an idea he was working to implement at his church:

> *"I want to be able to have people send us their self-made testimonies recorded via Webcams or personal video cameras so that we can select a few that are gripping, emotional, and compelling enough to make an impact upon the listener. Then we would make these accessible to the public via our Web site, and/or YouTube, Podcasts, etc ... For instance, we have a ministry called* Journey to Total Freedom, *which is a women's ministry for the abused. This would allow other abused women in our church to connect to women in the videos. I feel that it is a MUST to have these women's videos be self recorded. I feel that they would not be able to totally open up if they had anyone else recording, viewing, or listening while they told their story. This would allow them to speak freely, cry if they needed, have runny mascara, all of the things that show emotion. No cuts, no retakes, no scripts, just real women telling real stories. And I will have everyone do this, abused males, people addicted to porn, drugs, alcohol, and people who have broken marriages. I feel that those videos we use must be of people in our community, and who attend our church regularly. Why? Because if you are struggling with an addiction I feel that it would help to be able to look a few rows over and see this person that has been freed from addiction and be able to relate. This will also be a great tool for our other members who might know someone that is struggling and say, 'Hey I want you to check out this video. I think you can relate.' They can take them to our site, show them the podcast, or send them the YouTube.com link. I feel that within our church we have*

some people that have life changing stories that need to be shared. And if we post them to benefit our local ministry it would also be a great resource and ministry for everyone in our neighborhoods, state, country, and world."

Notice that Aaron is not just talking about putting up testimonies of his membership, but seeking those from his membership that can apply Christ to real life problems of addiction and abuse. He is seeking to use the bridge strategy.

I have seen several churches use different formats to encourage its membership to post testimonies to its Web site. I remember one church that had laid out its Web site similar to an online magazine, with articles written by their membership about how they overcame ordinary struggles in life, and they averaged twice as many site visits each month as they had people in their entire membership. Their site was ministering to their community, and to the world.

Connection and Opportunities for Feedback

For evangelism to be effective, you need to consider the nature of what is presently working on the Internet. People like to hear from other people, not authority figures. This is why testimonies from your membership can reach a different audience than a video stream of your pastor's sermon (although this should be done as well, and will be covered later).

People also need the ability to connect. If they are going to connect to your message, they must have the ability to respond, to leave a comment, to engage in a conversation, or be a part of a discussion. Look at the popularity and growth of sites that allow people to post their own videos. Videos on YouTube can reach an audience of millions in just days, and people have the opportunity to post comments, praise and criticism of any video posted.

Relationships are an important part of any communication, and are at the center of what is successful on the Internet. Your site cannot just proclaim the message of Christ, even using personal testimonies, video and the latest technology, without giving people the opportunity to respond. In the past, relationships were created by face-to-face connections and were kept alive by personal meetings or via letters or phone calls. Now people meet via the Internet and can not only develop relationships, but lasting friendships and romantic relationships as well.

Relationships and connections are at the heart of the Internet. Before the Web, a person's circle of relationships were usually initiated by face-to-face contact, and then sustained by personal communication tools. If you use your site to present the Gospel of Christ you must provide a way for people to respond, to ask questions and personalize their needs.

There are many ways to do this. You can provide a 24-hour help line for seekers to call, or you can set up a contact form on your Web site for those seeking to respond to your message, or to ask questions.

Although I haven't seen it used in a church application for discipleship, there are several different free conference call services that work via the Internet. For example, TalkShoe allows you to set up a conference call that can be open to the public, and is easily accessible to anyone by simply calling in using a pre-supplied phone number and code to insert themselves into the call.

Pastors, or lay leaders, can set up an Internet conference call and then promote the subject and time throughout their community. The calls can encompass all kinds of topics, including discussions for those that are having problems with their children, or people facing difficult health problems, or those seeking help with addictions, or people trying to save their marriage. Callers don't have to identify themselves when joining the conference call, while others may decide to just log in and listen. The service also offers a live chat room were attendees can ask questions or leave comments without having to say anything on the phone. I would LOVE to see a church use this tool, and I would love to hear about the results!

Another suggestion would be to create a FAQ page (frequently asked questions). These can certainly include questions and answers about what the church offers, but you could also include questions like, "What can I do to save my marriage?", "How come I don't seem to feel God is listening when I pray?", "I am afraid but don't feel I can tell anyone.", and "Where should I turn?" Then have your pastor or other ministers provide short answers, with links to additional information and ways to contact someone for more help!

USING YOUR WEB SITE FOR FELLOWSHIP AND COMMITMENT

There are a lot of ways to include content on your site to promote fellowship and/or commitment. An important part of fellowship is connection. We have already discussed social networking services, and mentioned how some Church Management Software programs are starting to include applications to work within sites like Facebook. This is an excellent example, since Facebook encourages connections, the sharing of photos, various links to entertaining videos, the ability to let others know what your status is, and the opportunity to ask for prayer.

There are also other ways to use the site to help encourage connection. One is to provide areas on your site for information that is specific to your different age groups. For example, have a page for the children to visit. At the same time, however, don't forget the parents of the children too.

Here's a great example of this I came across several years ago. The leaders of a children's church ministry would scan a picture from a coloring book (or, to prevent copyright infringement, they might have just employed a member to draw a basic black line picture suitable for children to color) and posted this picture on the church's children's site about mid week. They made sure the picture coincided with the Bible story the Church would be speaking about during the upcoming service on Sunday. They would encourage the children to have their parents visit the site and print the page, and then color it and bring it to church the next Sunday. They also provided the scripture references for the upcoming service and encouraged parents to spend some time sharing the story with their children before they came to church. This way the children were exposed to the Bible story from both their parents and the leaders of the church. Additionally, each week they would give a prize to the best colored picture for each age category. You know what the prize was? The winning picture would be posted on the children's Web site with praise to the children for doing such a great job.

I remember the children's pastor sharing with me that the program had an unexpected blessing; parents were sharing with him that they didn't have to get their children up to go to church because the reverse was happening. If the parents were tempted to stay home, it was the children that wanted to attend because they had worked so hard on the coloring project and wanted to submit their work for review!

Use Your Imagination

Create a list of trivia questions about your church and post it on the Web site with a way for people to take the test and see their score. Questions can be related to the actual church building, such as the number of chairs or pews, or the number of doors, or how many fire extinguishers. You can also ask questions about the membership. Who is the present chairman of deacons. Or chairman of your board? Questions can also be historical, like "What pastor served the longest?" Promote the contest from the pulpit, your bulletin and newsletter. Allow them to take the test online and let them post comments about the things they learned. There's a good chance people will get to know other members of the church they previously didn't know.

Promote a "Why I Love Our Church" essay contest. Have a place on the Web site for people to post their comments. Limit it to 500 words so that it is easy for people to read other people's submissions. Design the page so you can read the newest ones that are posted, and encourage your people to go to the site and express their feelings. Your members will get to know each other in new and exciting ways, and everyone will leave feeling excited about learning or being reminded about how their church is helping to touch lives.

Set up a Web page on your site to allow people to post their favorite YouTube videos. There are some fantastic videos being posted every day, and people like to share them with others. It helps to share a laugh or a tear with others. Also let them post their names with the videos, and create a section for comments. I saw this being done on several of the Christian social networking sites, and I am sure a clever Web site manager can figure out a way to make it happen. It will bring people to your site, and it will help them to better understand the humor of other members, as well as share what touches them.

We offer a "CCMag Video of the Week" on the *Christian Computing Magazine* site. We don't allow others to post videos, but we routinely post YouTube videos that feature things like new technology. I mention this because one of our staff members set up a Constant Contact signup box on our video page and invited people to join a broadcast email group, which allowed them to receive an email whenever we posted a new video. So far, approximately 2,000 people have signed up to get emails, and you could easily do the same for such a page on your site and quickly have the ability to reach out and touch people. When you send them an email notice you could also send additional information about your church, like times of services, new ministries, etc.

USING YOUR WEB SITE FOR WORSHIP

Last February one of our older pastors shared a fantastic message about love and marriage. It was one of the most beautiful sermons on the subject of husband and wife love that I have ever heard. Yet I don't think it would have had the same impact if I had simply read a transcript of the message. Actually, I don't believe it would have touched me as much if I had heard anyone else give the same sermon. My first thought was that I wanted a video of this sermon by this man. At the present time, however, our church doesn't videotape sermons, or posts them on the Web, although we are currently working to make it happen.

Does worship have to be collective within the walls of your building? Can you provide a worship experience from a Web site? I believe you can. I find myself worshiping God in lots of locations other than while in my church on a Sunday morning.

You could post thoughtful videos from YouTube, GodTube and even church video sites that allow you to post to your Web site, such as SermonSpice.com. Many short videos can be very inspiring or thought provoking. Many Christian music artists and bands now post videos of their songs that you can then link and place on your site as well.

I am not suggesting that you place or post any of these worship materials, videos, podcasts, etc., on your home page. But I think it can certainly be an extension of your ministry to use such content, especially posting your own videos. There will be more information on how to record, capture, encode and stream your own videos later in this book.

USING YOUR WEB SITE FOR SERVICE AND MISSIONS

When it comes to service there are many ways Christians can be challenged while online. Here are just a few ideas:

Spiritual Gift Assessment

I have seen several of these programs on the Web over the years. The Church Growth Institute provides a FREE Spiritual Gift Assessment tool (http://www.churchgrowth.org/cgi-cg/gifts.cgi?intro=1) that you could link to from their site. After people take the questionnaire they will be presented with a bar graph of their scores for each gift, a description of their dominant gift and several pages of personal analysis. They can print it out and bring it back to a church staff member for further consultation. Or you could teach a class on Spiritual Gifts and then encourage your members to go to your church's site, click on the link, take the assessment, print out the results and then meet back next week for a follow up on what the assessment showed.

(There are other spiritual gift assessment tools available on the Internet. Do a search in Google to find the one that best fits your needs.)

Online Giving

I strongly encourage churches to initiate a program for online giving. Many Church Management Software programs provide this service, and many independent companies as well.

Even though I have been endorsing online giving for many years, I always hear objections to it whenever I bring it up in the various conference sessions I speak at. "It's not really giving," some say. "It's encouraging the use of credit cards," others complain. And, some believe that electronic giving is somehow associated with the end of time and the antichrist. The fact is that our country has accepted credit or debit cards as the method of choice for monetary commerce. Most people simply no longer carry cash or a check book. We can buy gas for our car directly at the pump using our debit cards, or purchase a hamburger at the fast food restaurant using debit cards. My wife and I purchase our groceries on our debit card. Even the Salvation Army will let you swipe your debit card using electronic card swipe devices in some of their locations across the country. How is it at we have the nerve to tell people that when they join our church they can't use their debit card?

I think the number one reason some church members object to establishing an online giving program is because they have to establish a merchant account. It is not hard to set one up, and most banks will be happy to accommodate your church's needs. For some, it's the small transaction fee that bothers them most. If a person gives $100 through an online giving program, a small fee of a couple of dollars will go to the bank. I find this argument trivial. I'm sure there were people that objected when checks started dropping into the offering plates, as banks would require them to open an account to deposit checks, and there were bank fees involved. Yet by now, all churches that I know of are happy to take checks!

The other objection I hear is that it takes the giving of one's tithes and offerings out of the worship service. One pastor explained that he feared that those that gave online would be observed during the worship service as people that don't put anything into the offering plate. He was worried that this might set a bad example, although I am not sure I agree that this is a valid fear. There have been times in my life that I budget for my tithe and pay it once a month. I never thought about those that might be watching to see if I made a contribution on the Sundays that I didn't put anything into the plate. Frankly, giving is personal. And I feel it should be based upon my own conviction and not as a result of parroting my actions. However, if you share this concern then be aware that some churches have begun issuing a piece of paper in the bulletin for people to use if they gave using the online giving program. They write down the amount they contributed online for that week and then drop it into the offering plate as a testimony of giving their offering during the worship service.

Churches and Christians have the habit of being very conservative. While this serves us well in areas of doctrine, it has hurt is in many other ways. I am sure the first time someone put a dollar bill into an offering plate it raised an eyebrow. After all, a dollar bill, or silver note as they were called, was just paper. Real money was made of silver and gold, just like in the Bible. I would have loved to be at a church the first time someone dropped a check into the offering plate, as I am sure there was a ruckus because it was a promise of payment, and not really "giving" during worship since the church would have to take the check to a bank and have money transferred to their account later on during the week. After all, many hold that the giving of our tithes and offerings MUST take place during the worship service, and that a check is just a promise of that gift later on that week. Of course, these objections would seem silly today since checks are a traditional method of payment.

In fact, debit card payments are more direct than a check! And yes, to accept such funds you have to have a merchant account, but to accept checks you have to have a bank account, and normally there is a charge associated with having an account and ordering checks for it.

Young people and old now use debit cards, and it is unthinkable for a church to tell them that they can't give or tithe using this widely acceptable method. We risk making our message and our association with our membership irrelevant if we decline to accept it.

Some churches have been bold enough to install electronic banking kiosks within the narthex or lobby of their church. To them I say, Bravo! But since my subject is Web sites, let me stick to online giving.

Once you set up an online giving service, it should be displayed fairly prominently your site, although I don't suggest you post it on your home page unless you make it clear that this is in a "members only" part of the site. You don't want to give the appearance that your Web site is about soliciting funds. On the other hand, you want to be sure your members CAN find the location where they can sign up and make their offerings.

Once a member sets up an account to give electronically, they should have a variety of options. They should be able to give whenever they come to the site, or set up a regular payment plan just as they do for online bill payment services or other financial matters. If they set a figure to be automatically taken from their account each week, and something unexpected happens and they can't make the payment, they should also be able to simply visit the site and adjust the amount.

In setting up your church with an online giving service you will have the option to list various funds. When a member prepares to give they will be presented with the option to give a set amount to the general offering, as well as any or all of the various offerings you might be promoting at the time (such as a building fund, missions, etc.).

There are several different sources that quote pretty good increases in the percentages of monies received when they began to offer online giving. However, most of those sources making the claims are from companies providing the service, so I am hesitant to present such information as fact. I can tell you that I have spoken to many church leaders who have told that online giving has definitely increased their cash flow, though few would present accurate percentages.

WEBSITE MINISTRY SPECIFIC TO YOUR MEMBERSHIP

A "live" Web site is designed to meet the needs for those seeking a new church after moving to a new area, and those seeking information about God. But don't forget your present membership! If you have a static site your members will never need to visit the site, and it will not serve any of their needs. However, to really begin to offer ministry to your membership you need to set up your Web site so that it can have sections that are private and accessible only to your members. This takes some clever programming if you are going to do it alone. However, most of the services that provide Web site creation for churches have included the ability to allow your membership to log into your site for access to exclusive materials.

Earlier in the chapter I mentioned five items to make your Web site a live site. Here they are again:

1. Content
2. Community
3. Contribution (missions)
4. Connectivity (to ministry)
5. Construction

As we have looked at content in regards to a church's mission statement, you have seen examples of the many opportunities to develop a community as you find ways to include content to encourage fellowship. In the area of contributions and worship I have already discussed online giving. In the discussion of evangelism, as I have pointed out your members can contribute content such as their testimonies, either in text form or as a podcast or video. And in the area of connectivity to your ministries I have briefly covered some possibilities, such as participating in online discipleship classes. As we enter the area of Web site construction and look at the options available, we will again address many of the applications and features of Web site products and services and you will notice that they relate back to opportunities to accomplish a church's mission statements, as well as fit into the areas of providing content, creating community, and providing opportunities to contribute and connect to missions and ministry.

CONSTRUCTION OF YOUR WEB SITE

To build an effective Web site, my recommendation is that you need to use one of the many Content Management Systems that are on the market.

What is a content management system? Here's the definition according to Wikipedia:

"A Web content management system (WCMS or Web CMS) is content management system (CMS) software, usually implemented as a Web application, for creating and managing HTML content. It is used to manage and control a dynamic collection of Web material (HTML documents and their associated images). A WCMS facilitates content creation, content control, editing, and many essential Web maintenance functions. Unlike Web-site builders like Microsoft FrontPage or Adobe Dreamweaver, a WCMS allows non-technical users to make changes to an existing Web site with little or no training. A WCMS typically requires an experienced coder to set up and add features, but is primarily a Web-site maintenance tool for non-technical administrators."

I will cover three different options in the area of Web site construction. First, I'll take a look at the many companies that provide content management systems designed specifically for churches. Second, I will cover add-on services that can be hosted separately, yet linked from within your home page that allow you to offer additional services that might not be available from your content management system. And third, I will cover several options for those that do desire to do it alone. I will review Joomla—probably the nation's most popular free Web site service—as well as some programming directions for those that are really brave!

For most churches I feel that using one of the many content management systems available on the market is the obvious way to go. And there are several reasons for this. First, using a template from a content management system will help you avoid some of the mistakes people can make in setting up their Web sites. CMSs provide you with a consistent, acceptable menu system, as well as an organization flow for your site. Their services are setup up as a SaaS (software as a service) so there is no coding to learn, and everything you want to do concerning style, content, posts, and features, you do via the Web itself. This also means that multiple people can be involved in maintaining the site or posting content.

When you move into the construction stage for your Web site, you will need to revert back to your intended purpose, mission and goals. For example, do you want interactive communications? Will you require the ability for users to view or download documents, videos or audio files? And will you provide content that is only available to people that register or subscribe, like RSS feeds or Podcasts? Do you want to display a church calendar and, if so, who and how many do you want to have administrative access to post events? After reading through this chapter, and looking at examples of how people have used Web site features to expand their ministry, make sure that the direction you aim for in the creation and construction of your Web site can deliver the features you want.

David Gillaspey has the best site on the Internet for information on content management systems for churches, and has made available to me his comprehensive list. If you are in the market for a new Web CMS provider, want to remake your Web site, or are one of the churches that are just getting started, I encourage you to print the list and go through it, and select the items you think will fit the purpose and ministry goals of your Web site. Then use the list to help shop and compare between the different Christian Web CMS services. You will find that there is no one company has every feature, and you will probably have to sacrifice some features to go with the company that best meets your needs and your budget. However, later on in this chapter I will also provide information on services that can be added to anyone's Web site, regardless of which one you pick.

I know, this is a long list, but I feel it is important to provide it for three reasons. Number one, it can serve as a valuable tool to help churches shopping for a new service. Number two, it can help educate you to the many features and ideas that can be incorporated into your Web site—ideas you might have never thought of up until now. And number three, it will help many realize that the best solution for meeting their Web site needs is to use one of these services instead of doing it all on your own.

CONTENT MANAGEMENT SYSTEM FEATURES

Again, this list was compiled by David Gillaspey of Great Church Websites http://www.greatchurchWeb sites.org after receiving input from more than sixty different Web site vendors. The list is not final, and will always continue to grow as new features are added to the services of different companies. (NOTE: In this list, CMS refers to content management systems. References to Church Management Software will be noted as such and not abbreviated.)

Address book/contacts manager tool is built in

Ads manager tool is built in

Alerts/messages manager tool is built in

Announcements manager tool is built in

Articles manager tool is built in (refers to a specific type of content)

Audio gallery manager tool is built in

Bible readings/verses tool is built in

Bible search features are built in

Bible study/devotionals tools are built in

Blessings manager tool is built in

Branding collaterals (beyond Web site) options are available from vendor

Calendar manager tool is built in (not the same as an upcoming events list tool)

Calendar subscriptions capacity is built in (allows synching with Outlook, etc.)

Capacity to integrate with external email clients is built in

CAPTCHA (anti-SPAM) integration is built in

Church management (non Web site-related) features are built in

Church marketing resources (beyond Web site) are available from vendor

Churches can host their own Web site or use a third-party hoster

Churches can migrate to CMS from existing site without starting from scratch

Classified ads tool is built in

CMS allows content channels to be created and managed by site editors

CMS allows for members-only content

CMS allows site editors to hide pages from menus

CMS auto saves content during content creation or editing

CMS can automatically optimize or resize images

CMS can automatically parse (convert to verses) Bible citations in text

CMS can be used with an existing Web site design

CMS can encrypt data

CMS can import data from another database

CMS can synchronize different content types during presentations

CMS can track and log users' access and activities

CMS can track and record changes to content (being edited) to a log file

CMS creates friendly (human-understandable and -recallable) URLs

CMS enables an editor to edit multiple pages simultaneously

CMS enables content tagging and/or can create tag clouds

CMS enables end users to have personal devotional journals

CMS enables individuals to create and manage blogs

CMS has specific features to integrate sites of multiple churches/campuses/ministries

CMS includes a built-in online Bible

CMS includes a specific tool for creating Top 10 lists

CMS includes a specific tool for displaying local sunset times

CMS includes a specific tool for managing parish or organization directories

CMS includes a tool for creating and managing a pastor's (specifically) blog

CMS includes features specifically for churches with multiple campuses

CMS includes features specifically for denominations

CMS includes features specifically for small groups

CMS includes specific tools for creating and publishing HTML forms in general

CMS includes specific tools to add entertaining content such as cartoons and games

CMS includes specific tools to create and maintain church membership directories

CMS includes specific tools to promote community and world issues

CMS includes virtual filing cabinets for end users

CMS is based on open-source software

CMS is based on the Adobe ColdFusion® architecture

CMS is fully based on Adobe Flash

CMS is fully Web standards compliant

CMS offers ability to have printer-friendly pages

CMS provides chat rooms

CMS provides document libraries for end users

CMS provides options for content to be viewed on mobile devices

CMS requires Filemaker Pro (third-party software)

CMS supports sub domains

Code can be customized by church and parish customers

Comment (or other) SPAM protection in general is built in

Comments (by end users) manager tool is built in (for example, to approve comments)

Confessions manager tool is built in

Contact staff and; leadership forms (specifically) management tool is built in

Content (for example, articles) for site is available from vendor

Content approval system is built in

Content can be filtered or personalized by site editors for different groups

Content can be password protected or restricted down to content block level

Content editing capacity is built in

Content scheduling (publish or unpublish) capacity is built in

Content versioning/archiving capacity (to save older versions of content) is built in

Custom database programming by vendor is available

Custom site design by vendor is available

Custom Web programming by vendor is available

Design consultation by vendor is available

Design templates, themes, or skins are available from vendor

Document galleries (for site editors) are built in

Documentation (print or online) for CMS is available from vendor

Drag-and-drop layout capacity (for site editors) is built in

e-Cards manager tool is built in

e-Commerce (storefront) features are built in

e-Giving features are built in

e-Invitations manager tool is built in

e-Learning features are built in

e-Newsletters/campaigns manager is built in

Email a friend (about the church, an article, etc.) feature is built in

Email SPAM/virus filtering is built in

End users can create and manage a personal profile

End users can personalize content and pages

Event registration system is built in (not the same as an upcoming events list manager)

FAQs (for end users, for example, about the church) manager tool is built in

Feedback (specifically) form creation tool is built in

File sharing (by end users) capacity is built in

File uploads (by site editors) capacity is built in

File/media manager (for site editors) is built in

Files or media downloads (by end users) capacity is built in

Filtered Web search capacity is built in

Find members like yourself tool is built in

Flash tool is built in (allows site editors to create .swf files from within the CMS)

Forums or message boards capacity is built in

Free trial of software is available from vendor

Google Analytics support or tool is built in

Groupware features are built in (allows collaborative work on non Web-related projects)

Guestbook features are built in

Header/banner manager tool is built in

Hospitality/visitations tool is built in

Image editing tools are built in (not the same as image optimization capacity)

Image/content rotation manager tool is built in

Inline content editing capacity is built in (allows editing content on a live page)

Instant messaging (by end users) capacity is built in

iSpeak (virtual spokesperson) integration is built in

Library/book (for end users) manager tool is built in

Links checker tool is built in (checks for bad links on pages)

Links pages/links manager tool is built in

List server features are built in

Live streaming (for example, of worship services) capacity is built in

Live training on how to use the CMS is available from vendor

Local weather info can automatically be generated/displayed by CMS

Locator maps/directions manager tools are built in

Mailing list manager tool is built in

Media archives (for end users) manager is built in

Media center (for end users) for finding and; playing media is built in

Media player(s) are built in

Meta tag manager tool (for example, to customize tags by page) is built in

Ministries+volunteers matcher tool is built in

Ministry or groups can have their own sub sites or sections

Ministry profiles/descriptions (specifically) tool is built in

Multi-language support is built in

Multimedia support in general is built in

Needs and services tool is built in (matches people with needs to people who can meet those needs)

News manager tool is built in (refers specifically to content labeled as "News" on Web site)

Online help/tutorial files for CMS are available from vendor

Online newsletter manager tool is built in

Other graphic design services are available from vendor

Other marketing/branding services are available from vendor

Page error redirect tool is built in

Pages can be previewed by site editors before pages are published

PDF file creation (by end users) capacity is built in

People in the spotlight (specifically) feature tool is built in

Personal media library (for end users) capacity is built in

Photo album/gallery manager tool is built in

Pledge manager tool is built in

Podcasting capacity is built in

Polls/surveys manager tool is built in

Prayer requests manager tool is built in

Print catalog creation or editing tool is built in

Printed bulletin creator tool is built in

Privacy/security statements (specifically) manager tool is built in

Private messaging capacity is built in

Private subgroups/sections capacity is built in

Product pricing is based on church size

Quote of the day (specifically) manager tool is built in

Randomized content manager tool is built in

Redesign of CMS-based site (by vendor) is possible

Relationship management tools are built in

Requests (prayer, ministry need, etc.) manager tool is built in

Resource libraries (for end users) capacity is built in

Rooms and resources (e.g., projectors) scheduling tool is built in

RSS features are included in CMS

Schedule (appointments) manager tool is built in

Scrolling newsflashes tool is built in

Secure forms/pages can be created in CMS (not the same as password protection)

Sermon notes manager tool is built in

Sermons manager tool is built in

Services (worship, prayer, etc.) times/description manager tool is built in

Site backup capacity is built in

Site backup capacity is provided through vendor hosting

Site design can be customized by church and parish customers

Site map (for end users) manager tool is built in

Site search capacity is built in

Sites based on this CMS are accessible to people with disabilities

Sites based on this CMS are search engine optimized

Slide show management tool is built in

Social networking features are built in

Special navigation features are included

Spell checker (for site editors) is built in

Splash screen creation tool is built in

Staff and amp; leaders profiles/directories can easily be created using a specific built-in tool

Stock artwork library is available from vendor (not the same as templates)

Streaming media capacity is built in

Tech support (in general) is provided by vendor

Testimonies manager tool is built in

Text messaging (to mobile devices) capacity is built in

Third-party modules can be used to add functionality to this CMS

Ticket tracking is built in (tracks requests from end users not tech support requests)

Upcoming events list manager tool is built in (not the same as calendar manager tool)

User permissions management capacity is built in

Vendor hosting of site is not available

Vendor hosting of site is optional

Vendor hosting of site is required

Vendor offers option to manage Web site for church or parish

Video conversion capacity is built in

Video gallery manager tool is built in

Visitor stats/reports are available with this CMS

Visitor/attendee assimilation manager tool is built in

Workflow features are built in (refers to tracking of tasks to be completed)

As you can see, there are many different features used by these companies in helping to provide the most useful Web site for your church and congregation. Hopefully, as you go through the list, you will be inspired with ideas to add to your Web site, or you might realize that you need to scrap what you have now and move to one of these innovative content management systems for your church's Web site!

WEBSITE SERVICES SPECIFIC FOR THE NEEDS OF A CHURCH

There are many companies out there seeking to provide services for churches to use in setting up their Web sites. Companies such as faithHighway.com, Elexio.com, SiteOrganic.com, Ekklesia 360, Extend and Cloversite.com are just a few of the companies I am familiar with. But if you do a search for "Church Websites" on Google you are going to find that there are a lot of choices.

Regardless of the size of your church, there are solutions available to fit your budget. Obviously smaller churches with small budgets will be limited in the many services that most of these companies can offer (at additional fees, of course). But even a small church would be ahead of the game if they use the services of some of these companies that provide a low-cost or entry-level product. Design is vital. Most people will give a poorly designed and unattractive Web site a few seconds before they will click away to another site. So even the basics are important if the design, color scheme, and important information is communicated from just the top half of the home page.

Finding the Right Service for Your Needs

Here are a few tips to help you determine which company might be best for your church:

1. Define your ministry goals and list the features you want to include on your site, such as blogs, online giving, presentation of media, etc. Realize that all of these do not have to be provided by the original Web site service, since some can be added via other services (see more below). Form a committee of people who use the Internet. Include young people. In just a few years, they will be your young adults with families and be the ones you are seeking to involve. Get opinions about what people are using (blogs or discussion boards, Twitter or Facebook) and use them to help define your list of features. Certainly do not exclude ministry staff from the process. Even if they need to be educated as to how a Web site can marry with ministry, take the time to get their input.

2. Define your budget. However, realize that the more you spend, the more features you provide, the more you can actually accomplish the ministries your church was

established to perform in the first place. If you create a "live" Web site with good content, the opportunity for people to connect and communicate, and features specific for your membership (such as online giving), you will most likely have more people visit your Web site each week than walk through your doors. So don't under-budget for this important aspect of your ministry.

3. Prioritize your list. As you begin to shop and compare features with costs, you will be sure to limit your compromises and not be tempted to give up the very reason you want to establish your site (or rebuild your old site).

4. Most services offer testimonies from their users, and links to various sites that use their service. Visit these sites, and, if possible, make contact with the persons at the specific churches that use the services you are considering.

When you get your decision narrowed down to one or two companies, ask them for references in your area. The Internet is certainly borderless, and viewing churches that use their services will give you an idea of what they can accomplish, regardless of where it is located. But I recommend you make a personal connection with other churches that use their services. If they are in your area, you can visit with the person in charge of the church Web site and find out first hand if their experience has been positive.

CMS Testimonies

Here are a few quotes from some of the churches that are using the services of those I mentioned above. I encourage you to read through them and also visit the sites of those that seem interesting. By doing so you will gain some great insight concerning what is available, and what each company can offer!

faithHighway—www.faithhighway.com

Here are a few comments from some of the customers of faithHighway, including the Web addresses of the churches for you to check out:

> *"You guys have been just tremendous. From your customer service to sharing in our vision, to exceptional creative design . . . The way you provide feedback to us to let us*

know you really care about our vision and what we want was great! We gave you our vision and you told us what we needed, not just what we wanted."

Wanda McClure, Oasis Church, Loganville, GA
www.theoasischurch.org/

"As the Web Communications Coordinator I would like to say 'well done' and know that by being so kind, helpful and patient with us . . . you all will have additional jewels in yours crowns in heaven. Praying for God to bless faithHighway as we partner with you to bring God's Word and promises to cyber space."

Margie Brinker, Fellowship Bible Church,
Little Rock, AR—www.fbclr.org/

"Our church has tripled in size in only 4 months from having our media accessible online through our faithHighway Web site."

Pastor Tim Woodson, The Well Church, Grand Rapids, MI
www.thewellchurchonline.com/

"One of the most extraordinary outcomes we've seen through having a custom-fit Web site is when we did a direct mail campaign. We went all out . . . purchasing billboards around town and placing the campaign all over our Web site. We had a couple who started attending our church because they saw one of our billboards. They went to our Web site and were looking for a church . . . and that is what brought them to faith! We have testimony after testimony of experiences just like this. "

Pastor Kent Elliot, Faith Tabernacle, Manchester, CT
www.faithtabernacle.com/

"After about 4 years of having just a Web presence, we decided as a ministry that it was time to turn our focus outward and use the site as a means to really draw people into the church, and so far it's worked! faithHighway has been tremendous in helping us focus and streamline the site to make it relevant. "

Pastor Jermaine Keller, First Christian Church,
Napa, CA—www.fccnapa.org

Elexio—www.elexio.com

Here are a few comments from some of the customers of Elexio, including the Web addresses of the churches for you to check out:

> *"What a pleasure it is to work with Elexio! This highly professional team of developers and designers is very creative and thoughtful; I can count on the entire team to offer sound solutions for our Web site requirements. In addition, Elexio's content management system is easy to work with and has greatly simplified the task of developing and maintaining our Web site. Selecting Elexio as our Web site partner is one of the smartest business decisions we've made."*
>
> Cynthia Terpstra, Director of Communications,
> Advent Life Ministries, Boca Raton,FL
> citerpstra@adventlifenet.org

> *"I just wanted to let you know that I am being inundated with praise for our "new" Web site. Everyone is calling and emailing me to tell me how inviting it is, how easy it is to see and use, and how beautiful! I want to thank you for all you help. I really feel I got enormous value for my money! We are actually having a lot of visitors sign up for our events and we never had that before! What a blessing! I am so excited about the possibilities!"*
>
> *"Our Elexio Web site solution is an interactive partner that actually has our own 'personality.' With so many staff members contributing, I love having complete control over the content and being able to decide who can contribute and how. I never have any surprises!"*
>
> Judy Shedd, Isle of Faith UMC, Jacksonville, FL
> www.iofumc.org

> *"Everybody's really happy that we chose Elexio. It was like divine intervention. We were looking for a new Web site provider and had researched a lot of companies. My son attended a church in Richmond and they happened to be unveiling their new Web site, which was with Elexio. "*
>
> *"I had no idea how to do anything with a Web site and now everyone is very happy with the site."*
>
> Donna Hatfield, First Baptist Church, Hopewell, VA
> www.fbchopewell.org

"Just a quick note . . . I have been very impressed with the Elexio Support Team that handles the Support Requests. The timeliness of their responses has been great and gets our questions answered quickly, which was my first hesitation with that whole system. Not being able to pick up the phone and call someone with questions was a little unsettling, but I have been very pleasantly surprised with the whole process and want to pass it along."

Annie Helms, First Baptist Church, Orange City, FL

www.thejourneyoc.net

"We spent months researching and comparing options for our Web site. Elexio certainly stood out from the rest. We have been more than satisfied with the value. We had a very clear idea of what we wanted our site to look like and Elexio's designers went above and beyond to ensure that our site was exactly what we wanted."

Dan Leverence, Constance Free Church, Ham Lake, MN

www.constanceonline.com

SiteOrganic—www.siteorganic.com

Here are a few comments from some of the customers of SiteOrganic, including the Web addresses of the churches for you to check out:

"I just wanted to let you know that the more I use our site and the editing tools, the more I like it! Also, I have heard great reviews about the design from the people in my church. Thanks for all you did."

Patte Martin, Woodbury/Peaceful Grove United Methodist Church—www.wumc-pgumc.org

"We are still aglow with joy after reviewing the designs for our new site. We are so very pleased with the work that you and the design team have done and are so glad that we were finally able to take the leap with SiteOrganic. The work that you are doing will truly bless our congregation and the community at large. Thank you."

Meagan Block, Highland Oaks Church of Christ

www.hocc.org

"You all are a great company to work with. Thank you for not only getting our site looking good, but standing behind your product with great service."

Don Jaques, Christ the King—www.ctkonline.com

Ekklesia 360—www.ekklesia.com

Ekklesia 360 is created by Monk Development. Here are a few quotes from some of their users along with links to their Web site:

"As a person who has overseen the production of eight Web site overhauls, I have never used a CMS so easy and sophisticated as Ekklesia 360. All you need to figure out is what you want your site to do and how you want it to look and it takes care of the rest. It's an exceptional product for churches because it was built by pastors and church planters."

Eric Brown, Pastor, Imago Dei Community
www.imagodeicommunity.com/

"Ekklesia 360 is incredibly easy to work with, and I am constantly amazed at the flexibility their system offers. What continues to impress me the most, however, is Monk's staff. All of the staff I encountered are knowledgeable, gracious and fun to work with. They are willing to work with anything I can throw at them from the mundanely simple to the incredibly complex. I honestly cannot imagine working with a better team of people on this project.

I cannot recommend Monk Development enough. They have exceeded our expectations, and I look forward to the continuing relationship between our two organizations. When it's time to grow and expand our site again, Monk will be the company we turn to."

DJ Turner, Director of Communications,
Denver Seminary—www.denverseminary.edu/

"Monk Development has by far exceeded my expectations of what a Web site development company can and should be! We've had new visitors to our church as a result of our new Web site and the body appreciates how easy all of the features are to use. From a Ministry Director

standpoint, I appreciate how fast and reliable the site is in communicating with the body. I know Monk Development has been a blessing to my ministry!"

Kerri Sadigh, Director of Community Life Groups, Creekside Church —www.creeksidechurch.com/

"Every person I spoke to, and I went about two levels beyond the people on Monk Development's reference list, raved in their praise for the company. I don't know if there is something in the water out west, but I have rarely heard such praises for any organization. I only hope people speak as highly about me. I heard that the company surpassed each organizations expectation in the development phase. The art, graphics, and overall presentation was much better than the customers ever expected. More importantly, I heard that the company had a real passion for Christ and for spreading the gospel. And as a client, I found that all these references were spot on."

Greg Penna, Pastors Edge—www.pastorsedge.com/

"Launching our new site with Ekklesia has been great. The process was simple and fast. Since we've launched we already seen a significant increase in visitors both online and on Sunday. I highly recommend it to everyone!"

Russ Kapusinski, Pastor, Harbor Presbyterian Church
www.harborchulavista.com/

Extend—www.extendplatform.com/

Extend content management system is provided by ACSTechnologies. Check out some of the comments from some of their users:

"Reaching people for Christ requires multiple approaches for sharing the gospel. It's about Web ministry, not just a Web site. When we're working with churches, we can point them to the Web and help them with their online evangelism strategy. We value the relationship with ACS Technologies and the Extend staff, and all they do to serve us as clients."

Roger Orman, Associate Executive Director, South Carolina
Baptist Convention, Columbia, SC—www.scbaptist.org

"Extend has been a lifesaver for Revolution Church. As a young church plant, we made the decision early on to pursue a high technology driven outreach and we knew our Web site had to be the hub for information. Extend has allowed us to easily convey information to people both inside and outside of our church. We were able to easily integrate our contact management system, Facebook, Groups, and Twitter accounts on our Web site. With Extend, there is no need to learn coding or html. The ease of use reduces the time it takes to manage our site which frees us up to spend time with our congregation and community. The phone support for Extend is phenomenal. They have always been there for us to help if we should need a little guidance."

Chris Reeder, Lead Pastor, Revolution Church, Florence, SC—www.RevolutionChurch.me

"The beauty of Extend is it takes people with NO Web abilities, and gives them the tools to have a functional communication tool. "

Jeff Suever, Business Adminstrator, First Presbyterian Church, Pompano Beach, CA—www.pinkpres.org

Cloversite.com—www.cloversite.com
Here are a few comments from some of the customers of Cloversite, including the Web addresses of the churches for you to check out:

"I was impressed with how easy it was for a guy like me to manage my own Web site. I was able to use the demo link and email it to my senior, associate and other pastors to pitch to them why I needed "my own" Web site, separate from the church Web site. They were all so impressed with what I was able to do on my own that I was granted permission, granted the money, spent the money and now am in love with what we have been able to do in Children's Ministry because of Clover . . . seriously!"

Zack Grelling, Children's Director, Grace Church of Glendora—www.skitministries.com

"You guys have made it pretty easy for us. Just FYI—We're literally saving thousands of dollars over what we were doing before, plus the quality of the site and ease of use are much better than in the past. Thanks for helping churches."
Daniel Harris, Pastor of Discipleship, First United Methodist Church—www.firstmethodistmidland.com

"I've probably never emailed a company I've bought something off of, but there's a first for everything. I just have to say how impressed I am with your product. Everything from the ease of use, the quality of the sites, how easy it was to purchase and get going on it—it is one of the most intuitive things I've ever used. Well worth the money!! I've showed several people already who are considering getting their own site from you! Thanks!"
Matt Carder, Commonway Church
www.commonwaychurch.com

"I am a pastor with very little Web savvy, but I was able to purchase one of your sites and go live with it with 2 hours of work! It took me longer to decide what photos to use than it did to edit the site. I'm still working on it, but it is 100x's better than our old site. You guys are awesome. Thank you."
Kyle Turner, Life Church of Bartlesville
www.lifechurchok.org

ADDITIONAL SERVICES, SOLUTIONS, AND LINKS TO EXPAND YOUR WEB SITE'S MINISTRY

Now that you have decided how to create your Web site, and who to use to do it, realize that you are not limited to what they alone can provide. The beauty of the Internet is the ability to connect. You may have picked a Web content management system because you liked the price or certain features that you found enticing. But what if they don't offer the ability for other features that you want? Check around and you will find secondary services that you can easily connect to your site, and most have the ability to incorporate your logo and color scheme so the site has a connection to the overall look and feel of your site. Some even have services that can be displayed within a content window on your site so you never lose your branding.

Elexio Infinity—Ministry Website Plug-ins

Even though Elexio is one of the Web content management systems that many churches pick to handle their entire site, they also offer Elexio Infinity, which is presently made up of four different stand alone SaaS services that you can acquire and link from your site, regardless of who handles your home page.

Elexio's MediaRush—First, if your present site doesn't have the ability to post your audio, video PDF files or podcasts all in one place, you might consider checking out MediaRush. Some services simply do not have the bandwidth to stream large numbers of media files, especially video. With MediaRush you can have a site set up in minutes, and you will be ready to present your members and visitors with a clear menu system for finding your media files. MediaRush actually installs in a content window within your site, so there is no worry about people feeling like they left your site.

Use descriptive words to describe your media. That way, when you post your sermons, in either audio or video format, or your articles, lessons, etc., in Word docs or PDF files, people visiting will find the media they are seeking. People will come to your site seeking answers to today's questions. They will need to find sermons and materials on how to handle stress, or find peace in the midst of a disaster. You don't want to just list your media files using titles like "Sermon, May 3, 2009".

If, while listening, watching or reading materials in your MediaRush library, your members or visitors find something that meets their need or touches them in some way, they can click on the option to email a link to a friend.

MediaRush supports many different file formats including mp3, flv and mp4 (mp4 files can have many different extensions such as .mpg). They will also provide your site with built-in audio and video players in case some of your visitors don't have one already installed. So what does it cost after your 30-day free trial? How about $1 a day! MediaRush is a great service, and I encourage you to check it out at www.elexioinfinity.com.

Elexio's Higher Giving—Want to offer online giving on your site, but your present Web site provider or Web content management system doesn't have the function? No problem, you can use Higher Giving from Elexio to add the feature to your site in no time. You will have to obtain a merchant account to use the service (you will have to do this to initiate any online giving program), but once you set it up (normally in 2-7 days) it takes only minutes to get Higher Giving set up on your site. If you don't know how to obtain a merchant account, call Elexio and they'll put you in contact with someone that can you help you set it up.

Once installed on your site, your administrator can set up the different funds you have established to receive donations (e.g., general fund, building, missions, youth trip, etc.) When your members go to the site they can simply pick the amount the wish to donate and designate different amounts into the different funds that are available. They can make donations whenever they wish, or set up reoccurring donations on a regular schedule. Of course, if there is a problem they can simply visit the site and adjust their giving. And of course the church will have to pay whatever fees are associated with the merchant account, and these will vary depending on the credit cards you choose to take. The actual cost for using Higher Giving from Elexio is $10 a month, regardless of the size of your church or the number of transactions per month.

Elexio's SmoothEvents—If you want to ad events to your Web site, but don't have the feature available to you at present, once again Elexio has made a separate service that can be inserted directly into any content page on your site. You can create an unlimited number of events, each with their own pricing models (cost to attend an event, for example) with the ability to offer discounts. You also have an unlimited number of user-defined questions. When a member signs up for an event, the service can send them a confirmation email that you can customize, as well as a reminder email that you can set up to go when you desire. Once people have registered for your event online, SmoothEvents allows you to export the registration data in CSV format, ready to import into Microsoft Word or Excel. SmoothEvents uses the same security as their Higher Giving service. If you want to take payment for events that have a ticket price, you will need to set up a merchant account. It is only $20 a month for the tools, and if more than 30 people register for any one event then $1 is charged for registrant numbers 31 and up.

When your members or visitors come to your Web site to sign up for an event, they will see a listing of upcoming events, number of remaining seats, and the date and time for each event. They will be required to register to use the event manager, but only once. The next time they come back to the service they will just enter their user name and password. Once they have logged in they will see additional information, such as the location, contact information, a description/promotion for the event, and the cost. They can click to register or view other upcoming events. And, it is easy to set up an event. You simply go into the administrator menu, select "create an event" and fill out the form with the name of the event, start and end date, maximum registrations if there is a limit of attendees, cost, location information, contact information, etc.

Elexio's AnswersCafe—This one's pretty unique. Elexio has teamed up with HomeWord, which is a team of Christian experts in family, parenting, youth and relationships led by Jim Burns. They are on the radio in more than 800 U.S. cities. Peoplecall in and ask questions and HomeWord provides Biblical answers. Well, they have now taken many of those answers, audio files, and even videos and put them all in one place. And the content is constantly expanding as new materials are added. Sign up to use AnswersCafe, and in about five minutes you will have it up and running on our site. Visitors can simply go to the site and search for answers to their questions. They will also see subjects arranged by categories, including;

- ▶ Addictions
- ▶ Faith
- ▶ Money
- ▶ Relationships
- ▶ Entertainment
- ▶ Healthy Living
- ▶ Parenting
- ▶ Teen Life

Any person can search for specific words, as well as the format they would like to use, i.e., audio, videos or documents. When you add the code to your site, it will again fit directly into any content page so you are not taking people off site to use the service. The resource page is very inviting, with a rundown on where the information is coming from, as well as interesting information about your topic of choice.

One exciting feature of this service is that you can create your own resources and add them to those already provided by AnswersCafe. Do you have a sermon on marriage enrichment? Or audio recordings on substance abuse? Or has one of your ministers written an article for your newsletter on handling stress? As an administrator, you can go to the "Create a New Resource" feature and ad your media, including information that gets posted to AnswersCafe to help describe it and make it searchable. Fantastic! You can even use videos that have been posted on YouTube or GodTube, which makes it easy to create your own video chats with answers to today's questions right from your computer using your camera and microphone. Post them to YouTube, and then use that service to include them in AnswersCafe! The cost is less than $2 a day, and it's an amazing resource for your church and community for only $50 a month.

There are several services that allow you to organize and present your media to your church through your Web site.

SermonFlow from faithHighway

FaithHighway provides their SermonFlow feature even if you are not using their service to host your site. It allows you to post your media files—audio, video and text—in one location where you can present them in an exciting way. If you have ever been to iTunes, you will have noticed how media content is presented with the visual impact of being able to flip through album covers. The SermonFlow presentation is called CoverFlow. It looks similar to the way albums used to be presented in the old jukeboxes. So using SermonFlow allows you to present your media files in an exciting way, instead of having your visitors scroll down a long list of files. In this application, you can create graphics images like album covers, representing a particular series of sermons, sermons from a particular pastor, sermons presented during a specific time period, etc. You might use a picture of the pastor leading the series, or a logo.

SermonFlow will also encourage you to do something I think is important: provide media in a variety of formats, and not just the one you like. I call it "media the Burger King" way! Let people have their media the way they want it. For each sermon you might post, give people a choice of viewing it in video format, or taking it with them as an audio podcast, or even a transcript in the form of a PDF file. Then put an entire sermon series under one logo and allow your visitors to see the titles of each sermon and have three different ways to find and utilize the media.

SermonFlow also allows you to add descriptive tags to your media, so when people use the search feature they will find the content that will meet their needs.

ServiceU Provides Several Add-on Services to Your Web Ministry

ServiceU Corporation (www.ServiceU.com) was founded in 1997 to meet a common problem churches and nonprofits were experiencing with scheduling events and managing resources. They were one of the leaders in providing Web-based services that would work in conjunction with a church's Web site. However, founder Tim Whitehorn recognized the needs of the church and anticipated technology advancements in the software industry.

EventU—EventU is a Web-based event, resource and facility management tool that utilizes calendar scheduling software to help churches manage and streamline events in a completely hosted solution.

As you can see from the sample screen shot above, it is easy to provide online registration information, accept payments and any other critical information for any type of church event online.

All of the information that a church would input into the scheduling system can be automatically published to the church's calendar online in real-time. Also, because the system is Web-based, events can be set up, rooms can be reserved, and everyone members and staff alike can be kept in the loop 24/7, regardless of physical location.

TransactU—Once ServiceU had established itself in the market with their EventU product, there was a need for churches to be able to take registrations for events and pay online if there was a fee. So they created and released TransactU, which allows churches the opportunity to take payments for online registration, as well as online giving. TransactU also gives churches the ability to take registrations for online for Bible studies, Vacation Bible School, and any other events, along with accepting payments and one-time and/or weekly tithes and special gifts.

TicketU™—In 2005, ServiceU released TicketU, the company's solution for churches that sell tickets on their Web site to Christmas events, Easter Celebrations, summer concerts, or any other large ticketed event. From the convenience of the church's Web site, visitors are able to select the seat they wish and pay for tickets online. In addition, the church can offer print-at-home tickets, tickets by mail, and will-call service.

It is also worth mentioning one of ServiceU's latest ventures. If a church is using EventU to schedule all of their events, and thereby their building space, ServiceU added EventU Green™ to their list of solutions for churches. EventU Green is an add-on to EventU which allows churches to automate their heating and cooling HVAC controls online in real-time, which can ultimately save energy and costs associated with temperature control. As events and meeting are booked, changed, or canceled in EventU, EventU Green works to control heating and cooling accordingly. Churches average a savings of 10–20 percent in costs per year.

For more information about any of ServiceU's services and solutions, visit www.ServiceU.com.

Small Group Web Solutions from Upper Room Technology

Max Lucado is one of our generation's most popular Christian authors. He has written a host of books and materials that he has specifically marketed for small groups, and is a leader in the concept of churches establishing small groups that can meet in homes across the community, helping members connect with each other and expand the church's ministry of training and discipleship. Do a search using Google on the subject "Why Small Groups" and you will discover a sizable list of books, magazine articles, blogs and articles promoting the creation and use of small groups in today's church. This is especially vital for larger churches. The car has unfortunately destroyed the concept of the local church. Most people living in a city admit that they drive by many churches on their way to the one that they have chosen to join. My wife and I drive 20 miles to attend the church we worship and serve with. Unfortunately, large churches with members driving from outside communities risk losing connection within their membership. By establishing small groups that meet in homes throughout the week churches enable members to connect with fellow members of their church that live in their community. And, because you meet as a small group, the development of community allows people to open up and have the opportunity to support each other in personal prayer and ministry. Small groups enable a church to expand their discipleship ministry as people gather to study a Christian book or join in a Bible study.

Many Church Management Software programs have provided some ability to manage your groups, but many are lacking in the features required to meet the technology connection tools that are needed. Some groups turn to services like Yahoo Groups to help stay connected, or set up a group using one of the popular social networking sites, such as Facebook. However, there is a better solution!

Remember Max Lucado? He is the pulpit minister at Oak Hills church in San Antonio, Texas. Oak Hills was also blessed with some computer programmers who had an inspiration, and in 2006 they were asked to examine commercial solutions for Oak Hills to use to help provide Internet tools to help their small groups connect. Unfortunately, they didn't find a solution that worked. But since they were programmers with experience in creating multi-million dollar applications for other industries, they decided to create a special Web solution to enable all of the small groups at Oak Hills to have their own site to connect, and all of the sites would be connected to a central point where new members of the church, and visitors, could see the available groups and request a connection.

Groups Interactive—The company, UpperRoom Technologies, was developed and the product they provided Oak Hills was called Groups Interactive. And after using it at Oak Hills for two years, they brought it to the market in 2008 for other churches to use. Church members could now come to a location on a Web site and find several ways to find and connect with the available small groups the church was providing.

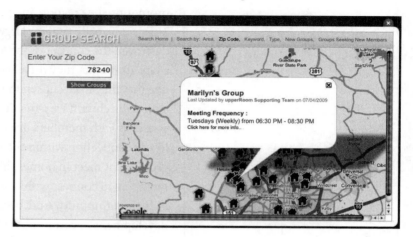

Groups Interactive (GI) provides you the ability to present a list of available small groups on your site, sorted by name, type (men's group, singles group, parents, young couples, general, etc.) location, etc. If a group is full (a small group is only effective if it remains small enough for communication and connection to be intimate), it can be noted that it is presently full (time to start a new one in that community!). However, one of the ways GI developed to present small groups to your members is through a mapping system. Click on the small group link they provide for your site and you will see a map of your city with a little flag in the locations around the city where your small groups meet. This makes it very easy for people to find and connect with a small group in their area.

GI also allows users to use a search features to find the group they want. Visitors can search for key words such as "woman's group," or using a zip code. You can even search for groups within your neighborhood by using the name of your housing development. And, just recently they added the ability to search for "groups that are just forming."

Once a member finds a small group that is open, they can request a connection. GI doesn't give out the addresses of the homes where your small groups meet. Instead, interested parties can click on the group they are interested in and fill out a small "request information" form, providing their email address, phone, or other contact info. This goes directly to the group that they requested information from. The group leaders receive an email informing them that someone has requested information about joining their group. If the group leader does not get back with the prospect, the email is then moved up and flagged for immediate attention. No one falls through the cracks . . . Fantastic!

Besides just providing great contact information and connection tools for your members, GI also provides an incredible online home for each of your small groups. Each site allows your small group members to have a pictorial directory, with each having the options and freedom to decide if they want their personal contact information displayed for the rest of the group. From within the site, the leader or ANY small group member can post an event, a prayer request, or a message. Now there is no need for everyone in the group to maintain each other's email addresses. You can simply go to the group and invite everyone over for lunch after church, or quickly inform everyone of an urgent prayer request. Even members who are not willing to post information such as their email address will be able to receive emails from the group.

In addition, GI allows each small group to manage their own calendar, book study information, and post upcoming events with the ability to request RSVP, and more. Each site also has the ability to pull church calendar information, church wide prayer requests, event announcements, messages and more, all from information the church's small group leader can push out to all of the small group sites in his church.

GI has a clean user-interface with a color scheme that will compliment any church logo or graphic presentation. They also incorporate your church logo and look throughout the program, even in the "welcome" and "find a group" windows.

A studies section makes it easy to create studies for groups, either by the group's leader or by the small group administrator. This is a great way to coordinate church-wide studies or sermon series, and administrators can monitor what each group is studying. GI even provides a special administrator's page where tools are easy to access and use, including reporting tools necessary to manage a dynamic small group ministry. It is in this area that church-wide events, prayer requests, messages, etc., can be pushed to all the individual small group Web sites.

Remember ServiceU mentioned above? Groups Interactive has partnered with their service. Churches using both will discover that when an event is scheduled in EventU, administrators have the option to pull the church calendar straight into Groups

Interactive. Users can then take events off of the church's calendar and add it straight into their personal events calendar. In fact, users can easily subscribe to their small group calendar through third-party calendar systems such as Outlook, iCal, Google Calendar and Yahoo Calendar.

Using GI, groups can take and report attendance, which are then pushed up to the small group administrator.

GI has a robust report function, and can provide reports such as:

▶ Users report
▶ Group approvals report
▶ Groups report
▶ Inquiries report
▶ Interested parties report
▶ Invitations report
▶ Members without groups report
▶ Remove members report
▶ Search results report
▶ Staff members report
▶ Study reports
▶ Users login report

Groups Interactive has the ability to work with large and multi-site churches, with the ability to designate, monitor and report on different campuses within the same church body.

UpperRoom Technology is also working with several of the Church Management Software companies to make their system integrate with church databases using these CMS products. For example, if a person visited their small group Web site and updated any portion of their contact information, that information would not only be updated to the GI site but also to the CMS product in use at the church office.

GI is working to complete mobile integration and release an iPhone application as well. They are also working on an application for Facebook.

One final note about Groups interactive is that it can help promote the start of new small groups. Within each small groups' Web site, there is an opportunity for information to be entered from the small group pastor that can provide details on how to start a new small group. Hopefully, many small groups will realize that they need to divide. By accessing this information, members may decide to start their own group and fill a need, and have the information they need to get started, and who they need to see to gain approval to launch.

ChurchRides.com—Another example of a Web service that you can plug into your present church Web site is a service called ChurchRides.com, which was also created and brought to the market by UpperRoom Technologies.

Basically, ChurchRides.com uses the same mapping software to allow members of your church to connect if they are seeking to carpool to church with other members in their neighborhood. As the price of gas goes up and down (mainly up!), and economic times fluctuate, such a service could really help many of your members. Members who live around the city and travel a bit of a distance to attend church could benefit by this service by clicking on the link on your church's Web site then entering information about where they live and the number of people in their party that need transportation to church. They can also enter information on whether they're willing to have others join them in their ride to church, or if they wish to take turns driving. They can click on the flags (represented on a map of their city) and request to be connected with others also looking to work out a carpool plan.

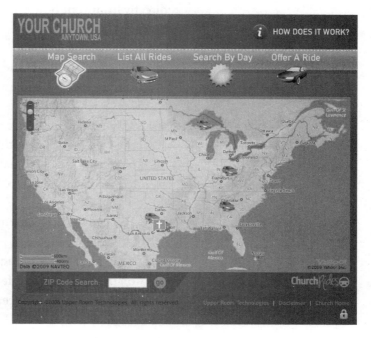

In the screenshot above you can see the different options available to a visitor. In this case, the map is zoomed all of the way out showing the entire United States, but once a person enters a zip code they will see a map of that city and can select from other available options. Doing a map search would show the location of those around the city willing to provide a ride, or a user can request a list of all available rides to peruse. You can also "Search by Day", or volunteer to provide rides for others by selecting that feature.

This will not only provide a needed service for those wishing to attend your church, but it will also cut down on your parking problem, especially if you happen to be a growing church that is quickly running out of parking spaces. Obviously, by encouraging your membership to use the services of ChurchRides.com, you will have less cars in the parking lot come Sunday. An added benefit is that membership will also have the opportunity to get to know each other better during the rides to and from church each week.

Add a Powerful Calendar to Your Site

There are a few Web calendar programs designed to work specifically with church Web sites, and here are a few:

CalendarCompanion.com This is a nifty little Web add-on I reviewed a year ago. It really provides a lot of functions to a church's Web site that goes a bit beyond just providing a calendar for our site. And it's easy to get started, allowing you to upload events directly from your browser. Here are some of the cool features of this must-have program:

▶ You can customize the calendar to have your look and feel, adding your own logos and color scheme.

▶ Visitors to your site can switch between views, displaying the calendar in monthly, weekly or daily views. They also have easy navigational tools to move forward or look at previous days on the calendar.

▶ You can set up recurring events.

▶ Your members can request an email reminder of an event on the calendar. This feature alone is why they made my list of Web add-on services. Very cool feature.

▶ Expanded content for each event is available, providing text with more information, graphics or Web links. You can also provide contact information for each event such as name, email address and/or phone number.

▶ Hide private events behind a password, since you may want to use the calendar for staff planning, but don't necessarily want the rest of the congregation to be aware of your schedule.

▶ Multiple administrators can be set up, so more than one person can help maintain the calendar.

▶ Your calendar can provide the ability to display a list of events that are scheduled for the next few days on other locations on your Web site using RSS. You would be able to provide a link to the complete calendar services from your Web site, yet also have a window displaying your next few upcoming events automatically in a section on the home page.

▶ Cost is $11.95 a month with a three-month free trial period.

MyChurchEvents.com—Ok, here's the skinny on MyChurchEvents .com:

▶ You can be set up and running in about 10 minutes simply by using a browser to access the functions of MyChurchEvents.com over the Web.

▶ You can enter recurring events once and it is set to show up in the calendar for the rest of the year.

▶ MyChurchEvents.com allows you to search for events based upon a special interest group. So if your church's calendar is pretty full, this will enable someone to select, for example, events held by the singles ministry, and get a clean clear calendar of those events.

▶ They provide an event plug-in that allows you to pull information from special occasions from the calendar and display it anywhere else on your Web site.

▶ They also allow you to customize your calendar with your church's logo and color scheme.

▶ MyChurchEvents also provides the ability to input door-to-door driving direction to events that are held at any location. If visitors wish to attend an event at a park, another church or at a member's home, they will have the driving directions along with the event details. Very nice!

▶ When your membership is viewing the calendar they can select the format that works best for their needs, viewing the calendar as a full month, a week at a time, or even having future events in a list format.

▶ MyChurchEvents provides a library with thousands of clipart pieces that can be inserted into one of your events to help people instantly recognize certain events.

▶ Members interested in a specific event can request an email reminder be sent a few days in advance.

▶ MyChurchEvents also provides a clever feedback form so that your members can give you valuable feedback about an event so you can improve it in the future. The forms tool can also be set for other uses. For example, you could set up a pre-registration form for an event!

▶ And finally, MyChurchEvents also uses a secure system to protect your calendar, only allowing administrators with access to set up events on your site, and also restricting some of the information on the calendar so that it is only viewable via a password.

▶ The cost for using MyChurchEvents is only $59.95 a year. Visit www.mychurchevents.com for more information.

WEBSITES MARRIED TO CHURCH MANAGEMENT SOFTWARE

Since many realized that the best church Web site would utilize content, develop community, offer opportunities to contribute and connect membership to ministry, it seemed only natural to combine a Web site with a Church Management Software program, and one of the first to do this was a company called MyFlock.com.

MyFlock.com

MyFlock.com was launched as a combination of services that included integrated content management, church management features and social networking tools. And it was considered innovative because their product began as a social networking tool at least two years before MySpace or any of the popular social networking tools were introduced. MyFlock.com was one of the first to include the church member as an active participant in the church management process by providing each one with a member profile on the church Web site. Additionally, every member profile feeds and helps maintain the integrated Church Management System member records for the church administrator. Member activities are also reflected in the church Content Management System by automatically showing updates to blogs, profiles, friend invites, who's online now, photo uploads, etc., right on the church Web site.

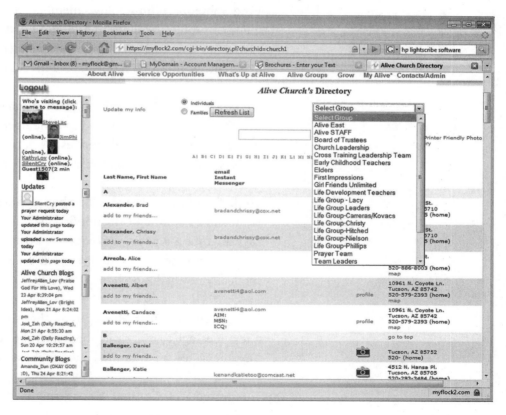

As you can see from the screenshot above, MyFlock provides a church directory with many options, including the ability to define the directory to a specific group.

In the area of developing community and fellowship, MyFlock.com also created some fantastic tools, and here are some of them:

Top 10 Most Like Me—Automatically analyzes every member profile to allow the member to see what things they have in common with other members in the church. This was sort of like some of the singles matchmaking sites that were hitting the Internet, but in this case it was designed to help church members and their families connect with other Christians that had similar interests. As we continue to see the decline of the small church and the growth of larger churches, an Internet application like this is a great way to help new people connect with others that have similar interests.

Find Someone Who—Allows members to search on all the member profile attributes to find those that share common recreation interests, common music tastes, common life experiences, common family elements, common hobbies, etc.

Google Member Map—The Church Management Software membership data is integrated in a member map viewable by all members to see where all families reside, where the small group leaders are located, where the elders live, etc.

High Tech Prayer Board—Members can sign up for the prayer team and be automatically notified via email and/or text message anytime a new prayer request is posted to the prayer board. Whenever someone responds to your prayer request, you're automatically notified as well.

Integrated SMS Text Messaging—The administrator can send a text message to every member using the admin control panel. Text messages are unlimited and incur no additional charges.

Integrated Web Content Management—They provide over 500 professionally designed templates and dozens of automated tools and pages for use in the integrated content management system.

Forums, Blogs and More—Every church member has a personal blog that they can design by selecting from the more than 500 design templates. Every church site has an integrated church forum where all the members can post.

Twitter Integration—They have created the ability to integrate your Twitter account. So when you post to your church Web site, it's automatically posted in your Twitter account too. They are currently working on a Facebook integration as well.

When MyFlock.com first hit the market, they created a dilemma but also defined the future. At first it was difficult to define what they were providing. They had some Church Management Software features such as membership data tracking, contributions, etc., but were also Web site providers for churches. Both attributes were combined into one offering and as a result, they were on the cutting edge in providing features and innovative applications. For example, if your church was using MyFlock, you could log into your church's site using a secure username and password and immediately see a graph of your recent contributions. Churches are required to send out a financial statement at the end of the year to its members for tax purposes, and some churches discovered that if they sent out a quarterly statement it would serve as a reminder for their members of their giving commitments. Most actually saw an increase in giving as a result of going to quarterly contribution statements. With MyFlock.com's posting of a member's most current statement, any member could immediately see where they stood as far as their yearly financial contributions were concerned, and could make adjustments as needed.

ChurchCommunityBuilder— www.churchcommunitybuilder.com

You have to love the name ChurchCommunityBuilder. Their name implies you "get it" when it comes to picking a service for your Web site and church administration needs.

Church Community Builder (CCB) was birthed out the need to build greater connectedness within the church. While leading a service at NewSong Community Church in Oceanside, Calif., the founders of this product became intimately familiar with the challenge of getting new people connected to the church and deepening their involvement and commitment. Leveraging the advantages and access of Web-based technology, they developed a solution that originally was designed to help churchgoers identify and commit to volunteer opportunities that matched their personal gifts, passions and abilities.

Over time they included membership data in the process and the original tool grew into a Web-based church management solution. However, as you can see from the title of their service, the community focus of CCB still remains a core focus and value for the firm. In their view, the church Web site is first and foremost a portal into the church community. It is often the first place people go to "check out" a church for the first time, and thus a critical and strategic place to make a good first impression. For that reason, CCB provides five different integration points that encourage traffic to the church Web site, and helps people connect with the ministry and other people once they are there. Here they are:

Community Login—CCB encourages the churches using their service to give every church member access to the church "database" at the appropriate level. The service uses the church Web site as the place where people go to log in.

Group and Ministry Search—CCB provides each church with a simple, yet powerful Web tool that allows visitors to browse the various connection opportunities that are available within a church. Whether its ministries, small groups or new visitor gatherings, CCB allows people to filter, search and locate opportunities that meet their needs and then connect with the leadership right from the church Web site. CCB does an excellent job of facilitating communication between visitors and members seeking to connect with ministry leaders, whether they are paid or volunteer. If a person sends a request for more information, the service can be set up to have it routed to the right person. However, it will also monitor if a response is given, and if it is not, after a set time, the request goes on up the ladder to a paid staff member.

Calendar—Every group within the CCB database is provided with a unique calendar. As group leaders create events, administrators can then elect to manually or dynamically post these events to the church-wide public calendar. This calendar can then be integrated into the church Web site so that Web visitors get a real-time view of what's happening in the ministry at any given time. Using calendar synchronization capability (ICS) churchgoers can also easily synch church events in CCB with Google, Yahoo, iCal and other Web-based calendars.

Online Giving—CCB offers integrated online giving to its churches which is securely facilitated through the church Web site. A major distinction of the CCB approach is that they do not require someone to create a login before they give. That removes any barrier for people to give, especially those that support the ministry but may not have become a member yet.

Forms and Registration—CCB also offers a flexible and automated Form-Builder that allows their churches to survey their audience, apply for service opportunities, register for events and provide other valuable information all from the church Web site. These forms may or may not be configured to accept payments, but all the necessary code is provided by CCB so that the church can easily add the form to a page on their Web site with little technical expertise.

All of these benefits are designed not only to provide meaningful integration between the church Web site and the CMS, but also to enhance the ability to promote community, and increase connectedness to that community through the Web.

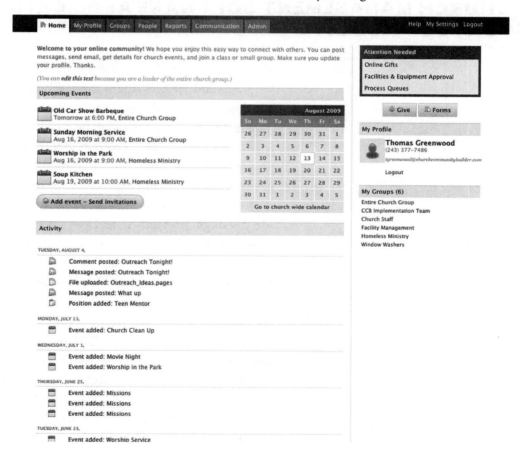

As shown in the screenshot on page 183, the CCB personal dashboard provides a quick summary of critical information such as snapshots of upcoming events, group lists and conversations, as well as links to other areas within CCB that require their attention according to their unique roles within the church and privileges in the system.

In addition to these key integration points, CCB also facilitates a Web-driven community by allowing people to respond to volunteer opportunities, event invitations and even congregational needs via the Web. With "Needs Management," CCB allows individual tasks or needs to be assigned and accepted by people within the church community. If a family in your Small Group just had a baby, the group leader can create a "Need" whereby the family receives two meals a day for two weeks. Each meal can then be assigned or proactively accepted by people even if they aren't in the same small group. The ability to notify people and accept tasks within specific needs is all facilitated via email and the Web.

CHURCH MANAGEMENT SOFTWARE APPLICATIONS FOR YOUR WEB SITE

Most church management software companies began by creating programs and services (many now Web-based) designed to help the church office with their administrative duties. However, most have realized the need to integrate data from their products into applications that can be accessed by church members. Since these programs now seek to serve the community and connection needs of the entire congregation, many have created and marketed Web site solutions that work in conjunction with whatever Web site you might presently have. Here are a few examples of church management software companies that provide such connection:

CDM+ Web Ministry Tools—www.cdmplus.com

CDM+ Church Management Software now provide widgets that can inserted in a church Web site, providing real time information or interaction with their CDM+ database. All of its tools offer optional password protection to limit access to church membership only, or even a defined group within the church membership.

The beauty of CDM+ Web Ministry Tools is the ability to "set it and forget it." Once the church Webmaster has installed the application on the Web site, the office staff only needs to keep the CDM+ database up-to-date to keep the information on the Web site current.

They currently offer five different tools:

Event Listing Tool—Dynamically lists information pulled from the CDM+ Roommate facilities manager's calendar, thus eliminating the need to re-enter information in a separate calendar program.

Directory Tool and Search Tool—These two tools provide access by church members (with optional password protection) to CDM+ Membership information, either the entire membership or groups, such as a class or youth group.

Stats Tool—Displays selected list or event statistics for one day or numerous days. For example, it can serve as a stats board for Sunday school or worship attendance and/or giving.

Current Account Balance Tool—Displays the current balance for any account (both balance sheet and income/expense) in CDM+ Accounting. This tool provides a convenient way for committee chairs and other church leaders to keep in touch with spending and available funds.

Single Event Registration Tool—This interactive Web Ministry Tool allows church members and others to register online for an event that has been set up in CDM+ Event Registration. If the church has an account with a payment processor, the tool can be set to accept credit/debit card payments.

More CDM+ Web Ministry Tools are currently in development, such as an online giving tool for CDM+ Contributions users, and a monthly calendar tool for CDM+ Roommate users.

For more information about CDM+ Web Ministry Tools, visit www.cdmplus.com/Products/CDMPlus/WebMinistryTools

eTapestry—www.etapestry.com/

The eTapestry Church Management Software program provides several functions that will work with your church's Web site. You can connect an online giving page, which can be built with the look and feel of your Web site, and processes the transaction and automatically update your eTapestry database. You can do the same with an event registration page, which is ideal for dinners, golf outings, or other activities where people need to register. Again, all registration information is automatically captured in the database. If it's an existing record in the database the information is added to their record, and if it's new a record is created.

Some churches also use their Web site to sell items (CDs, DVDs, books, etc.) so there is a shopping cart feature that again integrates to the database. Its donor login/member lookup module allows group members to login to see their current giving totals, update contact information and even search for other members (all based on security permissions).

And finally, its newest module is called Personal Fundraising. It allows a member to create their own Web page for soliciting funds from their own network of contacts. This can be used for event fundraising, especially those were sponsors are solicited such as walk-a-thons.

eTapestry also has a Web-services group that can build and host complete Web sites for organizations that need someone to manage the entire process.

Fellowship One, Fellowship Technologies— www.fellowshiptech.com/

Fellowship One (F1) refers to this application's features that connect its data to a church's congregation through their Web site as a WebLink, which is a coined marketing term that encompasses online giving, event registration, volunteer sign-up, contact forms (for everything from prayer requests to just general information), and small groups. The benefit of using these modules from a Church Management Software provider like Fellowship One is that they are already connected into your membership data. So for example, when a member logs in to make a donation online they can also see their entire giving history, including cash and check contributions.

Fellowship Technologies officials tell me they have a few churches that have purchased F1 just for online giving but they don't market it that way for the reasons stated above. They believe there is a greater advantage in using an online giving service that can connect with your Church Management Software product.

The integration of WebLink with your Web site ranges from very easy to complex, depending on what you want to do. However, it doesn't matter who's hosting your Web site, what content management system you're running, or its programming language.

MemberConnect, Concordia Technology Solutions—www.ctsmemberconnect.net/

MemberConnect takes the member information part of church management and puts it online, and makes information available to church members, which then allows ministry leaders to effectively and easily manage their ministry communications. There is an extensive array of security levels and settings that give each staff member the ability to access their own data to input events, prayer requests, documents, etc., into the MemberConnect system.

MemberConnect has additional features not typically found in most church management software: items that make sense because everyone in the church can view and participate from their Web browser, at anytime, from anywhere.

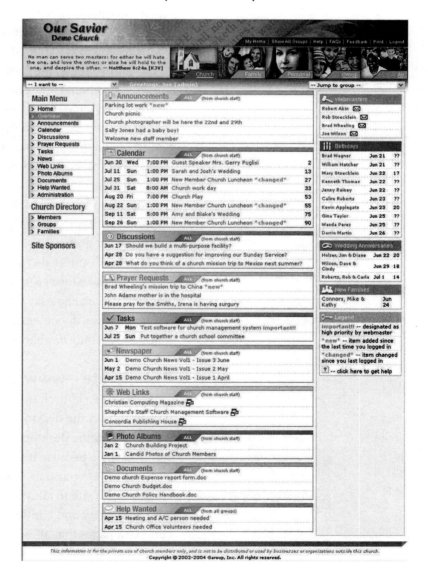

I first saw MemberConnect when it was demonstrated by the programmer who envisioned creating a service that kept members connected with the information they were wanting from their church. When a church uses MemberConnect and logs into its Web site, they can view a variety of different content like prayer requests, various documents, calendar events, online discussions, photos albums, announcements, and much more. MemberConnect refers to these as "Features" and you can see them listed on the left side of the screen shot above. Additionally, notice in the screen shot the icons listed along the top, such as "Church," "Individual," "Group," etc. MemberConnect refers to these as "Views" and allows the user to customize the content accordingly. For example, by selecting to view information that relates only to their family, the calendar feature would only show events pertaining to their family members. So if they had young people in the family the calendar would show events related to the youth department. On the contrary, if no one in the family sang in the choir then the calendar would not include information about choir practice. A very clever idea!

The individual can also select from several options on what materials they wish to view. If they select "church" then they would see all of the prayer requests, announcements, calendar events, photos, and other items related to the entire church. If they select "group", however, they would only see information pertaining to the groups that they are involved in, like prayer requests, announcements, photos, and other items related to their specific group.

MemberConnect also has fantastic administrative features with a variety of password protected access levels. With MemberConnect, though, you can allow lay leaders to have access to entering data, events, pictures, documents, prayer requests, etc., with the assurance that they will only be able to input such content in their own areas.

Excellerate—www.excellerate.com

Excellerate is a church management system that leverages the power of both the desktop and Web environments. Excellerate runs right on the desktop, which they believe is the best CMS solution since because it gives you the fastest user experience, and control of your data. However, it extends key features to the church's Web site to allow many people the opportunity to help with data entry and administrative tasks. For example, you can add extra pages that allow church members to administer their small groups and perform tasks such as visitor follow-up, or new volunteer signups, all from the Web, and thus from mobile locations like homes or offices.

In the case of online small groups, leaders can log in and view contact information for their group members, as well as track each person's spiritual development. And, after each meeting, they can log in and submit their reports.

With online follow-up pages, the members of your visitor follow-up team can go online to get the contact information for those they are to contact, and they can also submit reports about each follow-up attempt. This makes it easier to track who has and has not been contacted.

ACSTechnologies—www.acstechnologies.com

ACSTechnologies provides a host of different Web applications, including small group support, online giving, contact management, volunteer ministry solutions, event calendars, and more. Information can be published to the church's Web site—such as a listing of available small groups or volunteer opportunities. Church members and guests can also alert leaders of their interest in various ministry areas, and a follow-up sequence is then initiated electronically to be sure that the right ministry leaders know of someone's interest. Church staff also have oversight tools to make sure that the follow-ups occur on a timely basis.

Recently, while attending the ACS national conference, I was able to see their new Facebook application, which allows members in specific small groups to connect among each other, and the overall membership to connect with the entire church directory (Of course, each member retains control of the information shared with other members). ACS created this unique Facebook application, but it is branded to the church that uses it, which reinforces the church's role in being "front and center." Administrators do have control over who can join groups, however, and does provide the codes for churches to include on their sites that allows its members to find and install the application from a specific link, instead of having to search through thousands of applications while on Facebook.

As you can see from the screenshot on the following page, church members using the ACS Facebook application can easily select from the tabs to access their church's directory.

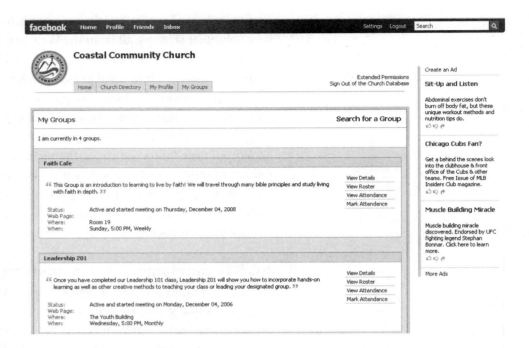

Making data available through API's (application programming interface) enables information to flow across multiple platforms, including into other specialty applications. From Google Gadgets you can download to your Google homepage to full custom-designed Web sites that integrate data, ACS Technologies offers a wide spectrum of solutions to meet the individual needs of churches. Even core Web functionality of a Web site is not taken for granted, nor left as a silo. Extend, from ACS Technologies, is a Web-based content management solution designed to help churches manage a Web site effectively. Whether it's a simple Web site with service information—calendars and staff—or a sophisticated site with data integration, every church needs both applications and a plan for managing their Web site.

ParishSOFT—www.parishsoft.com

ParishSOFT has launched their "My Own Church," which is part of the ConnectNow product series. My Own Church provides anytime, anywhere access for church members and families for online registrations, changes to their personal data, and much more. Every aspect of this program is designed to connect people to the church.

Another application from the ConnectNow product series is their Online Giving service, which provides a direct link from your church's Web site to its financial contribution data.

Icon Systems—www.iconcmo.com

Icon Systems partnered with Vanco Services to provide electronic donation services for churches using their church management software products. Add the login logo directly to your Web site to provide a direct link for your members to make online contributions, with the data being updated in the contribution records within Icon Systems. In addition, the service can give you access to your own information as well as an online pictorial directory.

Shelby Systems—www.shelbyinc.com

Shelby has two different levels of church management software solutions for churches, and each has the ability to connect with a church's Web site to provide ministry opportunities for your membership.

Shelby v5.x is Shelby's most popular offering. It allows a membership to update their information anywhere, anytime. They also offer:

e-Give—An online giving application that allows members to make donations directly to your Web site.

e-Groups—A group manager for small groups that allows members to log in and view photos and an online directory, while leaders can post events, announcements or send emails to the entire group.

e-Registration—Allows online registration for your upcoming events, including the ability to accept registration fees, with transactions processed into Shelby v.5.

e-Calendar—Provides a church with an online calendar that is password protected and displays information by categories such as events, dates, and birthdays of members. If a church is using e-Registration, members will also have access to register for an upcoming event from the calendar.

e-Survey—Allows for the posting of online survey forms to help members indicate their interest in volunteering for service within the ministries of the church. Churches have the ability to customize the survey to reflect their organization and ministry needs.

Directory—Allows members to keep their personal contact information current by logging into the church Web site.

Arena—Finally, Shelby provides Arena, which is a Web-based church management software that is customizable to fit any church's specific needs, although it comes ready with many features for any and all customers to use right away. For example, Arena allows for small group leaders to log in and manage their own small groups, send broadcast emails to their groups, add people to their groups, and more. Arena comes with the ability for churches to create customized pages to match the look and feel of the church's site. It also provides each member specific information of interest to their needs. For example, if you are a single adult and you log into the church's Web site, you will see information as it relates to being a single adult. Likewise, if you are a senior adult logging in, you would see information as it relates to senior interests. Since Arena is able to customize their service for each individual church, there are a host of possible applications, including some fantastic tools for groups with rich social networking content, and the ability to connect with other social networking sites such as Twitter and Flicker.

RDS Advantage—www.rdsadvantage.com

The RDS Advantage application provides a variety of forms that can be added to a church's Web site, including:

▶ A Debit Authorization form that can be filled out by contributors to automatically deduct recurring contributions from their bank account and deposit to the church bank account.

▶ A Prayer Request form that automatically sends information to the church.

▶ A Volunteer Application form individuals can complete and send to the church to show their interests and availability to help with specific ministries.

▶ A Membership form in which individuals can enter information about each family member. It also allows members to edit their contact information.

▶ A full-featured Event/Facility/Equipment Scheduler is included with RDS Advantage. Events recorded in the Scheduler can be automatically imported into church Web calendars by either .CSV or .iCal formats. It can also automatically send e-mail messages to those responsible for room set-up, food, child-care, and equipment, etc.

▶ All accounting modules (Payables, Receivables, Payroll, Contributions) support electronic banking, without the need for third party applications, and all banking information is sent directly to the bank. The newest banking technology, Remote Deposit Capture (RDC), is also integrated with Contributions and Receivables so that deposits are made as part of the accounting data entry process.

▶ Remote Internet data processing is supported through several technologies, including Remote Desktop, Terminal Services, wireless, and other remote applications.

JOOMLA!

If for some reason you really don't want to use—uh, buy—any one of the many services on the market designed to provide a feature-rich Web site, you do have one option other than going back to square one and writing your own HTML programming. Joomla! is an award-winning content management system that allows you to build a Web site using a variety of templates and powerful online applications. Joomla! is an open source solution, which means it's available for free. And that means that you can use many of its features, templates and applications for no charge. However, since it is open source, there are many third-party templates, applications, video training programs and add-on utilities, and some of them do charge a fee if you wish to use them. Additionally, unless you have your own server, you will have to pay someone to host your site.

But don't make the mistake of underestimating the power of Joomla! just because it's free. Once again, I think most churches would be best serviced by using one of the companies that have specifically designed CMS programs for churches, as their services take much of the work out of creating and maintaining a site, but if you do like to "do it yourself," then Joomla! is right up your alley. Here are some of the companies, products and organizations that use Joomla! for their Web site service:

▶ IHOP (Restaurant chain)—www.ihop.com
▶ Harvard University (Educational)—www.gsas.harvard.edu
▶ Citibank (Financial institution intranet)—Not publicly accessible
▶ Outdoor Photographer (Magazine) www.outdoorphotographer.com
▶ PlayShakespeare.com (Cultural)—www.playshakespeare.com
▶ Senso Interiors (Furniture design)—www.sensointeriors.co.za

Joomla! Features

The advantages of using Joomla! over going it alone is that Joomla! will provide you the features you need to keep your site updated and prevent you from making many design errors you see on sites that are being independently created. For example, Joomla! provides "breadcrumbs," which is a navigational aid so that as visitors go deeper into your Web site, they can see where they are in the overall construction of your site. Using this navigational aid, they can immediately click back to any part of the site they've already visited, at any time.

Joomla! also provides the ability for users to log into the site using a username and password, which allows you the option to set different levels of security on each page of your site. For example, you probably don't want all visitors to be able to see your membership directory with pictures and contact information. You can also increase or decrease a visitor's access level depending on their function within the church. For example, some visitors may need access to basic discussions boards, while others may need access to other discussions boards reserved for, say, the church staff only.

Joomla! also provides the ability to add a search feature to your site, which then allows visitors the ability to find any specific information they are seeking on your site. You can also set up the module to allow your visitors the ability to display the most recent content that has been added to the site, or to display the most read content.

Here is a list of some of the many features you can add to your Joomla! site through either the use of modules or plug-ins:

▶ Free templates in a variety of color schemes and menu layouts.

▶   Attractive polls that allow you to survey your visitors.

▶   Random images from a library of pictures you provide, which can include photos of your church members rotating at any rate you specify.

▶   Syndication of your articles using RSS .

▶   A "Who's Online" that lets you to see who is online at the same time you are.

▶   The ability for visitors to rate your content using stars, which will direct visitors to the most popular content.

▶   The ability to manage banners.

▶   The option to pull newsfeeds from other online services, which puts keeps your site fresh with new content being pushed from other sites.

If you want to give Joomla! a try, start by visiting http://docs .joomla.org/Beginners.

HELP THE SEARCH ENGINES FIND YOUR SITE

There are several important techniques that will enable your church's site to show up in search engines. Here they are:

1. In your HTML code, include meta tags. These are descriptive words and phrases that will be used by the search engines to find your site when people are searching using those same words and phrases. Here is an example:

<META name="descriptive" content="A friendly church that is open to meeting the needs of community and neighbors.">

<META name="keywords" content="church, meeting needs, community, neighbors, friendly:>

2. Submit your Web sites directly to Google and Yahoo by visiting www.google.com/addurl and http://search.yahoo .com/info/submit.html

3   Text is king! Some services or Web designers love to use as much Flash applications as possible. The problem is that search engines can't search a Flash picture or video and read the text. You must put descriptive text into your

code at the top of each page, and be as descriptive as possible, and include as many different words to describe your content and services as possible.

4. Encourage others to link to your site, including members who have their own Web site or social networking page. The more sites link to yours, the more important you appear to the search engines, and the higher up you site will appear in search results.

5. Consider using Google AdWords. Google is the most popular Web search engine in use today, and by paying a small fee your church's site will appear on the right site of a search results list as a sponsor. Here's what you'll have to do:

▶ Pick the search words you want people to use to find your site. You might wish to use the word "church," or your city name, or some other distinguishing words that would help identify who you are and what you offer on your site.

▶ You get to pick the price you are willing to pay for every word, and AdWords will tell you where you will be listed for that word, at the price you are willing to pay. In some cases it could be pennies.

▶ Use as many words as you wish, but be sure they are appropriate. Don't have your site come up when someone specifically types in the name of another ministry.

▶ You also get to determine the region of the country you want your AdWords displayed. If you are a ministry, then you might want to be found by people searching the whole world. Most churches, however, will simply want to be found by people searching within their region.

One of the churches I know that uses Google AdWords only spends about $25 a month. But they feel the results are well worth the expense. You can get started with Google AdWords by going to Google.com and clicking on the "Advertising Programs" link.

BLOGGING

The word blog comes from a combination of the words "Web" and "log," and principally refers to any text posted in an ongoing chronicle of information (newest information at the top) on a Web site. It is frequently updated and normally personal, although many bloggers sometimes operate on one site centered on a specific topic. It normally contains information from a person reporting on his or her own experiences, thoughts or general comments. People are invited to leave comments of their own. Blogs are not limited to just text as content, but can also contain videos, podcasts and links to other media.

There are several reasons why blogging has become so popular, one being the fact that we are what I commonly refer to the "personal communication age". People like to comment. We saw the beginning of this trend during the second Gulf War when it was noted that 45 percent of those with Internet access visited news sites with breaking information about the war. Another survey around the same time showed that 75 percent used the Internet to express their opinion about the war. It showed people don't just want to "get" information; they want to share their opinion too.

A blog site meets the needs of three groups of people who are on the Internet. First, there are those that host a blog site because they have always wanted to be a writer. Before the Internet, it was much harder to get something "published" since it would typically involve some degree of financial investment; paper, ink, postage cost, etc. Therefore, if a magazine published your article, it would actually mean something. It put you in a different class of society. You could tell people that you were "published," and it sounded good. With the advent of the Internet, however, the door to self publishing wasn't just opened, it was kicked open! Closet writers came from everywhere, and those first bloggers discovered they had the ability to cause an incredible impact on society even though they were not officially "published" in a print journal.

As noted, many of the content management systems provide churches an option to blog. However, there are many other services available as well, with features that are unique to the blogging experience. Here is one of the most popular:

WordPress

Probably one of the most popular blogging services is WordPress. Here are a few of the features that help to make them so popular:

▶ It can be installed locally

WordPress is designed to be installed on your own Web server, or shared hosting account, which gives you complete control over the Weblog. WordPress brags about the easy of installation, claiming it will take less than five minutes to install.

▶ UTC friendly

WordPress uses Universal Coordinated Time (UTC). Many blogs can be time sensitive. As such, many blogs post the time all content is made available on the site, so with UCT your content will display the correct time on your blog, even if the host server is located in different time zone.

▶ User management

WordPress uses user-levels to control user-access to different features. Users log in using a username and password, so as an administrator you can restrict the ability of individual users to create or modify content on your blog.

▶ Template driven

WordPress uses templates, allowing you to control the look and feel of your blog by using the template editor.

▶ Password protection

You can require your users to log in before they are allowed to leave a comment. Another benefit of this feature is you can then set levels on certain blogs, requiring a security level to be required in order to read certain posts.

▶ Timed release

You can write a blog and prepare it to be posted, but then set the time that you want it to go live. In fact, your posts don't go live until you are ready to make them live, so you can work on a post and then save it if you want to polish it up later before posting.

▶ Post via email

Want to keep your blog going even though you don't have access to the Web? With WordPress that isn't a problem. You can post a blog to your site by sending it in via email.

▶ You can moderate comments. You may wish to keep some control over the comments that are left on your blog. With Wordpress you can select from several options, including:

Checking all comments before they are allowed to appear on your blog

Have WordPress flag and hold comments with specific words in them

Have WordPress hold specific comments posted from a particular IP address

Have WordPress hold comments that contain a specified number of links

▶ WordPress provides a blogroll

A blogroll is your list of blogs that you like to read, presented on your site for your visitors. These can be presented in categories, or listed in your favorite order

▶ Inter-blog connection

WordPress comes ready with PingBack and TrackBack, which are two ways to connect your blog to others, and enables them to do the same.

▶ WordPress feeds

WordPress is ready to be set up for feeds, allowing your visitors to subscribe and have new content pushed their way.

▶ Application plug-ins

There are many plug-ins available for WordPress. For example, one can send you an email whenever someone new leaves a comment on your site, while others can help with navigation for your visitors, or help promote blogs that relate in subject to the one a reader has just finished.

Of course there are many sites that offer great blog services. Some charge a fee, but many are free. One of those is provided by Google can be found at www.blogger.com. Several of my friends use it and recommend it. While some would recommend using a blog service such as WordPress because it can be installed on your server and you retain some control, others chose to pick a blog service that is not tied to a server, especially if the service is a ministry and/or church, and they wanted to make their blog personal. For them, there was the advantage of keeping their blog completely separate from the ministry they were associated with.

Realistically, either scenario would work for our purposes since a blog designed for ministry needs to be responsible in its content. Again, there should be a purpose to blogging if it is being done to advance ministry. In the book *The Blogging Church*, the author says, "Blogging is all about connecting communities through conversation. Churches have traditionally excelled in one-way communication. We are more comfortable modeling our ministries after television, broadcasting our message to passive and silent viewers. There is a new generation, though, that is no longer satisfied by the one-way relationship. They have grown up in an Internet-driven culture that celebrates participation. The passive consumer has been replaced with an active engaged and empowered contributor."

With that in mind, I would challenge every minister and pastor to blog. By doing so you make yourself available, and in a way vulnerable. There will always be a place for preaching and instruction from behind the pulpit (or, if you have removed your pulpits like many churches, there is always a need for the preacher to be in front of a congregation presenting the Gospel). However, if you give the appearance of being untouchable, the effect of your Sunday message will be impacted. If, on the other hand, you are available to express commentary and are open to comments, questions and even criticism, you will have closed an important gap, which I believe will be evident even when Sunday rolls around and you are once again using one-way communication through preaching.

Use Your Blog to Reach a Seeking Community

Here are just a few suggestions on how a minister could use a church's blog to build community.

▶   Blog about news stories that are on the minds of those in your community. They might know how you stand on doctrinal issues, but they also need to know what their spiritual leader thinks about the events that dominate local and national news.

▶ Blog about humanity. People in ministry sometimes seem too aloft to be approachable. If your car had a flat and you had to deal with the frustration of being late, or having to deal with unexpected costs that weren't in your budget, share it in your blog. Stories like this probably would not make it to your sermon or Bible study, but in sharing how you deal with day-to-day frustrations you invite and inspire others to live life in a positive way (I am assuming here that a pastor, having a flat tire, missing an important meeting, and having to pay a heavy fee to have his car fixed, would have handled it with grace and patience, right?).

▶ Blog about basic issues regarding your church. Why does your church have the ministries they have? Remind people, members and visitors, about your church's mission.

▶ Answer questions. Ministers are always being asked their opinion about how to deal with life situations. Use your blog to answer those questions so that others can benefit from the same information.

▶ Start conversations. Remember, you want to encourage comments and community. Ask questions in your blog. Every teacher worth their salt knows that you have to ask questions if you want your students to learn the material. Ask questions, start conversations, and then your replies will provide a way to help disciple and teach as people become involved in the discussion.

▶ Blog about others. Use your blog to introduce the ministry of other staff members. In fact, blogs can be a great place to spotlight the contributions of your many volunteer leaders. Use a blog once a week to show your appreciation for specific people in your church that partner with you in service. Others can then comment and have an opportunity to show their appreciation as well!

A Few Other Blogging Tips

Be honest. Of course, I don't think most ministers would even think about telling stories that include lies, but I encourage you to honest in the area of really being open. While President George Bush (the first one) drew some heat for his statement about not liking broccoli, I admired the fact he was honest. It seems that the very nature of politics means that you have to seek the approval of everyone, leaving you in situations where you can't take a stand against anything. You end up learning the fine art of being a waffle! If you get asked something in a blog that is uncomfortable, whatever you do be honest.

Be brief. Blogs are not intended to be articles like those in a magazine. They need to be a short read. Many people are probably following other blogs from other sources. They don't spend all of their time reading, and if yours get too windy they might be tempted to drop you from their daily reading list.

Speaking of daily, don't feel the need to blog every day. If you don't have anything to say, don't push content that wastes everyone's time. However, try to remain consistent. Don't blog once or twice a week, and then go silent for a month before continuing.

If you seem to go dry on blogging materials, do some reflecting. What are you reading? Blog about it. What did you watch on television that impressed you, inflamed you, touched you, blessed you, or offended you? Blog it. With all of the holidays that come around, find something to share about what makes the day special to you. Heard something funny? Blog it. Or, just sit back and be observant. The trick is to be open to what is going on around you. There is always something to blog about, and again, people will gain insight into your life and develop a great connection that will open doors for ministry.

Use Google Alerts, or the site www.Technorati.com, to search for information about yourself, your church or subjects related to your local community that others might be blogging about. This will enable you to be up-to-date on issues of interest that you might wish to address in your blog.

CHAPTER 6
Podcasts

For the purpose of this book let me define what I mean by a podcast. I am aware that the actual term refers to a digital media file, either audio or video, that is designed to be downloaded via a Web syndication process, such as RSS. A podcast ends up on a Web site for people to click, stream and listen to. However, when talking about the theory of ministry or suggestions for using Podcasts, I will be using the term in a looser manner. For our purposes, a podcast refers to any audio or video media that is clickable, streamable or subscribed too, for the purposes of listening to or watching something via the Internet. And in this chapter, I will concentrate on audio files. Video is addressed in a later chapter.

WHY PODCAST?

Many churches have been recording their services for some time and making them available to shut-ins (elderly members who can no longer make it to the church building to attend services) via a cassette recorder. I have actually encouraged pastors to begin podcasting their services and have heard the reply, "Why? Don't our shut-ins have access to the Internet?"

There are so many, many reasons for churches to be podcasting their worship services, sermons, class recordings and more, up on the Internet.

Who is podcasting? Visit Apple's iTunes site and do a search in the business category. You'll find podcasts from the following:

- ▶ ABC News
- ▶ BBC
- ▶ *Business Week*
- ▶ CBS News
- ▶ CNBC
- ▶ CNN
- ▶ ESPN
- ▶ Fox News Channel
- ▶ HBO
- ▶ NASA
- ▶ *National Geographic*
- ▶ NBC News
- ▶ *Newsweek*
- ▶ *The New York Times*
- ▶ *The Wall Street Journal*
- ▶ *Time Magazine*

It is obvious that those in the business of communicating a message create and post podcasts. And I would think it is obvious that they are not just seeking to reach out to shut-ins.

In checking iTunes under the category of "Religion and Spirituality" I found the following podcasts under the sub heading of "Christianity":

- ▶ Max Lucado Daily Devotions
- ▶ Joel Osteen Audio Podcast
- ▶ 1 Year Daily Audio Bible by Brian Hardin
- ▶ Mars Hill Church: Mark Driscoll Audio
- ▶ Joyce Meyer Radio Podcast
- ▶ North Point Ministries by Andy Stanley
- ▶ Desiring God Sermon Audio by John Piper
- ▶ Renewing Your Mind with R.C. Sproul
- ▶ Insight Into Living Daily Broadcast
- ▶ Rick Warren's Ministry Podcast
- ▶ Creative Pastors Blog and Podcast by Ed Young

And this is just a partial list of those that came up. Don't be intimidated by the content that is already available. There is definitely room for your message from God. If he has called you to share his Gospel, and you have the opportunity to stand in a pulpit or lead a Bible study, it should be recorded and made available. God uses all of us to reach specific people that we are gifted to connect with when we speak—podcasting included!

For starters, you can podcast your worship service. However, you need to think past the "cassette to shut-in" mentality. You can record audio podcasts easily; anywhere, anytime, whenever remarkable opportunities arise. At your next church function, picnic, or activity, take a recorder and a microphone and ask people to share how they are enjoying the event. Do a "man-in-the-street" type interview about whatever the topic of the event is centered around. Make it available to your members and I bet they will enjoy listening to what others in their church have to say. Remember, we are in the "personal communication age," where people like to hear from their peers.

Here are a few other ideas:

▶ Interview new members that have joined your church.

▶ Interview new staff members that have started service at your church.

▶ Interview members of your church whenever they have a special event such as the birth of a new baby, an important anniversary, or returning from a trip abroad.

▶ Interview your young people about their summer camp experiences.

▶ Interview some of your older members, centering on their observations about how things have changed in the church today.

▶ Interview those that are preparing to go on your next mission trip, and then do an interview when they return.

▶ Interview your children. Ask them what they like about coming to church.

▶ Interview special guests that have come to speak or teach at your church.

▶   Interview a small group about their book or Bible study, asking what they have learned.

▶   Do a series of interviews with your lay ministry leaders, helping others understand what their area of ministry accomplishes.

▶   Interview people in your narthex or lobby as they prepare to enter your worship service.

If you can get your congregation to do it, you can try some serious podcasts. Ask your members to share their testimonies with you. You can do this interview-style, which can help you and them present the information in an organized way. Besides the testimonies from people that came to discover God in their lives, encourage those that have overcome addiction, found peace in times of anxiety, survived financial disasters, have lost their marriage but kept their faith, to offer their testimonies as well. If you can post these on your site, it will serve to invite and inspire others to a closer walk with Christ. Even beyond this, if you can help make them available to those in your community, they will serve as a fantastic opportunity for evangelism.

Podcasts can be used in a variety of ways. They can be posted to your Web site for people to click and listen. They can be syndicated using RSS from you site (RSS is short for Really Simple Syndication and is the Internet standard for pushing audio, video and text based content), or post to a service (even iTunes) that allows people to subscribe to your podcasts and have new content downloaded to their computer, their iPod or MP3 player, or their smart phone.

Podcasts can be sent as links in emails and text messages. Earlier in this book I talked about evangelistic opportunities in sending out broadcast emails to your membership that contained content that they would find appropriate to send to their unchurched friends. I would imagine a podcast of children sharing what they learned at church would have a cute enough appeal to get forwarded to a few new people. Testimonies from your people could also have the same impact. People are touched by the human spirit whenever they hear someone—especially "real" people—share about their connection with God.

A TRULY NOVEL IDEA TO PODCAST—RADIO DRAMAS

Want a creative way to combine many of the things I have been trying to suggest in this book? Give this idea a try and you may end up providing content in an audio podcast format that involves your membership in an area of ministry for evangelism and/or discipleship, and in the process increase fellowship. See why I like it?

Ok here it is. Many churches have started drama teams, but not everyone is willing to get up before the congregation and perform. How about taking these same plays (many are available on the Internet) and adapting them into a radio-type format?

Many church dramas are designed to help teach a Biblical point, or to help introduce people to a relationship with Christ. Find a few creative volunteers who may be shy, and involve them in a small group to create audio versions of popular Christian dramas. If the drama says that "Tom" is to enter from stage right, just change it and have a narrator say, "Tom entered the room from the south door." Then have Tom and the other characters in the play do their dialog. If the play calls for something visual to happen, either have the narrator explain what has happened, or develop some fun with sound effects. If someone was to enter from a door, get something that is squeaky to simulate a door being opened, or slap too books together to make the sound of someone slamming a door. Large sheets of metal, when shaken, can mimic thunder. And there are a host of sites on the Internet where you can download your own sound effects if you can't find ways to make up your own. Even those who are too shy to talk into a microphone or become a character in your audio play could find a place of service in helping to create and cue the extra sound effects. Can you imagine the fun, and the end result? You can post these on your own Web site and create an audience of people around the world who can be both entertained as well as inspired by the messages. Personally, I think this idea alone is worth the price of this book!

SO, HOW DO I CREATE A PODCAST?

First, consider your content. If you want to record a worship service or discipleship class, you probably already have a system in place to do it. However, if you are going to go mobile and record interviews outside of a controlled environment, try different equipment to see what gets the best results. There are simply too many recommendations and too many ways to accomplish these basic recordings to make individual recommendations, but getting a clear recording is not that difficult.

For example, you may want to invest in one of the new high-quality digital recorders on the market, which make it much easier to transfer your music into a podcast. The Zoom H4 hand-held recorder from Samson comes highly recommended. They cost about $200, but it will save you money in the long run, especially if you are still recording with an analog tape machine.

If you are going to do an interview:

▶ Know who you are talking with and what you will be talking about. Do some research. If they have written a book, read it. If they are a musician, listen to some of their music. If it is a member of your church, talk to them before you start recording to learn a little about their situation.

▶ Have your questions prepared in advance, and have them follow a logical progression.

▶ Prepare twice as many questions as you'll need.

▶ Never worry about a stupid question.

▶ Don't panic if the interview goes off in a different direction than you'd planned. Go with the flow. You can always simply suggest going back to one of your questions.

How Can I Get My Recordings to Stream from My Site?

To put your recordings up on your Web site, or to send a link out via an email is very simple. There are four steps:

1. Create your recording
2. Get your recording into your computer and convert it to an MP3 file
3. Upload your MP3 file to a server using a FTP (File Transfer Protocol) program
4. Post the links to your Web site, or include them in an email.

Now let's look at each of these in a little more detail.

Create Your Recording

One of the easiest ways to record is to use your computer. If you are using Windows XP or Vista, you should encounter no problems. Again, if you are recording something like your Sunday worship service, ask the person running your soundboard for a connection that can go into your computer. You can connect directly into your microphone or line-in jack. If you are creating content such as an interview, you can always use another recording device such as a cassette recorder or digital recorder and input it into your computer using similar connections. Use the headphone or line-out jack from the cassette recording and run it into the microphone or line-in jack on your computer. If you get a hissing sound as you input your sound, there are two solutions. First, consider obtaining a USB soundcard. Since they sit outside the computer the quality is normally better. You can find these many places. Creative Labs has a few models that start as low as $40.

The other way to remove any background hiss is to use a program on your computer designed to help edit audio files. Frankly, this is the best way to go for everything, since it will also give you a source to send your audio input too. A free program that seems very popular with people is Audacity, and you can find it at http://audacity.sourceforge.net.

Audacity can record live audio using a microphone, or take your pre-recorded source such as from your cassette tape. You then run your audio through Audacity in order edit it, or combine it with other files or new recordings. Here's how it works:

▶   You can cut, copy, paste and delete parts of your recording.

▶   Make a mistake and you can hit the undo feature.

▶   Edit and mix an unlimited number of tracks. This means you could put background music behind your message.

▶   You can fade the volume up or down smoothly.

▶   Change the pitch without altering the tempo.

▶   Remove static or hiss from your files.

▶ Adjust the volume, so if one person is too quiet you can turn them up without increasing the sound of the entire file.

▶ If you want to have some fun you can add effects such as echo, wahwah, or reverse the sound.

And, most importantly, you can use Audacity to convert your audio file to a variety of formats, including MP3, which helps accomplish the next item on our list.

Getting Your File on the Internet

Now that you have your MP3 file, all you need to do to make it available for your Web site, or link it in an email or text, is to get it up on a server. If you don't know if you have a server, check with those that run your Web site or blog, because these are run on an Internet server. I have access to several servers through Christian Computing Magazine. If I wanted to make MP3 files available for people to click and listen too, I would use an FTP program to send the file from my personal computer up to the server. The file name would depend on where I put it on the server, but let's say I had a subdirectory on the CCMag server named "audio,, and I named the audio file "bookreport.mp3" and put it in that subdirectory on the CCMag server. I would simply tell people to click on www .ccmag.com/audio/bookreport.mp3 to listen to the file. When you look at the features lists of Web site providers, one of them should be "linking files." This means that on my church's Web site I can post put something along the lines of, "Listen to last week's report on my book by clicking here." I would then link "click here" to the address www.ccmag.com/audio.bookreport.mp3.

So What is Podcasting?

Real podcasting is more than just streaming your audio files from a Web site or email. Real podcasting allows people the ability to download your audio file to a mobile device such as an iPod or other MP3 player. And it allows your audio file to be made available on sites like iTunes and a host of other podcast sites, where people can subscribe to automatically receive future content from you as a provider.

Why is Podcasting So Popular?

When you allow people to subscribe to your podcasts and download them to mobile devices, it touches on the popularity of personal communications. For example, if you were to take a recording of your service and broadcast it over radio, it is considered mass media. If you take the same recording and make it available as a podcast for people to download, you have moved into what is now called "narrowcasting." Podcasting gives people the opportunity to pick and chose what and when they want to listen to something.

If you broadcast your message over a mass media like radio, you are forced to pick a time and a place that people must tune into in order to listen to your message. When you podcast, the person listens to your message whenever they choose to, which means the message is perceived as personal, and thus increases the value of the message.

So How Do I Turn My MP3 File Into a Real Podcast?

You can turn your MP3 file into a podcast, which allows others to download it to their mobile devices and subscribe to new podcasts that come from you and your church, simply by using one the many podcast services available on the Internet, starting with iTunes.

However, you might consider hosting your own content on your Web site. Again, most of the commercial Web site content management systems have the ability to do this for you. All you have to do is upload your file and then identify the theme or content of your podcast so that others can find it.

If your Web site service doesn't allow you to do real podcasts then you might want to use one of many programs designed to help you post your media content to your Web site. In most cases, these also allow for RSS. I have already mentioned the MediaRush service from Elexio, and SermonFlow from faithHighway. Here are a few others that seem to excel in the area of audio files:

Podcasting Services for the Christian Community

SermonCompanion.com—www.sermoncompanion.com/ Using SermonCompanion is easy. You simply upload your audio files to the online library, which provides unlimited space so you can feel free to take all of your old recordings that have been saved on cassette and convert them (as we outlined above) and start an extensive library.

Your visitors can then sort through your audio files to find the one they are looking for based upon date, speaker, scripture, series or title.

You can add the code and run SermonCompanion right from your Web site, or they will host it for you. When you click on an audio file, there is the opportunity to view a picture that you might want to use to relate to the sermon, or have a picture of the speaker. In addition, they have a scripture window that will popup in the window with the scripture being used in the sermon. Your visitors will also see a button that will allow them to forward the audio file to a friend. This form allows you to enter their email, name, and your email, along with a comment.

The cost is $19.95 a month with a 30-day free trial.

SermonPodcast.com—www.sermonpodcasts.com/

SermonPodcast.com provides sermon hosting, podcasting software and a Web site player, all in one, and uses their Web service to upload your files, which avoids have to learn and use FTP. Once you upload a file to SermonPodcast.com, they immediately broadcast it to iTunes as well as to the player they provide for your Web site. Simply provide basic information such as the title, some basic details about the content so it will be found by those seeking your information, and click to submit.

Some of their features include up to 10 GB of storage (which translates to about 10 years of sermons, so feel free to put up some of your older sermons if you already have them recorded). They allow for around 4,000 plays of your files per month with their plan (additional plans are available for higher use by mega churches.)

Wonder if people are listening? SermonPodcasts.com provides you with some statistic reporting. Their basic plan costs around $15 a month if paid quarterly, $20 a month if paid by the month.

SermonDrop.com—http://sermondrop.com/

The service of going from cassette to podcast couldn't be any easier using SermonDrop, because if you really can't accomplish the transition, they do it for you. You can literally set up an account for their services, and simply drop a cassette of your sermons in the mail to them and they will do the rest. This doesn't mean that they don't provide uploading services like their counterparts, because they do. And, you can insert their little widget of code into your Web site, or link to a customized page hosted on their site.

SermonDrop also uploads your files directly to iTunes at the same time they are posted to your site. They also provide the ability to add additional resources to view if you are listening while sitting in front of your computer. They can add sermon notes, PowerPoint slides, and/or supplemental study materials.

I have to give credit to SermonDrop for being patient with churches. They believe strongly that a church should be podcasting their sermons, and they believe it strong enough that if you can't do anything more than drop your cassettes to them in the mail, then they will set you up. They also have the ability to help you stream and podcast audio files of your sermon even if you don't have a Web site. They will host your sermons on their site, and you can just encourage your members to go to their site via the address they give you, taking your members directly to your hosted page. And what if new people stumble across your sermons on their site and want more information about your church? Since some of their customers don't maintain their own Web site, SermonDrop will provide information about your church, including a map so if visitors listening to your sermons want to attend, they can.

SermonDrop.com offers several different prices depending on the plan you wish to try. The best plan runs $28 a month, but they also have a plan that will cost a church absolutely nothing. You only get to have 10 sermons in your library, but they still provide you the widget for your Web site, or host your library on their site. Once you hit ten sermons, the oldest one is dropped as you add new material.

SermonCast.com—www.sermoncast.com/

SermonCast provides many of the same features that the other services provide. You can easily upload your files and have them streamed from their site, or from your own player(s) on your Web site. I mention players, because SermonCast can provide multiple players that are coded to appear on different Web sites because some churches request this function since they have different ministries.

However, SermonCast is different from those I have already mentioned in that you can use their services for free, with unlimited access and an unlimited number of sermons. How do they make that work? They broadcast your sermons on their sister site, http://sermon.net/ and are dependent upon advertisements to make the business model work. You can pay a fee for their service and your site will be free of advertisements, but frankly I am impressed with the number of churches and ministries around the world that are using them. They have a variety of ways to find sermons, including a world map that shows where each of the churches using their service is located. I was able to listen to a sermon from a church in North Africa, and also found a church in my community and enjoyed listening to one of their sermons as well.

What Else Can I Do with My Podcasts?

Spread the joy! Don't keep your sermons, lessons, or those great audio plays (remember my idea?) just for your congregation. Podcasting gives us a great opportunity to spread our message to the world. This is a wonderful time to live, and the church has a unique opportunity to be involved in world missions. Spread your podcasts around the world! Here is a list of a few dozen great podcast directories that are being used by millions of people around the world. Sow your seeds and see what God can do!

AllPodcasts
> http://www.allpodcasts.com/

Blinkx Podcast and Video Directory
> http://www.blinkx.tv/

BlogExplosion Podcast Directory
> http://www.blogexplosion.com/podcast/

BlogUniverse Podcast Directory
> http://www.bloguniverse.com/radlinks/

Digital Podcast
> http://www.digitalpodcast.com/

GetAPodcast.com
> http://www.getapodcast.com/addfeed.aspx

Get reviewed at Podcast411
> http://sourceforge.net/projects/opda/

Gigadial
> http://www.gigadial.net/

IdiotVox
> http://www.idiotvox.com/

Internet Archive
> http://www.archive.org

iPodderX
> http://ipodderx.com/directory

Loomia
> http://www.loomia.com/

Odeo
> http://www.odeo.com/

OpenPodcast
   http://www.openpodcast.org/
Open Media Network
   http://www.omn.org/
Ourmedia
   http://ourmedia.org
Plazoo
   http://www.plazoo.com/
PodcastDirectory
   http://www.podcastdirectory.com
PodcastHost
   http://podcasthost.com
PodcastShuffle
   http://www.podcastshuffle.com/
Podcast Alley
   http://www.podcastalley.com/index.php
Podcast Bunker
   http://www.podcastbunker.com/
Podcast Pickle
   http://www.podcastpickle.com/?p=home
Podcasting News
   http://www.podcastingnews.com/
Podcasting Station
   http://www.podcasting-station.com/index.php
Podcast Tools
   http://www.podcasting-tools.com/
PodCatch
   http://www.podcatch.com/
Podfeed
   http://www.podfeed.net/
Podscope
   http://www.podscope.com/
PublicRadioFan
   http://www.publicradiofan.com/podcasts.html
RSS Network
   http://www.rss-network.com/index.php
SingingFish
   http://search.singingfish.com/sfw/home.jsp
Syndic8 Podcasts
   http://www.syndic8.com/podcasts/

CHAPTER 7

Creating and Using Video for Ministry

By the time you have reached this chapter, I will have already given you many examples of how to creatively use video in worship, and for your Web site. In this chapter I will expand on the need for churches and Christians to embrace the use of video for all aspects of their ministry. You might say that we have before us an incredible opportunity to create and use video for both worship and for studies, as well as distribution to our community, nation and the world. But this moves it far past an opportunity, and I believe we are obligated to use this medium as much as possible.

VIDEO AND WINDOWS

There has been a raging debate for years over whether a PC or a Mac is better for use with creative mediums. The prevailing assumption is that a Mac is the obvious choice, and is superior to Windows in this area. But I don't believe it. Macs may be a "trendy" choice, but Windows is a practical choice and offers a great platform for all of your video creation and editing needs. Whether for the creation of video projects, or for simply playing back videos on the screen or through a projection process, Windows is a very competent option, and one with many great benefits. One of them—a crucial matter for many ministries—is the cost.

Buying a computer that runs Windows exclusively is much more affordable than an Apple computer running Mac OS X, and you can accomplish the same level of performance, or even better. The purpose of these comments is not intended to incite a war over which is the best operating system (OS), but rather to point out that if you are running Windows you will be able to do a fantastic job creating and editing videos for your ministry. Apple has many great computers, but there are reasons why they only have a small footprint in the marketplace.

WHY CREATE OR USE VIDEOS IN MINISTRY?

A media ministry should not exist simply because it's what "other churches are doing." It should be born out of a desire to effectively communicate truth, and aid (not distract) the church member in their worship experience. A capable team of either paid staff and/or highly motivated volunteers should make up the core of this functional ministry, but should work in sync with the worship team and preaching minister. This is vital. Many of those that are worship leaders are not technical, and yet most churches can find members or other staff members with the creative and technical abilities to create, edit, and present video. However, there needs to be a close tie between those that are leading worship and those that create the videos.

Media and video technology are simply extensions of human functions that are replaced and/or made obsolete in other mediums. For example, a video that is created for use as an illustration to be played during the sermon can achieve the same purpose as a live drama on the stage. However, it allows for greater creativity and eliminates the possibility of error.

Live drama has been used by many churches for years, and it still presents an exciting element to any worship service. However, I have seen plenty that fail to make a desired impact because things have gone wrong in their production. Even if everyone remembers their lines, I have seen many dramas lose their impact because a microphone was not turned up and the message was simply not heard. If the same drama was prepared as a video, opportunities for error or mistakes are removed.

There are many other examples of how you can use video to replace elements of the worship service that are being handled live. For example, videos can be used for announcements, scripture animations, picture slide shows, countdowns, testimonies, baptism videos, and much more.

Of course, one of the biggest advantages of creating any of these elements of worship as a video, are the endless possibilities of distribution. Today, any video presentation can be posted on the Internet and the audience can be worldwide. We live in exciting times where the central message of the Bible can be transmitted freely in modern formats, and touch so many in the process.

Though the time has never been better to reach out to the world with the positive, uplifting, and convincing Word of God through video, it must be done with planning and a little prayer. Every medium has the potential to be a blessing or a curse. Video can be a wonderful addition to your ministry, and well worth the investment dollars if properly applied. It can greatly enhance your church services, Christian education, camps/ retreats, or conferences. The moving images, combined with thoughtful planning of organized thought, can evoke a wide range of emotions in the audience. Because video is planned, it has the potential to present the information you want to share in an organized and receptive way. A well-crafted video should solicit a desired response from its audience, persuading the audience to:

► Reflect or mediate on a thought
► Consider making a choice
► Cause an action
► Change a way of thinking

Moving pictures are a common language in this video saturated age. The written or spoken word could say, "The woman was anxious". Video, through good and realistic acting can actually show an anxious woman. It is easy to convey a message through video without dialogue. I wrote the script for a particular video that was released about two years ago. It was based on the passage in Romans discussing the struggles of dealing with the old and new nature that we have to struggle with. As the scripture was being read on the video by an unseen narrator, I designed different scenes with a central character that was trying to do his best, but in many ways failed. One scene, for example, showed the camera moving across people sitting in a pew, taking notes as you could hear a sermon being spoken in the background. As it moved from person to person, each was intent on the Word that was being preached. However, as the camera panned down the pew you found our hero fast asleep. This was one of four different scenes that were being shown while the scripture from Romans was being read. No dialog, just video impact that helped the scripture come alive. While some people have difficulty in conveying emotion in the spoken word, a video can be used to present an illustration and lay the foundation for response using emotion.

Also, the ever popular comedic element can be used in such a way as to drop the guard of the listener and leave him or her ready to encounter a message of truth. A creative comedy short can grab the listener's attention, and then it is the job of the speaker to build on that foundation. Video with humor can be an extremely effective form of communication.

TOO MUCH OF ANYTHING CAN BE NEGATIVE

If taken to an extreme, the use of too much video can be irritating, distracting, and have an opposite, detrimental effect. The goal should never be to use video for the sake of using video. In a ministry setting it should not be merely to entertain, but more importantly to educate. It is to be inserted into ministry when—and only if—it is appropriate and fitting.

We in ministry can take this simple but complicated medium of video and use it to proclaim God's truth in a powerful way. This art form should not be applied solely in the secular world. We as Christians (1 Chron. 12: 32; Eph. 5:16) should use it for the glory of God, and so redeem this technology, perfecting its powerful effect. Everything done in the name of God should be done with the best quality possible. Secular producers strive for excellence, and sadly in the church we tend to settle for what is mediocre at best. Hollywood, with all of its resources, has abused this power, and consequently has tainted the medium. The church should come in and turn the tide. Take, for example, the way the Kendrick brothers and Sherwood Baptist made *Facing the Giants* and, most recently, *Fireproof* a fantastic success. The success of these movies had a shocking impact on Hollywood. We must not be affected by our culture, but rather be an agent of positive change.

While the lack of knowledge and budget shortfalls in a ministry setting may be commonplace, this doesn't mean that creating your own videos is out of reach. Today, there are fairly inexpensive ways to achieve the goal of helping churches create and use video for their ministry. Videos can be made with consumer cameras and cheap lighting tricks, and video testimonies can be made for Internet evangelism with any Webcam, household light, and a free subscription to YouTube, Vimeo, Tangle, or any other of these types of sites. The really exciting thing is that God is raising up talented people to match the production standards of Hollywood. Entire MTV and YouTube generations await true meaning and significance in their lives. The church *does* have the message of truth. Is it being heard? Is it being understood through our methods? It is our task to be clear in our presentation of the gospel.

There are many, many ways to use videos, some you might be able to create, and others you can download from a host of video providers on the Web. Here are some of the ways to utilize video in worship.

BACKGROUND LOOPS

Most sites that provide videos for church use also provide background loops. These are especially great to use with text. Using video behind text, either scripture, lyrics of songs, or even announcements, is one of the key features that Christian presentation software can provide. See the previous mentions of EasyWorship and MediaShout in chapter two.

Background loops can be computer animated, graphics-based, or real video clips. Nature is always a popular choice for these functions. Short clips of one scene can be looped seamlessly. I have also seen video loops that combine multiple scenes and are still looped seamlessly. While most background loops have something to do with nature (clouds floating by in the sky seems to be a favorite) not all background loops center on nature scenes. There are an abundance of themes that should be considered when choosing backgrounds for songs, and one must be intentional about matching the message of the songs to an appropriate and complimenting background. For example, a song about the resurrection of Christ could have a nice background of an empty tomb or time lapse clouds, and not a loop of trees in a forest. Likewise, a song that mentions the roar of the seas should have video of ocean waves and not a loop of the cross. These considerations should not be an afterthought.

A youth service could have more upbeat and/or grungy back-grounds than a tamer corporate worship gathering. If you are using a presentation program, such as EasyWorship or MediaShout, these programs can typically allow the background to be changed by the click of a button, and applied to whatever song or scripture is live. You can, of course, also have a preferred background assigned to a certain song so that every time it is live it shows the same background.

You should also be able to easily read text. Its color should be something neutral, such as white with a black shadow. The font can be creative as long as it is plain enough to be understood without any struggle. One must always remember that the aim is to aid the worshipers, not frustrate them. If a video behind the lyrics is too distracting then it's better to have no background at all. A simple philosophy in selecting these loops would be a welcome attitude. Like with so many things, the "KISS" principle is a good one- "keep it simple silly (or stupid)."

Other examples of using videos in worship include sermon illustrations, calls to worship, using them while the offering is being gathered, for announcements (normally videos you have created yourself), and at the conclusion of the service. It would be a travesty to use videos for all of these opportunities in one service, but you can mix it up a bit and use a video almost every week to enhance the worship experience in some way.

COUNTDOWNS

A countdown video can be used before the service or program begins. It works similar to the slide show or other video information that takes place before a movie starts at the theater. These countdown videos keep the audience (at least those who arrive early) busy, and lets others who may be roaming around know that the service is about to begin. There are many types of creative countdowns; the options are almost endless. Some are trivia questions about the Bible. Others can be quiet, serene images with thematic Scriptures. Some can educate, but if since it takes place before the service then try to entertain with fun facts or plain craziness.

It is fairly easy to create your own countdowns. You could use a green or chroma key (Wikipedia defines chroma key as a technique for mixing two images or frames together, in which a color (or a small color range) from one image is removed (or made transparent), revealing another image behind it.) countdown to overlay over your video or your announcement slides. For a modest price you could download software at www. thecountdowncreator.com to make your own countdowns using practically any font installed on your computer.

CHRISTIAN VIDEO SERVICES AVAILABLE ON THE INTERNET

There are many different Internet sites available for churches to shop and download videos they can use during worship services or Bible studies. In most cases you can preview the videos on their sites, and most can be purchased for a very reasonable price. Here are few of my favorites:

www.sermonspice.com—SermonSpice is the largest provider of Christian shorts to date, with well over 1,300 producers, and many exclusive to them. They carry video illustrations, count-downs, and backgrounds, and offer special discounts on selected videos during special holidays.

www.worshiphousemedia.com—This is another great resource with lots of videos to choose from, and many clearance items.

www.theworkofthepeople.com—This site offers a membership program, including unlimited downloads for one year for $250. Smaller packages are also available, and many videos can be had for as low as $3 each. They have been praised for their refreshing slant on Christian short films, and have an edgy side to their "Visual Liturgy."

www.ignitermedia.com—This site often runs creative specials, and offers different types of products. Their bumpers allow for you to add your own text and build your series graphics using their great designs. Also, their igniter tracks are a neat feature, which like Integrity's "iWorship DVDs" come with a performance track as well as a click track or split track that is in sync with the visuals, in case your house band wants to perform to the video.

www.sermonvideos.com—Offers excellent work, and a subscription for $150 a year which gives you access to 250 resources.

www.midnightoilproductions.com—This site has lots of creative content as well as valuable insights in their "reading" section on the philosophy of metaphors and other worship arts themes.

Most of these Web sites, as well as producers' individual sites, offer free videos that change every month or so. You can stock up on freebies to use at a later date. You'll find a lot more free motions and other modestly priced content on www.organicvideos .com, as well. In addition, www.bluefishtv.com offers video illustrations for just $1.99 each, along with other teaching series on DVD.

When churches are faced with limited budgets, there are other Web sites that give away content. Here are a few:

www.muddyrivermedia.com—They have a good selection of different types of videos which are offered for free with the option to donate to the ministry.

www.sermonade.com—They offer all of their videos absolutely free as open source content.

www.stufficanuse.com and www.lifechurchtv.com—offer some of their sermon series media and other items as well.

It is good to collect freebies and search for good deals, etc. However, often times the perfect video is not available for free. Your other option, of course, is to use your PC and create your own video!

SELF-PRODUCED VIDEOS

Collecting video clips for worship is a great way to keep current with the times. There are some producers that excel in creating meaningful and relevant films that benefit many. From time to time, though, the perfect clip for your needs has simply not been created.

Many churches are producing their own videos. And the good news is that you don't have to expend your time and money to produce a video that you'll only use once. With so many services out there selling and distributing videos to other churches, the ones you create—if they are up to quality standards—could very easily be submitted to a distributing Web site, and a Windows PC makes for a fine video-making machine.

There are many programs that make the editing process a fairly simple one. Technology has advanced so much in the last several years that practically anyone can be a filmmaker. More advanced programs would be an investment, while other user-friendly programs provide an easy-to-understand approach and will certainly not break the bank. There are some basic rules of filmmaking that will assist you in helping to produce videos that look professional.

EDITING PROGRAMS AND SERVICES

When it comes to editing videos, there is a large selection of programs and services to pick from that can meet your needs. Here is a list of some of the more popular editing software programs:

Adobe Systems—This is a very well-respected company and always has software that is on the cutting edge. They have been absorbing and refining software from other manufactures and developing programs that are commonplace in many offices and enterprises. Their video collection and creative suite are a favorite editing option for many in the production business.

▶   Premiere Elements—a down-scale model of their powerful editing software
▶   Premiere Pro—the flagship of Adobe's video non-linear software
▶   After Effects—a must-have program for advanced graphic artists and filmmakers
▶   Encore—for DVD authoring
▶   Photoshop—though not directly related to video, indirectly useful for the creation of high impact text and other graphics for video, print and/or Web
▶   Avid Technology
▶   Nitris DX / Mojo DX
▶   Media Composer
▶   DS—for FX, compositing & graphics
▶   Symphony Nitris DX

Muvee Technologies autoProducer—This inexpensive program is quite useful. For example, whereas to create the Ken Burns effect (motion on a picture) can become very tedious using the key frame animations of Adobe Premiere, this program automates the process. It is intelligent in its selection of movement and effects. Its styles (some free and others affordable add-ons) can be a big time saver. However, automation can be frustrating to the advanced user. Artificial intelligence will never replace human intuition; the same goes in video editing. This program is great for photo slideshows, or a style of effects on an entire video clip. Perhaps the best practice is to use muvee for a part of your production and render it out as a DV-AVI to import into another program and have more control over it.

MAGIX Movie Edit Pro

MAGIX Movie Edit Pro Plus—powerful and affordable.

Pinnacle Studio (now by Avid)—very user-friendly, powerful, and fairly inexpensive. A good option, especially if you are new to video editing.

Sony Creative Software—Sony is a big name and well-respected for its quality products.

▶   Sony Vegas Movie Studio
▶   Sony Vegas Pro

Ulead Systems

▶   VideoStudio
▶   VideoStudio Pro
▶   MediaStudio Pro
▶   DVD MovieFactory

Windows Movie Maker—every copy of Windows should come with this program installed on it. Then no one would have an excuse not to create simple videos! For a free program, it really is a decent piece of software. It comes loaded with all sorts of effects, transitions, and title animations. It is really easy to use, and you can even render out to DV-AVI. The default setting for rendering is .wmv. WMVs are good quality and much smaller files. This program is also great if you wish to put your videos up on the Web, since it can take your full resolution movies and convert them down to .wmv for Web usage, or for transferring a smaller copy to another computer. The downside to this program is that on the storyboard there is only one video track. Titles can be overlaid, videos cannot be layered.

Quicktime Pro—This is an upgrade from the free player which enables you to convert video files to all of the most popular formats for PC or Mac.

Format Factory—This is one of many free video converters which allows you to convert to most video files, sound files, flash files, and even rips DVDs. It can come in very handy from time to time when completing a project that is giving you problems.

SOME AFFORDABLE STOCK FOOTAGE SOURCES

Stock footage is an often needed item in the realm of video. Most of the time you will create your own footage, but every now and then you may require a shot that you did not actually film yourself. Stock footage that you use in your own productions needs to be royalty-free so you avoid any copyright trouble. For a long time, stock footage libraries were pretty expensive, and some still can be. Fortunately for those of us in ministry, some Web sites have recently launched that offer a more affordable option for stock footage. Here are some of them:

http://www.pond5.com—They offer quality SD or HD clips at very reasonable prices. They also usually have great clips that they are willing to give away every week at http://www.pond5 .com/Free-Stock-Footage.

http://www.revostock.com—They too offer some great clips, music, sound effects, and After Effects projects that will not break the bank. And they also offer free weekly clips which can be found at http://www.revostock.com/Freebie-Empty.html.

http://www.istockphoto.com/video.php—Offers photos, video, and sound effects, and music with one monthly freebie.

http://www.footagefirm.com—Runs great specials from time to time offering entire collections for free on DVD for only $8 shipping per disc.

http://www.newdogdigital.com—Very inexpensive stock footage DVD collections, animations, transitions, and animated graphics, as well as sound libraries. One 10 Gig Collection is priced at only $10.

http://phoenixclips.com/—This is a site that is growing and adding more producers with inexpensive stock footage. They offer a couple of freebies every month.

You should not let High Definition (HD) scare you when downloading free or purchased stock footage clips. If you have not yet transitioned into HD editing, that doesn't mean that you cannot use these clips. You can still use them, but they will be larger on your screen. You can scale them to size, or even put some motion on them. Once they render out with your final production they will be standard in size.

SOME BASIC RULES IN FILMMAKING

From very early on in life we learn that there are rules to be followed. Some believe that rules are only made to be broken, however rules are generally accepted by all. Rules keep things in an organized, acceptable manner for the betterment of all. Bearing this in mind, there are certain rules in video which result in a more professional appearance. There are rules in crafting, editing, and framing your productions that will make them more appealing without compromising the art form. At times, cutting-edge filmmakers will push the envelope and break some of the "rules" for shock value, or some other desired effect. However, most would do well in following the rules that are commonly applied to film.

Setup

Obviously a camera is a requirement for video. What kind of camera you use is dependent on how much you want to spend. There are three basic levels: consumer, prosumer (refers to products that fit somewhere between consumer and professional levels), and professional. Consumer cameras can be purchased at any electronics store. Prosumer and up are usually purchased online or in a specialty store. Research the specs when shopping for a camera and try to get the best performance possible for your dollar investment. You can use Google to find your best match. Consider the differences of three CCD chip cameras and cameras with one CMOS chip. Other things to consider are how the camera will actually store your video (tape, DVD or to a hard drive or flash drive), and whether you should jump to HD (High Definition) with all of its benefits and challenges.

If using tape, be certain to have plenty of blank tape, and stick with one brand of tape—preferably the same brand as your camera. Switching tape brands may cause your camera heads to clog. Also, label your tapes to stay organized and not waste time searching for a blank tape.

Stabilize your shots. A steady shot is always desired, unless you purposefully have a frantic chase scene or something where you need to exhibit a chaotic feel. The outside edge of your picture must stay smooth in motion. Only the objects within the picture should be moving. The most obvious way to accomplish this is by using a tripod. Expensive fluid head tripods are the best option, however, even a cheap tripod sold at stores everywhere would be better than any hand-held footage. Even with OIS (Optical Image Stabilizer) enabled, hand-held shots will be shaky and appear amateur in nature. For hand-held shots, or shots on the run, a steady cam would be in order. On the Web there are many DIY (do-it-yourself) tutorials on building inexpensive versions of these costly rigs. More advanced producers may incorporate cranes, jibs, dollies, or rigs that combine these utilities.

Check out the ever popular "poor man's steady cam" at www.steadycam.org, and some more interesting DIY projects at www.softweigh.com/video *(site wouldn't load)*. Any video clip that you shoot must be stabilized, level and fluid for it to be taken seriously in front of an audience.

Tell a Story

Popping in a tape and filming to your heart's content does not guarantee a quality video. It could result in just the opposite. Before even pressing the record button, there must be a purpose and intent to what you plan to shoot. At times, our images will simply express truths in the art of metaphor. And more often than not, our video will need to tell a story. Random images cannot tell a story. Even a short film must have a beginning, middle, and end. All these components must be present. If not, your audience will likely not be satisfied. They may, in fact, be annoyed. This is how we communicate as human beings. When we talk, we do not utter meaningless words in any order. Imagine if you were reading along in a book and suddenly I wrote, "Truck by grasshopper delight with letter running tree happy." It is nonsensical. That is not how we speak or write. Imagine telling a joke but leaving out the punch line? It is useless. We are sequential and purposeful in relaying our story, and support it with facts and analogies. If this is how we understand each other, why would we not apply this method in our video productions? (Special note—you know I had fun with this paragraph. How many times do you get to write a book and put in the sentence "Truck by grasshopper delight with letter running tree happy!")

Even if you have been commissioned to do something as simple as videoing the highlights of your church's annual chili cook off, your production must tell a story. It must not simply show pictures and/or video of the event without some thought involved. Wouldn't it be a better plan to start by showing those contestants in the contest setting up, the decorations, the people arriving, the faces of those trying the spiciest of the bunch, and then finally the coveted trophy being presented to the winners? Add some bluegrass music or something upbeat and you have yourself a nice little video!

Storyboard

The story that is to be told must be told in a creative and interesting way. The technical term for planning out a film ahead of time is pre-production. Actors, costumes, locations, etc. are secondary to the actual story or point you want to convey. Storyboarding is a tool that filmmakers can use to help organize all of their thoughts and ideas. A storyboard is a scene by scene, shot by shot picture of what the camera will record. It is made ahead of time as the director imagines how the shots should be filmed. It is helpful for the day of shooting, as well as the editing process. It forces one to think in a sequential manner, and the range of different shots adds overall production value to the final version. A storyboard breaks your script down into all the separate shots that you will use. Even if you feel you are not artistic enough to draw out the scenes, anyone can draw simple stick figures in a storyboard. If you Google the term "storyboard" you will find printable sheets, and even software with 2D and 3D applications, to storyboard more efficiently.

Tell a story, and do it with the video shots but also with the audio. Video is a powerful medium. It can stir the emotions and, if done correctly, will lead the audience into the desired effect— be it action, appreciation, or compassion. Video can assist in letting down the guard and can heighten a person's willingness to accept the message. It is the metaphorical language of our culture today. With such power at our fingertips, we must take it very seriously, and never throw together a video with a nonchalant attitude just because other churches are doing this and having success. Be intentional about what it is you need to portray. Start with a plan. Storyboard it using a vast array of creative but tactful shots. Create a composition that will reach the goals you set out achieve. Then move out of the way, and let God speak to the hearts of people using your hard work.

Framing and Composition

Video tends to be more forgiving than still photography. Even so, a videographer must compose his/her shots. Those who have spent time in either photography or video should be not just familiar, but rather ever conscious of the rule of "thirds." This most famous of rules can be traced back as far as 1797, in relation to proportioning for scenic paintings. The goal should always be to make our productions as aesthetically pleasing to the eye and professional looking as possible. This rule tremendously helps us in achieving this. One might think that default framing of subjects (people or objects) should be to center them. It is not. The rule of thirds assumes that the frame is divided into nine equal parts. The subject is aligned according to these imaginary lines.

The four intersecting points are called focal points. Action sequences do not necessarily follow these principles so methodically because the camera will follow the action and the audience will naturally be engaged. However on more ordinary shots the rule should be in place. In an establishing shot, it is best for the horizon to be on the upper third line. The lower third line would suffice as well, for example, in a shot of a sunset, where the clouds need to be accented. This process will help you ensure that the framing is level as well. In an establishing shot, if there is something that you will be shooting close ups of in the next shot, be sure to keep them near one of the focal points.

In a tight shot, you should aim to have your talent's eyes as close to the top third line as possible. Watch tonight's news cast and you will see confirmation of this rule. This will give you the right amount of headroom. In even closer shots, keep the eye line on this line. Cut off part of the head instead of the chin. Otherwise, you will be breaking the most important and generally accepted rule. Keep the focal points and these lines in mind at all times. If you are shooting a lone tree in a desert, it is more interesting if it is on one the lines and not merely in the center of the frame. If it is a person standing against a wall, align him or her on the a third line as well. If your subject is walking to the right, move with them, but keep them left line within two-thirds of what is called "lead room" in the frame on the right side.

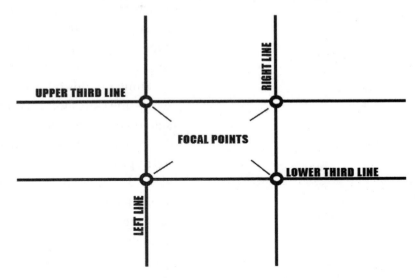

Once you have the rule of thirds in mind you can start shooting your scenes. Here is an overview of some of the most basic shot types. Their names do a decent job of describing their function and effect.

First there is the long shot, also known as the wide shot, or the establishing shot. What this does is reveal the subject's surroundings and other important details. However, these shots should be few and far between, mainly in the opening sequence so that the audience can truly understand what is happening more close up.

Next is the medium shot. If taken of a person, it will typically be from the waist up. While much more personal than a long shot, the background is still in plain view.

Then there is the famous close-up shot. All of these shots can be applied to people as well as objects. The close-up is an important shot in storytelling. It is where you can reveal things that your characters do not communicate (example: a stoplight changing to red that will play into the plot later on). The shots are also all relative (in that a medium shot of a tree may be a long shot of a bird in a nest).

The extreme close-up provides great detail, and at the same time provokes more emotion or visual excitement. Like the long shot, this shot should also be used sparingly and with good judgment.

A two shot is a comfortable shot of two people framed up like a mid shot or medium shot. Another popular way of shooting a conversation or interview is the over-the-shoulder shot. Be aware of the 180-degree rule (covered later) when doing this.

Here are some basic camera positions:

The high angle occurs when the camera is above the subject. Whether you use a ladder, or a hill, or shoot out of a window, it doesn't matter. The natural effect of this shot is that the subject appears smaller and therefore less important. The audience, being in a superior position, so to speak, has the feeling of power.

Similar to this is the bird's eye view or—a better Christian term—the God shot. This can be achieved from a tall structure, shooting straight down on the subject, revealing the big picture.

In contrast, there is also a low angle position. This shot is low to the ground. If the subject(s) is up on a balcony or something else, it is simply shooting from the ground up to them. These angles tend to make the subjects appear bigger and more powerful, even intimidating. Tripods typically will not let you get low enough, so a cheap way to achieve this is using a two-inch wide, three-ring binder to set the camera on, or even a bean bag pillow shaped so as not to be crooked.

The eye-level angle is the most commonly used shot. This is where the subject is shot straight on at eye level. This is sort of a neutral effect, good for reality. Another shot to consider is the point of view shot (from the subject's perspective, where you see what he/she is seeing).

180-degree Rule

Another classic rule is the "180-degree rule." It is also essential to maintain "consistency of screen direction." What this means is that you must not cross the "axis of action," another imaginary line that follows the main subject's action or direction of focus and cuts through the middle of the scene, from side to side with respect to the camera.

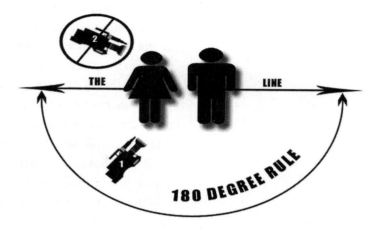

In other words, if the subject is walking down a street (the line), and the camera is on the right, it can cut to any other angle on a plane 180 degrees off of that line (right of the street). A cut to an angle on the left of the street would cause the audience to think the subject is going in the opposite direction. Unless the audience follows the camera's moving shot that crosses line, they will be subconsciously jarred and confused. Then the viewer sees how the perspective is changing right before their eyes. In that sense it is not confusing to them. Crossing the line (reverse cut) is something to be avoided.

An effect usually called "horizontal flip" may repair an inadvertent breaking of this rule if there is the same type of scenery on the other side of the line. If there are no landmarks or distinguishable inconsistencies, this effect may save the day. Gregory Fish, a producer for Sermonspice.com, and a regular columnist for *Christian Video Magazine* says, "When you get to the editing stage, there's nothing worse than the realization that you messed up by overlooking something, and it's not salvageable by crafty editing, so a tedious re-shoot is the only alternative." It is better to get it right the first time, than to have to repeat or fix an error later on. Keep these rules in mind at all times in order to produce the best videos that you can.

Cut-ins and Cutaways

Take some b-roll footage. This is footage that sets the scene, provides detail, or enhances the storytelling process. Always film more than you will use. You will also want to film a few seconds before the action or dialogue takes place. Along those lines, also shoot a few seconds after it is over before stopping the recording. This will be helpful in the editing stage, especially if adding transitions. The b-roll footage and multiple angles will help to keep the end product interesting. Cutting to a close-up of the hands, for instance, of a character showing something will allow you to retain the audio from one take and then cut to another take where the actor gave a better performance. Beware, though, of inconsistencies in similar shots. This is the rule of "jumping." Jumping is using the same camera set-up but showing two consecutive clips with a slight difference in the subject. This is to be avoided at all costs. Instead of opting to settle for incongruent clips, you could use a fade or cover the cut with b-roll footage. Always match the scene. When you take shots not filmed at the same time (i.e., different angles or takes), ensure that the elements do indeed match up, so that it appears to be one continuous scene. For instance, if your actor exits a room at the right, coffee in hand, make certain in the next room that you capture him coming in at the left, coffee still in hand. This also is taking into account the 180-degree rule previously discussed. Some people in your audience will pick up on the discrepancy with the coffee if he were to walk in empty-handed. They will immediately ponder this oversight and become distracted, missing the point entirely.

Another good editing rule (which is good to know when filming as well) is to try and cut on motion. Movement distracts the eye. So naturally an edit cut on motion is less noticeable and therefore preferred. For example, if shooting a book being put on a shelf, the close-up of the book would be much better if it is made when the action is taking place rather than after the fact (while it is simply a static image of the book on the shelf). It is also a good principle to edit together still shots with still shots and moving shots with moving shots. Otherwise it creates an awkward feeling for the audience and doesn't achieve the goal of keeping their interest alive.

Camera Movement

Movement is key in great filmmaking, bringing energy to the scene. Reasons to move the camera, besides the fact that the choreography makes it interesting, would be: to follow a character, to reveal something, to emphasize a character's reaction, or to create a sense of chaos or excitement. When there is not a budget or the means to pull off spectacular dolly shots (which move sideways on a track) or shots with a crane or jib, you can use some simple techniques with a tripod.

The most widely known and used moving shot is the zoom feature. This is always over-used, and ever-present, in home movies, and is to be used very sparingly in professional applications. There is simply no justification for back and forth zooming for no apparent reason. Our natural eye does not zoom, so in a point of view production it is very unnatural. Intentional zoom shots in a scripted plot should use zoom with tact. Generally the zoom in or out shots should be slow and always fluid in nature. The speed at which the zoom takes place must be consistent. Zooming at one speed and then slowing it down is usually not recommended. If it is jerky at all, it is always best to start the shot over, in order to edit in the whole shot at one speed.

Another classic movement is the pan. This is a simple horizontal movement left to right (best since it is the way we read) or vice versa. It is important that if you are filming a person who is walking, you want to leave about two -thirds of the space in front of them empty (rule of thirds). This is called lead room. As you pan, leave some walking room or lead room to give the audience a sense of where the subject is going. This is aesthetically pleasing.

Finally, we have the tilt. This is the vertical movement, pointing the camera up or down without moving the whole camera. Like in panning, practice the shot. Keep your feet steady and maintain a center of gravity. End at a comfortable position rather than beginning comfortable. Avoid any sudden jerks in your arms. Slow is always nice. Make sure your tripod is level and the movements are free and loose. These tips will help bring variety to your productions and help you to tell your story in exciting and effective ways.

Lighting and Audio

Most dead giveaways to the amateur video are bad lighting and bad sound. These things can be solved fairly easily. Until you have a good light kit, which you can purchase online, you could film outdoors in natural light. Aim away from the sun so as not to mess up your image. If you must film indoors, use as much natural light as possible. Open windows, and then turn every light on. Lamps can be pointed in a three point lighting manner. Another inexpensive but powerful way is to reflect light by using a halogen work light pointed to the ceiling, or diffusing its light with a glossy shower curtain in front of it.

Unless you have a proper microphone setup, music videos and/or voice-over narrations may be the way to go. Microphones that come onboard cameras are usually pretty good at picking up ambient sounds, but a nice condenser shotgun mic would definitely be in order to pick up a person or group of people speaking directly in front of the camera. One good and fairly inexpensive option is the Rode VideoMic (http://www.rodemic.com) which fits perfectly in the shoe and plugs in to the camera's stereo input. It is studio quality and even comes included with a shock mount.

For your soundtracks, you have to be careful with copyright laws. Royalty-free loops and sound libraries are a good way to go. However, one of the best solutions can be found at http://www.smartsound.com/. These high quality tracks come in any genre of music and can be resized instantly to any length, freeing you from the limited set of the 15-, 30-, and 60-minute lengths that you'll get from any other source. They will end when you want them to end, intelligently. If you stretch it out a few more seconds, it will find a different way to end the song. They can be expensive, but if you sign up for email updates you will find many good albums discounted from time to time ($25 instead of $99).

Advanced Video Techniques

This chapter is meant to be an overview and a resource for video enthusiasts in ministry. There are hosts of other resources available to go deeper into the world of advanced video techniques. You might wish to check out Christian Video Magazine (subscriptions are free) at www.christianvideomag.com. They have many articles of interest covering all things related to video in the church (and since I am the Editor-in-Chief and one of the founders, I can highly recommend it!). As a technical resource check out www.videomaker .com. Another great site for those who want to create great looking productions is www.videocopilot.net by Andrew Kramer. It is a goldmine of many free tutorials and nice products, all for sale. The presets and project files are free downloads and cater to users of Adobe After Effects version 7 or higher. However, the principles learned can apply many times to users of versions 5 or 6. For special effects, color correction, green or blue screen keying, 3D titling, there is no better (free) place to go and learn these techniques.

Informal Video

I know that I have just finished outlining a lot of information to help enable and encourage you to create the best and most professional videos possible. However, there is also an opportunity to use what I call "informal video." These are videos taken without a rehearsal, or without a script. Sometimes, real testimonies or something that doesn't have that professional look, can have an impact.

Jay Delp, (Jay Delp Productions) is one of the contributing editors at *Christian Video Magazine* each month. In talking about informal video, he says, "The explosion of affordable, even free, high quality pre-produced ministry video content continues to be a rich resource for all churches. But don't overlook the unmatched power and impact of your own 'home-grown' media and video content. It's usually not a choice between one or the other but a healthy blend of both based on available time, talent and technology."

A great example of informal video, or as Jay says, "home grown" video, is when you video your teenagers as they are returning from camp. Ask them how it went, what they enjoyed, what God did for them during the week? You will normally get some very energetic testimonies, un-rehearsed, yet with some fantastic impact. Show it at the next church service instead of giving a "report" on how camp went. And save the video for use next year when you are trying to promote and encourage young people to sign up for camp.

VIDEO ON-DEMAND

There are host of different services that will be happy to take your video files and help you to stream them from your Web site. Many of these have already been listed earlier in the chapters on content management systems and podcasts. The services of Elexio and faithHighway are two that I can recommend highly, and are both mentioned in detail in those previous chapters.

STREAMING LIVE VIDEO

There is one more fantastic use of video. And thanks to the Internet, every church can take advantage of the opportunity to stream their services live on the Web for the world to view and enjoy. There are several ways to accomplish this task, and many solutions to help you do it. Of course, the source of the stream and the available bandwidth can limit the number of people that are actually able to watch your live stream, so consider your intended audience as you select the solution that is right for your church or ministry.

The "How to"

A minimum setup would require a computer with lots of RAM, and big hard drive, and Internet connection, and either USB or firewire connections. A Webcam will work, although you may want a camera that works in low light situations and has a zoom. You'll also need some free encoding software on that computer, like Flash or Windows. Turn on the camera, fire up the encoder and hit the "Start Broadcasting" button on the encoder software. You are now streaming!

Of course, there are many versions, features, equipment and functions that can be added. For example, you may want to create a production of your service, requiring several cameras with operators that are equipped with headsets to hear the director. A switcher gives you the ability to switch from one camera to another, so that even during a production streaming live to the Web you can get different shots and angles to increase the production value. There are also several services that can help stream your service live.

Really, Really Simple? Churchon Video.com

Why doesn't someone just invent a simple box that can go between the camera, audio input and the Internet that would be simple to use and would encode and stream your video worry free? Well, actually someone has! A company called Tech-Werks has partnered with Church On Video, and combined a seven-inch touch screen encoder with Internet services provided by Church On Video.

It is so easy to steam live video of your services that when I describe it, it will probably sound silly. You take the encoder box (about the size of a loaf of bread) and connect any video and audio input device using the video/audio input cables (red, white and yellow). For live streaming this would need to come from your camera output or a switcher box. For other uses you could be hooking up a VCR, DVD player, etc.

After hooking up those three cables, be sure to plug in your encoder box to an AC outlet. You need to have a cable connection to the Internet because they don't allow the encoder box to work with WiFi as it is not reliable enough for live streaming.

Now turn your attention to the front. If your camera is sending a signal you will see it on the seven-inch touch screen. Above the video are a couple of touch screen button options. They are very basic. You can start recording and hit "stream." You have this option because many people use Church on Video to encode and post their videos up on the Web, but you don't have to use their service to stream live. If you want to just post your videos, hit record and start. When you reach the end of what you wanted to record, hit stop. If you were not streaming it live you will see the option to "auto publish." Hit this button and your recorded video is uploaded to your account on Church on Video where you can then view it or grab the HTML code they provide for your video and put it into a content box on any Web site. After your video has been uploaded to their service, you will receive an email notifying you that you video is ready. In the email they provide a link that you can click to view the video. This makes it handy for you to email to others so they can also watch the video. And if you don't have a Web site, Church on Video can also create one for you to use so that you can share your services or recordings.

If you wanted to stream the content you are receiving from your camera, hit "start" when you are streaming LIVE and the encoder automatically notifies the "SMART" on-line software, which then adds a "WATCH LIVE" link on your Web site. You are now streaming "LIVE" to the entire world. When you "Stop" streaming live, the "SMART" on-line software removes the "WATCH LIVE" link. The video is then automatically published to your Web site to be viewed on-demand, and ready for people to watch any time, any place.

If you are wanting to record and post something to the Web site at a later date, and don't have access to the Internet, no problem. You can hook up your camera and hit record. Later, when the encoder box is back at the office and you have access to an Internet cable, you can select the video and hit the "auto publish" button. The encoder box can also hold p to 900 hours of video recording.

The encoder records the files as a Windows Media Player file (.wmv) ready to post to your Web site. However, if you want to edit the video for any reason, simply connect the box to any network and you can access the directory of files and download them to your computer where they can be accessed via any editing program.

For more information, visit www.churchonvideo.tv. The cost is $1,500 for the encoder if you are a church, ministry or non-profit. Remember, with the encoder box you don't need a dedicated computer to stream your videos. There is also a fee for the services of Church on Video, with the monthly fee of $200 if you want to do live streaming.

Virtual Church

The MyFlock.com service (mentioned in chapter five) has a special service that only helps you stream your service live, but also helps you provide a virtual worship service for those watching your live stream. The service is called StreamingChurch.tv.

StreamingChurch.tv is unique in that it is able to closely replicate the experience members and visitors have when visiting a church in person, but in an online environment. For example, they provide an integrated countdown timer to the beginning of the service. As you enter the service online, it recognizes existing church members and displays them in the "who's attending" area with a photo and link to their profile. All attending guests show up automatically in an integrated "who's attending" area, and church staff and lay leaders are able to greet them (a virtual hand-shake) in the integrated chat room. Guests can choose to participate in the dialogue or hang back and watch. Everyone attending also has the ability to chat privately with individuals as they watch the integrated live video of the service.

The folks at AliveChurch.com report that their Web pastor will also pray individually online with whoever requests private prayer using the private messaging system. In addition the Web pastor (or other lay leader) can dynamically update the video service page as the service progresses. For example, when the worship team is performing a particular song, the Web pastor can push out a button link on the service page to the original artist of that song. Or when it's time for the offering, he can push a "donate online" button to every attendee's screen.

StreamingChurch.tv also provides an integrated Google map so you can see where everyone attending is from.

The sermon/teaching notes are also included in the online experience for every attendee to follow along or print at home as the service progresses.

Mike Gray, Web Pastor for Alive church says, "Our online campus has been a better outreach tool than I had expected. It has allowed people who are skeptical of church to try out church with anonymity for a few weeks. We have people coming in to a campus every weekend, after watching two or three weeks online, ready to make Alive their church home.

"Our Web campus has made it possible for attendees to stay connected to the body while out of town or sick. Every weekend someone thanks me in the live chat for making the services available so they don't have to miss."

VIDEO IS KING
. . . .

Regardless of how you use video, realize that it is a very important new form of communication. Video used to be considered one and the same with broadcast media, such as television and movies. Now, services such as TokBox.com allow you to have live video chats with multiple people at once, turning an ordinary phone call or conference call into a real communication opportunity. Take Apple's iPhone. While popular with over 20 million units sold, it was consistently criticized by many because it didn't have the ability to record video and share it with others or post directly to the Web. The new version of iPhone, however, now has these abilities.

Bottom line is this: USE VIDEO! It can give you the ability to broadcast an important message, evoke an emotion, and open the door to the mind for new thoughts and ideas. Use it because it is a great communication tool. It can make you smile or frown. It can show your feelings and emotions directly to the people you wish to communicate with. It is powerful, and it is direct. And now, it is easy to accomplish!

CHAPTER 8

Computer Bible Study

I go a long way back with computers. My first computer was a Radio Shack Color Computer with 16k of memory, and you had to load your programs via a tape recorder. There was no real monitor. Instead I had to use my only color television that my wife and I had at the time (And you can bet that if I wanted to be on the computer at night during prime-time programming, I wasn't a popular guy).

When I moved up to my first PC, one of the first things I purchased was a computer Bible study program. It arrived on floppy disks (those 5.25 inch floppy disks that actually still have some "flop" to them). I don't remember how many disks came with the program, but I can tell you that if you wanted to do a search through the entire Bible for a particular phrase, it took a long time, and a lot of switching in and out of floppies.

BIBLE STUDY SOFTWARE HAS COME A LONG WAY

Bible software for Windows has come a long way since the early days of using 5.25 inch disks to store, search and read a single translation of the Bible. Today you can have literally thousands of volumes ranging from Bibles to commentaries and books about counseling, fiction, and leadership, all available on your computer, easily searched, referenced and ready for your study.

Software helps Christians in almost any realm of studying the Bible. There are great programs that will help you stay on schedule with a daily Bible reading, keep track of where you left off, how far you have progressed, and where you are going. You can set up custom reading lists or use dozens of prearranged reading plans. And we're not just talking about going from Genesis to Revelation. If you are willing to go online, you can get involved with a community of believers and readers. You can share your thoughts on the passage of the day and read someone else's thoughts as well. Add to that the ability to keep prayer lists, post readings to Web pages, and read any of the hundreds of classic or recent devotional books. Your options are seemingly endless.

However, not everyone is satisfied with just devotional materials. Bible study software can help you prepare for your Sunday School lesson, read the Bible and other study books for a small group study, and prepare to teach a lesson. If you are a teacher you can create a lesson from scratch using the Bible study tools, or just work with something like LessonMaker, a program from WordSearch Corporation (http://www.wordsearchbible.com) that quickly creates an instant lesson with discussion questions, colorful images and maps, and exports it to PowerPoint for displaying purposes. Many software makers have added books and commentaries that will help you understand the Bible, apply it to your personal life, or help you apply it to the lives of your small group, church, family or class.

As beneficial as Bible study software is to lay people and small group leaders, it is quickly becoming a necessity for professional clergy. Most pastors over age forty will remember the days of preparing a sermon or study for their church using nothing but books, legal pads, and a pen. If you were super technical and advanced maybe you used something like a Brother word processor. I am old enough to remember what it was like to be a pastor, preparing sermons without the aid of a computer or the Internet. It was important to have a grand library at your disposal, including multiple translations, a large green Strong's concordance, and a Greek New Testament (I loved my Greek classes back in college so much that I took most of them twice). You also needed a lexicon or Robertson's Word Pictures, stacks of commentaries, Bible dictionaries, and maybe a Bible handbook and atlas. I also had a wall of other books that contained Bible and subject studies from a large variety of pastors that I respected. Taking such a collection on the road with you would make your chiropractor very happy. I never thought that much about the time it took to go through the basic steps of the Bible study process using all these books. At the time, I guess we didn't know any better.

Today, with Bible study software you can do all of that study in about half the time. Or you can access twice as many reference works in the same amount of time, thus adding to the depth of your studies and sermons.

HOW TO STUDY THE BIBLE

The basic steps of studying the Bible are the same whether you are learning for your own edification, preparing a Sunday school lesson, a small group Bible study, or a sermon. Bible study software just makes these steps faster and easier. Let's take a look at the process and see how it helps.

Studying Passages in Context

First, it is a good idea to read the passage you are studying in its context. All Bible study programs allow you to quickly find your passage. But if you know your Bible, you might actually be able to thumb to Romans 12:1 quicker than I can boot up my computer, start up the software and then type in the reference.

After the initial reading, you will want to read the passage in a number of translations. Using books, you'll have to look it up in two to four Bibles or more. This is where Bible study software really begins to shine. Using a Bible software package I usually just have to click a button or menu item to quickly display a few different translations. Some of those will also be in interlinear format, where the English translation is put above or below the Greek/Hebrew text. Still, it may be more satisfying for some to do this initial reading in a hard copy Bible. But for me, software wins because I can quickly access so many translations almost instantly.

Next, you will want to begin to study the passage in a more in-depth way. With software you have almost instant access to things like Strong's definitions or even more scholarly references. Using the Reverse Interlinear Bibles from Logos or WordSearch you can not only read the passage in a modern English translation, but also find the Greek or Hebrew words behind the complex English words. Without clicking your mouse button, you can hover over the word and see its basic translation and access the grammatical information about the word(s), called "morphology," which helps you see why the word was translated the way it was. Often Greek and Hebrew terms are more complex or nuanced with meaning that our English terms don't perfectly translate. Bible software helps you do this kind of study even if you never took a class in Greek or Hebrew. And if you did, then you will be able to very quickly access the words that will help you use your knowledge. The more advanced packages will give access to some very advanced scholarly works.

One of the steps some serious Bible students take is outlining the text. In the old days we took our Bible out and copied the words or phrases onto a legal pad in a visual outline . . . something like this:

For God so loved the world
        that he gave his only begotten son
that whosoever believeth
                in him
        will not perish
        but
        have everlasting life

Why do this kind of outlining? Because it helps me see the relationship between the ideas in the passage. If you are a student of Greek or Hebrew, then you can do it in those languages and see how the various clauses relate to one another. This often clears up somewhat complicated sentence structure that you find in some of Paul's letters or other places. Here it shows that God's love helps us have a choice between either perishing or having everlasting life. That contrast might help us decide how we will present John 3:16 to a congregation.

Without ever having to copy words in your horrible handwriting, you can do the same thing using software. At the most basic level, you can cut and paste the passage from your Bible study software into either the software's location for saving notes, or a word processor like Microsoft Word or the free OpenOffice.org Writer. You could even use Windows Notepad or Write/WordPad (depending on which version of Windows you are using). You get the the same result, but it will be cleaner and quicker.

A couple of the more advanced packages have built-in outline features complete with drawing tools so you can not only show the relationship based on the tabs and spaces you add to the lines, but also with lines, boxes, arcs, and circles. I also like to use bold or underline typeface to show important words or action words.

As mentioned above, one of the benefits of Bible software is that nearly all of the packages available today offer some way to add your own personal observations and collect information about the verses. There will likely be a dialogue box or window you can open that will show text and pictures that you have added to a verse, a chapter or even one word. The better ones will tie it to the reference and not the translation, so that you can see the collection later no matter which translation you are reading.

If you translate the passage from Greek or Hebrew, you can include it in the notes feature. Then you can give an explanation of the main words or theological concepts. Also, you can collect observations you have made from your general knowledge of the passage from past studies, or just common sense. Then you can type in some questions to be answered by the "experts" who have written commentaries or study notes on the passage. The old fashioned way requires you to keep a notebook of your observations. If you are like me, your handwriting is hard to decipher. Sometimes I am able to read what I wrote because my mind can still remember what I was thinking about at the time. However, when I look at what I wrote a week or a year later, it is sometimes impossible to understand. I have looked back at some of my handwritten sermon notes and simply had to scratch my head in wonderment before I eventually end up throwing the notes away. But now, using Bible study software you can keep this information in the notes feature of the software, giving you immediate access to it every time you read that verse. You can even copy and paste notes from passage to passage. And instead of sketching a picture you can copy a map, a picture, an illustration, or a hyperlink to a Web page with information. Some software will even let you visit the site without even opening a Web browser.

Consulting References

Answering questions recorded in the software's notes feature leads us to the next step of Bible study—consulting references. You will want to start with dictionaries, lexicons, or word studies. Next you will want to look up cross references. Finally, you will read commentaries. Always consult the commentaries last.

Using traditional means, these steps can take forever. You have to gather the different books from your library or borrow them if you don't have them immediately accessible. Doing a concordance search of the word "perish" in John 3:16 is simple enough. But what if you want to search multiple translations? You will need multiple concordances. The "Exhaustive Concordance" for the New American Standard Bible is about two feet tall and weighs nearly a ton (Ok, maybe not a ton but you get the picture).

Imagine carrying one for the King James, the New International Version, and the Revised Standard Version?

With Bible study software and the right tools installed, I can not only search for the word "perish" in each of those translations, but in all the translations I have on my computer. For some packages, that might be a dozen or more Bibles. Also, some English words are from a Greek or Hebrew word that is translated different ways. For example, one form of "perish" might be just that, but another might be "destroy," since the original Greek term means literally to destroy oneself. With some Bible study software packages you can look up the underlying Greek word for "perish" and then search the Greek New Testament with a simple right click of the mouse, followed by a left click in a "context menu," which pops up whenever you click or right click a word with your mouse.

The number of ways you can search and study the text just by right clicking a passage or word is vast. You could do the same thing with traditional books, but what takes you one hour to accomplish with books and a legal pad can now be done in a fraction of the time using software.

Wildcard Searches

Searching the Bible for the concepts of John 3:16 using a book concordance might not take a long time, but the power of these search engines is fantastic. You can search for one word, an exact phrase, or even parts of a word. What if you wanted to find every word that has the root idea of the word "believe?" That might mean finding words like "belief", "believer", "believing", "believeth", "believes", etc. With most software, if you search using something like belie* you will find all of those instantly. The asterisk is a wildcard, which means that it will find any word that has "belie" at the beginning of it. If you want to also find a word like "unbelieving," then simply add an asterisk to the front of the word too. Other "Boolean" searching tools include the ability to do searches using either the word "or" or "and". For example, you might want to find a specific passage that has the word prayer "or" mediation, or a verse that has prayer "and" mediation within the same verse. You can even do searches that would search for Peter "and" Jesus within three verses of each other. A couple of the very advanced programs have complex searching capabilities that would let you find a Greek word translated with a certain English word only in the past tense and the third person. Typical Bible students might not need that, but very advanced scholars might.

After searching for the words and concepts in various dictionaries and other sources, it is time to consult the "experts." One of the things you will find is that by studying the passage in context, you should already have a very good working knowledge of a passage. The primary reason for going to commentaries is to find the answers to questions you could probably answer on your own, and to confirm what you already have discovered. It is good to make sure you are not going off on a wrong theological path based on a single word that is only in one translation, or is based on a faulty understanding of a lexicon's entry regarding an obscure word. People who are trained and tested Bible scholars are the ones that write commentaries, and we should avail ourselves of the fruits of their study. But don't let that hinder you from doing your own personal study first. Read the passage, outline it, read it in context, study the words, search the scriptures, and look up key concepts in dictionaries and lexicons first. Then go to the commentaries.

Windows Reference Materials

Using traditional means, you might have a Matthew Henry Commentary, a set of commentaries from your denomination's publishing house, and you might be able to invest in another volume about a particular book of the Bible. For the price of your Matthew Henry, the entire set of commentaries, and that one volume, you could invest in one of the software packages and have access to a dozen commentaries, including two or three modern ones. And instead of investing in books that take up space on shelves and cost time, effort and sometimes money to move from church to church, you can carry a whole library in a computer that is smaller than that NASB Exhaustive Concordance mentioned earlier. Furthermore, you will be able to access that information with a few mouse clicks or key punches. You can then record your findings in the software's notes function and you won't have to look it up the next time you study John 3:16 because it's all right there, nicely stored from your previous study.

Other things you can quickly consult using many of today's Windows Bible study software programs are maps, databases of illustrations, hymns, art work and visual images, videos, and other sermons or studies that relate to any passage. Many packages also have a community feature like Internet forums and shared Bible study notes.

Benefits of Using Bible Software Over Books

Above we've summarized the way Bible study software can help you study and prepare for lessons or sermons. The chart below summarizes the steps to studying a passage and shows the specific benefits of using software instead of a stack of reference works and commentaries.

Bible Study Step	Software Step	Benefit
Reading the passage	Open software to passage by either clicking buttons or typing reference.	This is the one step that might actually be quicker the old way, using a paper Bible!
Compare translations	Click Parallel View Button or Menu Selection (May have to initially go into preferences to choose which translations to display).	Can quickly open multiple translations, have access to sometime dozens, use interlinear to see relationship between English and Greek/ Hebrew.
Make note of observations	Open notes function to record your observations.	Notes are always there instead of tablets or paper notebooks that you must file.
Outline the text	Either copy text into a word processor or open the outlining function of your software, then move text around on screen.	Faster and able to see it all at once and save for future uses more easily than saving paper notes; easily add markings like bold, italics and drawing features.
Consult references: to study the scripture in context, using dictionaries or Strong's	Usually right click a word and choose a context menu item or hover over a hyperlink to display a tooltip; click words to open dictionaries.	Instead of looking up a word in a lexicon or dictionary you can quickly click or right click and even hover over hyperlinks. This is where software really shines. Many references are available instantaneously.
Consult references: topical Bibles/cross references	Click on hyperlinked notes or footnotes to display verse lists or open a topical bible and either click verses or hover over these to display tooltips.	Instantly display references instead of having to page through a bible after opening a book or looking in margins of study Bibles.
Consult references: handbooks and maps	Open the work and often will instantly synchronize with related passages.	Takes longer to open huge books and find related content instead of instantly having it displayed and listed, many maps are online and updated often or shows in multiple views like satellite views.
Consult commentaries	Open the work and often will instantly synchronize with related passages, some have tabbed interfaces so you can instantly click to see other commentaries.	Multiple commentaries available almost instantly and immediately opened to the passage being studied.
Record findings	Either type what you learn from references and commentaries or more quickly copy and past, either content or links to content.	Instead of having multiple notebooks which are hard to keep up with, you can collect them digitally and always have access any time in the future you read that passage.
Decide on what the purpose, main idea, and lessons are of the passage you are studying.	Record ideas in notes or included word processor.	Not necessarily helped by software, but can spend more time here since other steps get you hear faster.

Bible Study Step	Software Step	Benefit
Write sermon or Bible study	Using word processor notes features included in most packages.	You don't have to open another program unless you want to, can save for future study of the passage, can often publish to external places like online communities or export for your own viewing in other software or to distribute for others to view.
Consult other sermons if stuck or to confirm your findings.	Open sermon collections and search for passage.	Instant access to thousands of sermons or studies on your given passage, this step might not even happen if you didn't have computer Bible study software.
Create teaching resources to help in presentation	Edit handouts or even instantly create a handout for your study if you don't have time for previous steps. You can also create picture files to display in presentation software.	Much easier than making posters, overhead transparencies, or mimeographed handouts typed or written by hand, more legible and faster and cheaper to produce.
General Uses of Bible Software	Search for passages using complex or simple Boolean methods.	Much quicker and you will find better results using complex tools that while powerful, are easy to learn and use.

As you can see, the steps to the actual presentation of sermons or lessons are faster, simpler, and richer. You will have more immediate access to a greater quantity and quality of information that will help you become a teacher who presents very in depth, informative and helpful lessons or sermons.

Basic Features of Bible Study Software

A mechanic uses different tools for different jobs. He doesn't use a crescent wrench to remove an oil filter. He doesn't use a screw driver to change spark plugs, unless that is all he has and he finds some inventive way to do it. A well-equipped mechanic will have the right tool for every job.

A student of God uses Bible software like the mechanic uses his toolbox. Some mechanics have huge, complex tool kits that have multiple versions of the same tool. Others have on adjustable wrench, one screw driver and a hammer. The more tools you have the more likely you are to find one that will help you quickly do the job. A Bible student will want the right tool for the right job. He or she will want to have a good toolbox with the right tools to effectively learn and present the lessons of God's word.

Like the mechanic's toolbox, all Bible study software packages usually do a few basic things. First and foremost is the ability to read the Bible using one or more translations of the Scriptures. What differentiates one package from another is normally just a few items:

▶   What translations are available?
▶   Search abilities
       Search Scripture
       Search additional books within your electronic library
       Search your notes
▶   What additional commentaries and books work with the program?
▶   Program features

There are some very expensive programs that include almost any translation you can think of. And they can include many different versions of the Greek and Hebrew text as well as the Latin Vulgate. They will also provide interfaces in multiple languages. It would not help a Spanish speaking person if the menus and toolbar titles were all in English. Some packages are not as complete. For example, they may only include an English interface, or may only have public domain translations. A public domain book is one that no one owns the copyright to, so no fees have to be paid. Examples of public domain Bible translations are the King James Version or the Young's Literal Translation. They are in the public domain and you can freely distribute them for free, or for a small fee as you are presenting them in a way that is useful and people are willing to pay for it. But you don't have to pay anyone for the right to distribute them.

Copyrighted Bible translations include the New International Version, owned and published by Zondervan, or the English Standard Version, owned and published by Crossway. Zondervan is very particular about who they let distribute their translation and they require a fee. Crossway is less particular and is often available free of charge for some software packages.

Because some publishers require payment for distributing their translations, they will not always be included if a distributor is offering a very inexpensive or free program. That is why many freely downloadable programs will not have translations like NIV, NKJV, or NLT.

A second basic feature of nearly all Bible study programs is the ability to search the Bible. Most will have either a toolbar button or even search boxes where you can type in key words you want to find in one or more translations. Many let you do simple searches by double clicking or right clicking words. A few programs let you do very complex searches that will let you find words in one translation, while at the same time finding a form of that word in Greek and/or Hebrew. One or two programs have much more complex searching tools, and using them would require some amount of training. For example, Bibleworks 8 has a very complex searching tool that lets you map out searches visually using boxes and drawing tools. Their search feature is the exception to the rule. All programs function like a concordance and let you find every instance of the word. Even with its very complex search tools, it should be noted that Bibleworks has simple search functions as well.

Some searching tools will also let you search other parts of the software, like reference works, books, and even your own study notes. This is one of the great benefits of doing your Bible study on a computer, because you can keep your findings and later read and search them.

A third basic function is the ability to consult more than just the Bible. Almost all programs handle reading and searching the Bible adequately. But some also allow access to other research books, like Bible dictionaries, topical Bibles, commentaries, Bible handbooks, and original language lexicons. Some have other books like the latest works on leadership, Christian living, or preaching from contemporary authors. If they do not offer contemporary authors, they will have public domain works from classic authors. One can amass huge digital libraries through add-on books, or by purchasing various collections.

I would like to note that you shouldn't overlook the value of those that provide public domain works from classic authors. A few years back, a small book by a notable author became very popular. I had a friend who published a Christian newspaper and wanted to use the popularity of the book to help draw attention to their publication. However, to reprint text from this book would have been very costly. Doing a quick search in classic works he discovered a book by Moody that, almost chapter to chapter, contained many of the same thoughts and outlines of the newer popular book. He simply ran a series of articles from Moody's book, and didn't place a lot of emphasis on the author. The subject of the series was very well read in his newspaper, and the few people that noticed it was from Moody commented on the lesson learned; that when it comes to writing about the Bible and doctrinal interpretation and application, there is not much new thought, just new authors that are popular because of their visible appearance in today's media.

Everyone who grew up in church remembers looking at the back of their Bible to study the maps during boring sermons. (This never happened to those in my congregation when I was a pastor, but others have related the experience to me). Most Bible study software gives you access to these as well. And aside from just having the same old maps you used to have in the back of your Bible, some will let you add your own markings, text, or notes to the maps. You can then copy or export them for viewing in handouts, sermon presentations, or to post on Web sites.

Along with maps, many programs will have charts and graphs of important data. Some will have timelines and even images of significant items found in scripture, like the temple furniture or archaeological discoveries from ancient Greece and Rome. Being able to see these types of items will help your congregation or class to better understand what the Scriptures are saying. Having images, and in some cases video, gives us a better "picture" of what the Bible is conveying.

After a student has amassed all this knowledge, he or she needs a place to collect it and save it for future reference. As mentioned above, most Bible study programs give you the ability to collect information in notes or documents that can be saved within the program. The benefit is you can attach them to verses of Scripture, and years later come back to that verse and instantly find the information that took you hours to collect at an earlier time. You can search all your references, and conduct cross reference searching, and the copy all of that into a note file, which you can then attach to either a verse, chapter, or even a single word. Your computer Bible study program becomes your digital filing cabinet.

Notes features also can become a digital filing cabinet for illustrations, anecdotes, and quotations. Maybe you were trained to keep files on topics or passages. Before computers, you could copy it and place it in a file. If you heard a good quote at a Bible conference you would scribble it down and place it in the file. After a few years of doing this, you probably had amassed a huge filing cabinet filled with this kind of material. I used to keep spiral notebooks of information with hand written notes and illustrations, and scratches in the margins trying to keep track of where I might have told each story so as not to repeat myself to the same audience.

With Bible software you can do the same thing, but digitally. This gives you instant access to all of it, and allows you to tag it by multiple topics and search within it. It would be like placing that magazine article in five different folders. But instead of making five copies you only have to enter it once. And then when you forget where you put it, just do a search for key words in the article and you can quickly access it again.

Today, many people are no longer just preaching or teaching the Bible with spoken word. Many are also using multimedia to communicate God's word. Bible software can help. All of the programs give you the ability to quickly copy and paste passages of scripture into handouts or presentation slides. As mentioned previously you can also copy the other content such as maps and pictures. A few of these programs even have links to online databases of video or PowerPoint slides and JPG files.

When you are studying you will want to access your information quickly and easily. Bible study software gives quick access through searches. But another feature of nearly all programs is the ability to quickly arrange the many books on the screen at the same time. This way you can have your Bible open to one or more translations at one time. You can also have a window with multiple commentaries open so you can read them quickly. Then if you need a word defined in English, Greek, Hebrew or some other language, you can also have a dictionary and a lexicon open. If you have searched for a topic, you might also have a list of the verses you found. All of this can be arranged on the screen at that same time. Some might do this in a tabbed interface, or have it hidden behind one of the windows ready to be viewed with a click of the mouse. But instant access to multiple Bibles, references and books is a key feature. It is like having all your books open on your desk, and being able to switch between them with the wave of a magic wand.

You can also arrange your desktop in any way you want, either by resizing windows or arranging them anywhere you prefer on the screen. Then you can save those arrangements for later use. Saving desktops is something that helps you quickly get access to the books you use for various tasks. You might save a particular desktop arrangement for doing your devotions. Then you might also save one for doing language study. A third desktop arrangement might be set up for consulting commentaries. You could set up a different desktop for all the different steps of your personal Bible study method. Saving and accessing these desktops might be as simple as clicking a toolbar button, a drop down menu or some other method. It is like being able to wave a magic wand and arrange those old dusty books in a new way for each step of the Bible study process.

If you are an advanced computer user, you will likely be able to jump right in and start using some of the more powerful Bible study programs with little help or training. But if you do need some help, most of these programs will have help included. What is really great the more advanced programs are the help files, which are not just technical documents about how to use their software. They go as far as helping you learn how to utilize various types of Bible study methods as well. And with the programs that include non-reference libraries, many have books on how to do anything from sermon preparation to devotional exegesis. Exegesis is studying the Bible in order to find the primary meaning of the text.

The goal of Bible study is to edify the reader. Most of these programs excel at helping preachers or teachers present the Bible to audiences. But they also help readers with their own personal worship time. We call this function "devotions," and most programs will have some method or system of presenting daily devotional readings. This can come in the form of a devotional book like *Morning and Evening* by Charles Spurgeon, or it might be a system of arranging the Bible into daily readings. Good programs will. at the very least, offer to let you read one devotional book and do a daily Bible reading. The better ones will have multiple devotions to choose from, and will also provide some method of creating custom readings with dates, along with the ability to record your progress with checklists. Many will even nag you to do your devotions every day by starting up with the devotional readings showing first on your basic desktop. After you read it you can check it off for that day and move on to your other Bible study.

The features I have shared so far will give you a basic understanding of some of the very essential things that all Bible study programs do. If you are planning to get a Bible study software program, here is a list of the minimum things you should require:

▶ Ability to provide multiple Bible translations
▶ Ability to do simple searches, and complex "Boolean" searches
▶ Ability to consult reference books and commentaries
▶ Study maps, charts and other visually presented information
▶ Ability to arrange books into windows and tabs
▶ Ability to save desktops for future use
▶ Ability to teach various Bible study methods
▶ Ability to read devotions and keep track of daily Bible readings

Four Great Bible Study Programs for Windows

Up to this point we have looked at the general benefits and features of Bible study software. Now we will focus on five different programs and show how they excel.

Understand that there is no one program that is the best for everyone. In fact, most pastors I know that use Bible study programs own several because some programs are better at specific functions. A program that excels in original language studies doesn't necessarily exceed at accomplishing simple fast word searches. Or while some like the functionality of one program for their Bible searches, they make the decision to purchase an additional product due to the large library of resources that can be upgraded. Of course cost is an important part of the purchase decision since some products are free while others offer many different levels of their product depending on the additional resources and commentaries that are included.

With that in mind, let's start our overview of specific Bible study products by looking at one that has some great features and is also offered for FREE!

e-Sword

Granted, there are some bad programs out there, but there are a few really great ones. And, interestingly enough, one of the great ones is also free—and one of the most popular.

Rick Meyers was a computer programmer who made good money doing what he loved. And as a Christian he wanted to give back, so he created e-Sword—a free, downloadable Bible software program available at www.e-sword.net.

This program has a lot to offer. The simple layout makes it easy to read, search, and study the Bible. It has all the basics listed above. In one pane you can view multiple translations through the tabbed interface. In the second pane you can view the many commentaries available. Finally, the third pane is for dictionaries.

With e-Sword you download the basic program and install it. It has just the KJV. If you want more, then you go to the download page, click on the various kinds of programs that are available, and download and install them. There are hundreds of different works, most of them in the public domain. There are a few that are copyrighted. For example the English Standard Version is free to download for e-Sword, as Meyers pays the license himself. However, if you want the more modern translations like the NIV, NKJV, or NLT, you will have to buy them from third-party publishers. They will give you an unlock code which you will use when you install their translation through with e-Sword.

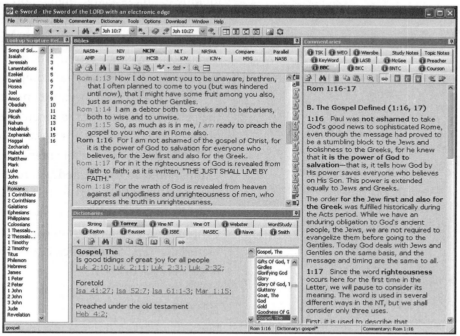

There are dozens of free commentaries, dictionaries, devotionals, visual graphics books, and other miscellaneous works, and e-Sword also has a STEP reader.

STEP was a nearly defunct standard for publishing Bible software books that was intended to help the user. Publishers could use the single standard format to publish their works, and then the various software makers could code their programs to be able to read the books all using that single format. It was kind of like PDF for Bible software. While it is now outdated technology and very few publishers support it, there are a lot of STEP files floating around and e-Sword has a reader that allows you to access them if you have an old CD or floppy disk with STEP books.

If you want some modern reference books, e-Sword also has a few available, again from third-party publishers.

What e-Sword doesn't do very well is help a student of Greek or Hebrew. You can download some Greek and Hebrew texts, and they have Strong's numbers, which are hyperlinks and tooltips. But if you do a lot of original language study then you will want to pay for one of the other programs that are on the market.

Unfortunately, there are not a lot of huge libraries of Christian books that will work with e-Sword. However, there is a feature to publish books in a topic-based way, and you can create your own commentary with a very simple to use notes feature. But if you are looking to amass a large digital library of recent Christian books then this is not the program for you. But it's FREE, so you should at least give it a try. If you like it and are willing to spend just a few dollars on some recent translations and references then this might be all you need to meet your computerized Bible study needs.

There is also a very mature online community surrounding the program if you want to receive help using e-Sword. A good place to start is located at www.e-sword-users.org.

Deserving an honorable mention in the free category is The Online Bible. It was created before the Internet, so its name does not mean that it is used "on-line," as some are. You can get it at www.onlinebible.net. Like e-Sword it does not have a lot of contemporary material, but you can order a DVD with more recent material and pay for unlock codes for translations like NIV, NASB, NRSV or NLT.

WordSearch

If after trying out the free programs you find them lacking, you may want to try a more advanced program with more recent works. One of the best at what some call the "library approach" is WordSearch, which is available at www.wordsearchbible.com. It is a library on your hard drive. The interface resembles the old Windows Explorer with folders on the left and content on the right. It has a simple interface and does the basics quite well.

One of the things that set it apart is the volume and diversity of the available library. Open the program and you can use the menu system to go online and buy hundreds of add-on titles in subjects ranging from Greek study to Bible study lessons to theology, history and even Christian fiction. The library is arranged in topics with folders. Open a book and it automatically arranges itself on the screen. If you want to find a book, you can click on the "filter resource" button and type the title. From the default opening screen you can click on the "browse add-on books" button and it will take you to the WordSearch site where you can order and download books.

As you can see from the screen shot on page 259, you can have multiple windows open at the same time to aid you in your study. In this case, the top left window shows Chapter 5 of Matthew from the *New International Version of the Bible*, with the screen below showing commentary on Chapter 5 of Matthew from the *Bible Exposition Commentary*, while the screen on the right displays one of the maps provided in their atlas.

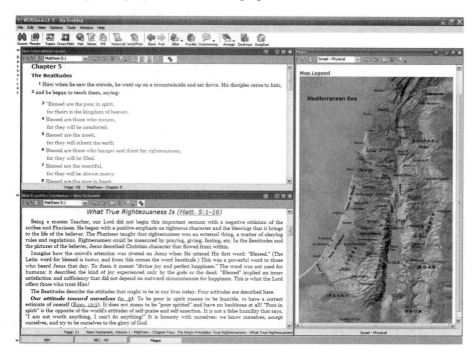

Among the great list of resources is a unique resource called the Holman Christian Standard Bible Reverse Interlinear. Only two publishers produce these unique Bibles, and interlinear is common. It displays the Greek or Hebrew text on one line, and below that the English translation of the text. What the Reverse Interlinear does is reverse it. It puts the English on top, such as in the case of the HCSB, a great new translation from Holman Bible Publishers. One benefit of a Reverse Interlinear is that it brings original language study and searching to an audience that is not very adept in using biblical languages. It is also more readable for English speakers than a traditional Interlinear. Finally, you can do easier searches of Greek or Hebrew words without really knowing Greek and Hebrew. Since you immediately see the translation above the corresponding word, you know that is what you want to find. You right click the word and choose search and it will give you a list of references with that word, or a form of that word. You can then open it in the Reverse Interlinear and see how else that word is translated in the Bible. This helps us understand the meaning of the word, even if we do not know Greek or Hebrew.

WordSearch also excels in product training. Aside from good help files, it also has training available through their Web site, which is accessible through its Help menu. On their Web site, registered users can access the two-and-a-half hour basic training lessons. Also available on the site are video tours. The default opening screen in WordSearch also has a link to video tutorials.

Another standout feature is the online community associated with WordSearch. From within the program a user can go into the discussion forums tab and learn about the program, get help with features or problems, and suggest new features, books or tips. Also, if you need, you can post a prayer request. There is also a community tab where you can upload documents created within WordSearch.

Document creation is another standout feature of WordSearch. Of course you can create notes that can be assigned to verses. But in addition you can create and share full documents such as Bible studies, sermons, papers or anything you wish. From the file menu, choose new document and then create it however you desire. The feature is a simple word processor. When you are finished, click the publish document button and it goes online. The benefit of using this that you can have the documents saved in WordSearch for searching and referencing at a later date. You can also create links to other books. And finally, you can publish them for your own use on another computer or for others' benefits.

The final standout feature of WordSearch is its ability to do what is called an "instant verse study." Open the dialogue box and choose the translations, notes file, and commentaries you want to use and it will copy the content to the clipboard where you can then paste it into the new document window or another Windows program like your word processor. So if you want all the information in your library about John 3:16, then click whichever translations you want included, along with whichever notes file in which you might have already created verse notes, and whichever commentaries you want to read. This is much faster than opening every commentary, notes file and translation.

Aside from WordSearch, you might want to give QuickVerse (www.quickverse.com) and PC Study Bible (www.pcstudybible.com) a look. QuickVerse has a lot of resources like WordSearch, just not as many. PC Study Bible is very simple to use and has a great content creation tool which might be better than WordSearch's. Neither of them have as many resources available for download as WordSearch, however PC Study Bible has some nice demo videos so you can get a look at the program before buying it. Both of them have varying packages ranging from simple and inexpensive to very complete but also very costly.

While all of the above have Greek and Hebrew texts and simple study tools like Strong's dictionaries available, none of them handles original language study and translation like the powerhouse BibleWorks.

BibleWorks

The makers of BibleWorks do not have the same approach that the other programs have in the area of features and function. However, they do not want—or ever plan—to be a large digital library with vast collections of resources. Instead, it focuses on helping users study the Bible in its original language, and in its ability to search the Bible.

BibleWorks does the bare minimum well. You can read, compare, search and copy/paste multiple translations of the Bible. Since it is a commercial program it has all the modern translations. It also does simple things well, such as taking notes.

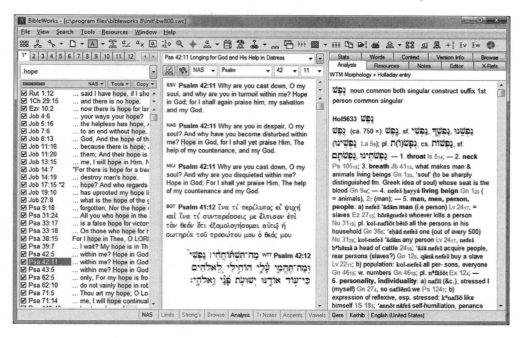

In the screen shot above the three panels in the standard BibleWorks interface allows users to do fast searches and quickly access information about the text under consideration. First, users can do a search and scan the results (left panel shows search results for the word "hope" with Psalm 42:11 highlighted).

The center panel shows "hits" in multiple Bible versions (Psalm 42:11 in five translations [ESV, NAS, NKJ, plus a Greek and Hebrew text]). The right panel shows the parsing information for the Hebrew word for "soul" as well as that word's lexical entry from Holladay's lexicon.

BibleWorks excels at language study. That is the primary function that sets it apart from the other programs available. It does Greek and Hebrew study well, but that's not all. If you are a translator and use other non-English languages then BibleWorks is for you.

The second thing that sets BibleWorks apart is the very complex search engine. Because it is complex, it is also a little harder to use. For example, you cannot simply type a word and hit "enter" or click a button. You have to enter what the program calls "command line shortcuts" to tell BibleWorks how to search. This is because the command line in BibleWorks does a lot more than just accomplish a normal search. This is where you tell the program what translations to display, or not display, what references to open, or a host of other complex search functions.

The command line in BibleWorks may be complex, but the program will help you learn how to use it with their very complete help files and tutorial videos. In fact, the first time you open the program, you are presented with a splash screen that gives dozens of learning options.

Since BibleWorks is such a good language tool, it also offers many language references, grammar, and other resources. One of the best features is their ability to right click a word and send the verse to what they call the "Lexicon Browser." This is a window that pops up and gives the definitions of all the words in a verse. This saves a lot of time compared to some of the other programs, not to mention the old-fashioned method of looking up words in a traditional lexicon. You also have the option of changing between the various lexicons you have installed, from within the browser.

A third tool in BibleWorks is the ability to create new translations. If you used all the language tools to translate the Bible, you could then create a translation that would have all the features of a commercial translation that comes with the program.

If you like to do outlines, as mentioned previously, BibleWorks has a very nice diagramming tool. It comes with a set of Greek New Testament diagrams produced by Randy A. Leedy. But you can also create your own in Greek, Hebrew, or any other language. With the ability to quickly import the text of the verses you want to diagram, you also have the ability to use the many drawing and marking tools included. This lets you use the rigid rules of diagramming that you might learn in a seminary level class, or you can be creative and do whatever helps you see the relationship of the words and phrases of the text. And if you really don't understand how to diagram a Bible verse, no problem. BibleWorks gives you the tools to learn how.

BibleWorks may sound intimidating to the average Bible student, but it is actually one of those great programs in that it is not only very mature and complex in its features and capabilities, but it is also very simple and helpful for less knowledgeable students. The way it is designed, you could easily make use of the more advanced language references, even if you do not know a lot of Greek or Hebrew. You may be more proficient in one language but elementary in the other. BibleWorks will help you excel at studying the language you know best, while holding your hand to help you learn the one you don't know as well.

The one thing that some would call a limitation is the limited scope of the program. Fortunately, while the makers have no plans of becoming a digital library, they do recognize the value of these other programs. BibleWorks, in its latest edition has a way of linking from BibleWorks to other programs, called the External Links Manager or ELM. It is a bit complicated to use, but if you are willing to spend the time to learn how to use the ELM then you can link to other software programs, including some of those that I am highlighting in this chapter. It also can link to Bible services that are found on the Web.

Logos

Another great tool for original language study can be found in the Libronix Digital Library System from Logos (www.logos.com). Logos is one of the early Bible software pioneers, and made a mark for themselves by being one of the first Bible study programs to hit the market that utilized Windows. Over the years they have continued to be innovative in providing a powerful Bible study program that is easy to use and connects the user to a large and growing library of resources.

What usually happens when a company tries to do it all is that it often does nothing well. That is not the case with Libronix, or as most users simply call it, Logos. Like BibleWorks, it has very good tools for original language study. Like WordSearch, it has a large library of books besides Bibles and reference works. And like QuickVerse, the basic package is free. You won't get much more than the basic package for free from Logos, but at least you can give the program a try and see if you like it before investing in a lot of resources, or one of the collections.

The two best things that set Logos apart from the other programs are the guides—the Passage and Exegetical Guides. These are available either from the menu or on the "home page," which opens when you first launch Logos. The Passage Guide runs when you enter in a passage in the dialogue box. For example, if you are studying the Lord's Prayer, you can enter Matthew 6. But maybe you don't know the exact verses, in which case Logos can help you by offering suggestions based on the sections of the various translations you have installed. These are called Pericope Sets. A pericope is a section of scripture that constitutes what someone considered a single message unit. For example, many translations will divide Matthew 6 up into sets, and the Lord's Prayer will be in Matthew 6:5-15. So if you have the NIV installed then the sections set apart by that translation's section headings or pericope will be shown in a drop down menu that offers suggestions once you start typing Matthew 6. You don't have to follow the suggestions, but you do have them available to help.

Once you click the big orange GO button, Logos does its magic and opens your favorite translation to the text. It also searches for commentary entries on that passage. After you have used the program a little, the program will learn what you like and it will show the commentaries you use the most at the top, with your less favorite commentaries listed below. If you have a large library it stops after it shows the first 10, but you can just click on the "more" option and it will show you the rest. The passage guide also shows other content depending on what you have in your Logos installation. For example, you get cross references based on that verse. You also have a list of passages that are similar to the one you are studying. An example of this would be if you are studying a passage in the Gospels, you will get the parallel Gospel passages. There are lists of passages either quoted in your chosen text, or that quote your chosen text. There will also be a list of important words with the ones used the most highlighted by bold or increased font size.

The Passage Guide is like having a research assistant at your seminary library. Tell them to go get everything on the Lord's Prayer and they will come back with a stack of commentaries, cross reference lists, multiple translations of the Bible, a collection sermon illustrations and sermons. They might also go through the stacks and find books that are not necessarily about the Lord's Prayer, but make references to it. The Passage Guide feature in Logos does all of that.

One other thing the Passage Guide will do is offer to do additional searches for you. It will search exegetical material, show the passage in multiple translations or every translation you have, and it will go through your entire library for you.

If you want to study the text in Greek (Hebrew for the OT) then you will want to use the Exegetical Guide. You can access it from the Passage Guide, from the menu system or toolbar, or from the Home Page.

Like the Passage Guide, begin typing your reference and the Exegetical Guide will suggest passages from the pericope sets you have installed. Logos will display the text in your default translation and Greek or Hebrew text. Then, going verse by verse, it will highlight the most important words, leaving out articles and less important words. If a word is highlighted, it will be listed in the content for that verse. Then, below the Greek or Hebrew text, each verse will be listed with the following items:

▶ Grammars that refer to the passage
▶ Visualizations, like the OpenText.org Syntactically Analyzed Greek NT which is a diagram similar to BibleWorks Leedy NT Diagrams
▶ Apparati like the Nestle-Alund NT Apparatus
▶ Lexical entries for each word along with a basic translation, the lemma form of the word, and an icon which when clicked with pronounce the lemma

Under each word is a list of the lexicons or dictionaries with that word in it. If you click the hyperlink, the book will open. If you click the plus symbol, that entry will open below the list of references. If you have a lot of them listed it will only show a few and give you the option for more, much like the commentaries listed in the Passage Guide.

If the Passage Guide and the Exegetical Guide were the only unique features in Logos, that would be enough to make it one of the most useful and complete Bible study software packages available. The Home Page mentioned above is another very unique feature. It is like having an Internet "home" page with quick access to your favorite sites, only in Logos it shows various tools in the program, as well as links to some Logos related Internet sites.

Most Bible study programs will have a Window Explorer style interface like WordSearch with a list of works along the left side of your screen, in folders based on types of books. The second most common interface is a multiple window or pane-style like e-Sword. That means that there will be a window open for Bibles with tabs or a drop down box. There will also be panes for dictionaries and commentaries. Logos can be arranged in panes, but by default it has the Home Page.

As mentioned previously, the Home Page has the section for Guides. It also has a section for Logos-related news and their Internet blog. The other sections on the Home Page are for Bible readings, devotions, prayer requests and books on prayer, the library section and the lectionary viewer. The library section shows you the book of the day and also flashes a slideshow of pictures of the books you have installed. Like the other programs mentioned, you can customize the interface and have certain books open by default in a desktop. But the Home Page is a very unique tool that makes Logos easy to use for beginners. Unlike any other program, it is accessible and easy to use from day one. Yet Logos offers so many powerful features that it would take a long time to become skilled at using all the unique features. This might be why the offer special "camps" for serious Bible students to attend, enabling them to learn how to use all of the powerful tools that Logos offers in their program.

Unlike any other program, Logos is quite innovative. We've only described three of the unique features. There are many more, and here is a list of some of them:

▶ Word Study Guide which searches the library like the Passage and Exegetical Guides
▶ Bibliography tool for researchers
▶ Very complete set of original language study tools
▶ Verb River and Bible Cluster which visually shows the differences between multiple translations
▶ Lectionary Viewer which shows the lectionary passage for that week in one or more lectionaries
▶ Timeline viewer
▶ Sentencing Diagram
▶ Bible Study and Sermon Add-ins
▶ Word Find creator

This list is not complete. But it gives you an idea of some of the features that makes Logos the leader in innovation in the area of computerized Bible study. Another innovation that is underway is their online tools.

Online Bible Study Services

One category of Bible study not listed above is the Bible study programs available over the Internet. One of the latest trends in computing in general is what is called "cloud computing." The term comes from the idea that software can be run over the Internet as a service, instead of installed onto your computer from a box. The benefit is that you can access your "applications" regardless of where you are, or what computer you are using. With another trend in computing being netbooks, often with much smaller local storage, the idea of having most of your programs stored externally on a Web site is appealing.

Can online Bible study programs meet all of your Bible study needs? Kevin Purcell, who reviews Bible study software for *Christian Computing Magazine* recently said, "I could see using [on-line Bible Web sites] to accomplish what I need to do when I am preparing for a sermon or Bible study."

It could be enough but is not nearly as useful and extensive at this point as what can be done with the software programs we have already featured. For some, however, it will suffice.

Online or cloud computing Bible study Web sites are a lot like the suites we have used. There are free sites that focus mostly on public domain works that may be out of date. And there is at least one subscription site that has a few more up-to-date resources.

Few of these sites will have very many modern translations. But they often have the most popular ones, like ESV, HCSB, NASB, NIV, NKJV or NLT. Nearly all of them have the KJV. You will be able to do most of the basic things you can do in programs, such as searching and reading the Scriptures. You can usually copy them into an online or local word processor as well. Some of them have original language study tools, as well as access to Strong's dictionary, and in some cases even more advanced resources. A couple of them even have modern commentaries, dictionaries, and handbooks. One thing that is rare, but available in a couple of sites, is the ability to save notes and bookmarks for future reference if you are willing to register for an account.

Maybe the best and most complete site is the Bible Study Tools site at Crosswalk.com (biblestudy.crosswalk.com).

Crosswalk is a wonderful Christian Web site with a wide range of offerings. You can read articles, movie reviews, and learn about the latest Christian music. Like everything else Crosswalk does, theie Bible study site is first-class.

It has a tabbed interface with some wonderful resources. Once you sign up for a free account and login, you will be greeted with a home page that offers quick access to site tools, as well as a section for customizing the site to your own needs.

When you personalize it using the options available, the My BEST tab will open your favorite translation of the Bible. This will allow you to read the Bible, study it, and then save your highlights, notes, and bookmarks.

Crosswalk has most of the major translations, including the NIV, ESV, NKJV, NASB, and HCSB. It has commentaries, dictionaries and topical Bibles, but they are primarily public domain books. It has a pair of lexicons to study Greek and Hebrew, and its maps come from eBible Teacher at www.eBibleTeacher.com. They also offer help for people who visually teach the Bible using PowerPoint or some other presentation software.

Crosswalk has a huge number of devotional offerings, and also many personal development articles, which makes a great site for the lay persons or clergy. They also provide Bible reading plans. There is a tab labeled "The Bible in a Year." With it you can keep track of your reading progress. You will, however, have to register separately for it.

Besides doing basic Bible study, Crosswalk offers other feature articles covering a number of Christian topics. There are also articles about preaching and sermon preparations, yet lay people will enjoy the wealth of topics just for them.

Crosswalk is not the only available site for doing cloud Bible study. Some of the others are listed below:

▶ Logos has a collection of sites including bible.logos.com, sermons.logos.com, wbsa.logos.com (standing for "What the Bible Says About" and has a topical Bible) and books. logos.com. And, as mentioned, Logos also offers www .reftagger.com, which helps you put the Bible on your site using special code.

▶ YouVersion (www.youversion.com) is a unique combination of social networking and Bible study. With it you can do Bible study and share your findings with a community of users on the Internet in a kind of Facebook for Bible study.

▶ BibleGateway (www.biblegateway.com) gives something few of the other sites do: The IVP NT Commentary series as well as an audio Bible with recordings by Shakespearean actor Max MacLean, who has made a career out of performing the Bible word for word in auditoriums across the country.

▶ BibleMaster's strength (www.Biblemaster.com) is the collection of studies. They are study articles ranging from scholarly articles and devotionals to small group resources that are user submitted.

▶ eBible (www.ebible.com) focuses on studying in a community. It offers more modern resources, but at a cost. There is a monthly, yearly and a lifetime subscription fee, which is said to be a limited-time offer.

▶ e-Sword (live.e-sword.net) is like having the free program available on-line with a limited number of translations, commentaries and references.

▶ The Greek Word Study site (www.greekwordstudy.org) has Greek study resources online.

CHAPTER 9

CHAPTER 9

Facing Our Anxiety and Implementation of New Technologies

When we are faced with the vision to move ministry forward and expand our options by adopting new technologies, there can always be some anxiety. And, as this book has revealed, there are many different ways to use technology to help accomplish various ministries. One of the fears of using technology is that you might not make the right decisions. Technology costs. What if you invest your money in a new direction only to find that it was a passing fad? Or what if you fear you do not have the knowledge to make certain technology tools, services and solutions work for you?

Should you podcast your services or stream them live as video to your Web site, or both? Do you increase the use of broadcast emails, or should you try to move your congregation into accepting text messages? Broadcast emails is an easier sell since even older adults have accepted email, yet it is slow and ineffective since so many go unread. Yet text messaging has a higher learning curve if you are looking to get older members to use it to receive important announcements from your church. Do you encourage using a popular social networking service such as Facebook, or encourage your members to connect via a private service? What do you gain in security, but risk losing as an outreach opportunity? If you start a blog, can you maintain it? What will you write about each week, and what kind of comments might you receive? And what if you invest in seeking to connect via Twitter and then something else comes along? Feeling stressed?

BE ANXIOUS FOR NOTHING

In George Barna's book, *Boiling Point*, he shares the story of a fictitious woman named Jill, and her potential stress when faced with new technology and the impact it will have on her lives and those in her family.

"*Jill loved technology. And Jill hated technology. Based on conversation with her girlfriends, she knew she was not alone in this state of suspended ambivalence over the true master of the universe: technology.*

"*A commentator she heard on the news the other day described her state perfectly: technostress. On the one hand, her life was all about managing the technological devices that made her existence more efficient, exciting, fulfilling and economical. On the other hand, the unfathomable speed at which the world of technology changed made her feel like she was in the ocean, sinking quickly, with the waterline almost beyond her line of sight. If she didn't buy the latest digital stuff, she'd feel like a dinosaur—her tech-crazed husband and tech-natured kids would see to that. If she didn't take the time to learn the new applications, she'd feel like an imbecile and be left in the duct of society. But who had the time or inclination t become a walking encyclopedia of software applications? If she even heard the term "killer app" one more time, she'd scream.*

"*In her calmer moments, Jill could list the numerous benefits that technology had provided to her and her family in the past decade. Brittan had grown a new tooth where there was none before through the use of some new-fangled bone-growing process at the university dental school. Jackson, Procrastinator General, had become incredibly adept at throwing together impressive presentations for school by musing together music, video clips, information, and color photos into automated presentations that wowed his professors (and probably did nothing to fool his classmates). Jill and Carl saved hundreds of dollars on travel each year by gambling on-line rather than at Las Vegas. (Of course, they more than made up for their travel savings their losses sustained at the digital gaming tables.) The smart house, the GPS in her car, the global shopping options, the instantly accessible and customizable entertainment alternatives—all of it was wonderful. But it still left her in a state of cybershock." (pg 119-120)*

So with the risk of technostress and cybershock, we are left with a dilemma. We face an era of technology where much of it is centered on communication, and we are the people with a message. No longer does it take billions of dollars to provide live video streaming of an event to the rest of the world. The ability is now available and affordable to individuals. For some, the temptation to keep up with the wave of new technologies seemed daunting and could best be avoided by simply "riding it out" until retirement. While that might work for our homes, our cars, and even our means of making an income, as Christians we can never just sit by and miss such a grand opportunity to share the message of Christ. Those that have gone before us set sail in wooden boats with limited supplies to explore new lands and new peoples, and took the time to learn new languages and cultures, just to share the simple Gospel of Christ with those that didn't have the good news. How can we dodge our responsibilities to adopt new technology tools in order to share the good news with those in our communities, our nation and our world?

Walt Wilson, in his book *The Internet Church* states:

> *"While there is no reason for Christians ever to be anxious about the future, being too casual about it is also a mistake. Dynamic tension is a fact of life, and it's good. There are always footsteps behind you. There is always the next Internet mousetrap that will be better, faster, less expensive, and more efficient that yours. Chances are your customers will leave in droves to try the latest service. Does this strike a chord for the senior pastor as well? Can the church learn from the fast-change models of the business community?" (page 113)*

I believe we don't have a choice. We must use the tools God is providing to minister. We could. We should. We must. To do anything less is to hide our light under a bushel!

Walt Wilson continued later in his book to ask:

"Is God big enough to place a global communications tool in the hands of the church? Does He alone have the authority to do such a thing, and is He willing to delegate His authority to His church? Will He empower the church to see new visions and create new models for communication to the lost world? Hasn't He already?" (pg. 116)

When I started *Christian Computing Magazine* back in 1989, our mission statement was to "Promote the computer as a vital tool for ministry." Back in the late '80s and early '90s we were simply trying to get churches and ministries to consider using a computer for their church administration needs and Bible study. In the mid '90s we changed the mission statement to read, "To apply tomorrow's technology to today's ministry." It was a bold statement since Christianity is normally conservative, and most churches were lagging behind in the adaptation of new technologies. Over the years we have seen many churches leap ahead in the adoption of new technologies, specifically in the area of communication and networking via the Internet. Yet, I am aware that most churches look at computer technology with a wary eye. For many churches, funds are always limited, and technology moves at such a fast pace that it is daunting to make a decision to invest time and resources to use a new computer tool that might not bring the return in ministry or funds to justify the investment. Yet, there is a growing communication gap between generations. And while each new generation seems to adopt different terminology and symbols for communication, the technology communication gap between the young and the old must be breached by the church if we are going to reach each new generation with the message of Christ.

I hope you will find inspiration and new ideas on how to apply computer programs and technology services to your ministries, in order to share the message and ministry of Christ with your membership as well as your community, nation and the world.

IMPLEMENTATION OF NEW TECHNOLOGIES

If you have read this book and have been inspired to try new technologies to implement within your ministry, how do you go about introducing them to your church and congregation?

Take Things One Step at a Time

First, take things one step at a time. For example:

▶ If you are doing broadcast emails from your server, you might wish to move up to a service such as Constant Contact in order to use many of the features outlined previously in the book.

▶ If you have a Web site that is brochure-style with no interaction, you may want to consider adding one of the many add-ons discussed in this book, such as online giving or a blog.

▶ If you are recording your services and distributing them via cassettes, you may want to start streaming them from your Web site or making them available as podcasts.

▶ If you have a class for your membership on how to share your testimonies, you may want to try to encourage them to record the classes and upload the videos to YouTube and then share the link with friends.

▶ If you already have a phone prayer chain in place, you may want to explore using text messaging to deliver instant prayer requests to your membership within minutes.

The point I am trying to make is that you can take baby steps. You don't want to be overwhelmed by trying to implement too much, too quickly. Not only will it exhaust yourself and/or your staff, but you will scare your members by presenting too much change at one time. However, if you look at the examples above you can see that what you are actually doing is building on ministries you might already have, and simply taking them to the next step by applying new technologies.

Add the "New" without Throwing Out the "Old"

Sometimes you might have to *slide* into new communication opportunities. For example, some churches are still create a print newsletter and mail it to their membership.

You can save a lot of postage if you start a full-color digital newsletter by converting your regular newsletter (if it's produced using desktop publishing software) into a PDF file and then distributing it as a link in an email. I wouldn't advise, however, that you make such a change overnight. You can start by creating your newsletter in a colorful format, converting it into a PDF file, and then printing it out in black and white. Continue to mail it to your membership, but give them the option to stop receiving the printed/mailed version and to start receiving the email—or "paperless"—version instead. Emphasize the fact that the email version can be in full-color, with pictures and photos (DO include these) and hyperlinks to online content. You can also emphasize the fact that if church members opt out of the mailed newsletter and sign up for the email version, it will be delivered faster, better, and save the church money! Members like to hear that churches are saving money.

After a period of time, you will probably discover that most of your members have opted out of the printed/mailed version and have signed up for the email list. If you approach it in this manner, you will have given them the "power" to accept the more colorful and practical solution. This works much better than to simply make the announcement that you are no longer printing and mailing the church newsletter, and that they must switch to the new format or risk not staying informed. A little diplomacy goes a long way in helping to keep the peace. And it gives everyone the chance to join you in an improvement, instead of feeling that new technology is being forced upon them.

You can apply this principle to the implementation of any new technology or communication tool. Sometimes the answer is in *how* you present it. As I shared earlier, when you ask people if they would be interested in texting, most of those over fifty will probably reply "no," because they simply don't text. However, this doesn't mean that you can't begin to use such services within your ministry. For example, if you have any type of a youth ministry you should setup a Twitter group for them to follow. Since there is no cost, you are not wasting any money—even if the group consists of only two people! Other options would be to use texting services, or Twitter, as an outreach tool. Promote your new Twitter or text service to your community. You could set up an account using a name such as "OurChurch" and simply encourage people within your church, or those in your community that are unchurched, to follow your group. You can then use the service to send special text announcements about upcoming events and ministries. If you introduce the service in this way you are not taking anything away from your present membership not interested in texting, yet you open a new line of communication to those members and prospects that would like such announcements. After you have advertised the texting option for a set time, and your members are comfortable with repeatedly hearing about texting options, you could then introduce other texting and Twitter options, such as using it for those interested in receiving text prayer announcements. Again, I would introduce a texting prayer support group as an addition to whatever methods you are presently using. For example, some churches publish the prayer requests of their membership in the weekly bulletin, or send out emails or make phone calls to a prayer chain. Don't eliminate the old in order to implement the new, simply offer multiple methods. Believe me, if you have a phone prayer chain in place it doesn't take any extra effort to establish a Twitter prayer group and encourage people to follow. Over time, most will draw their own conclusion about how much more effective the texting service is over everything else. With texting, an entire group—no matter its size—will receive your prayer requests within minutes, while prayer chains always seem to crash because someone is on vacation, out of town, or didn't get the message.

Did your church ever do a pictorial directory? Most churches have one sitting around somewhere. However, if it's one of those provided by a directory company that camped itself inside your church taking photos of your membership, the directory is probably already out of date. Many of today's church management software systems now connect your membership to an online database, enabling your members to log in and update their data as well as have access to an online membership directory. Use the "old" pictorial directory experience to encourage your membership to make the church Web site the ultimate community and membership portal. Encourage them to access their online membership information in a more accurate, up-to-date format that wasnever possible before with the old print directory. And remember, some will either not have access to the Internet or will be disposed to using such technology. Don't exclude them, but rather provide a printout of the same information that is available online. You can now do this fairly inexpensively right from your inkjet printers, even providing a limited number of color copies to keep those non-Internet users happy and connected to the rest of the membership.

Survey Your Membership

Remember we discussed how the "personal communication" age has impacted our society? As you consider implementing new technologies, survey your membership in order to gain important information that should help you decide the best paths to take. For example, if you are thinking of investing in improving your Web site, it would help to know how many people in your membership actually have Internet access. I am pretty confident that most would, but am also aware that many of them would probably assume it is not a high priority. But if you can produce survey data that indicates that most of your members would take advantage of new online features, you would be able to make a much better case for online improvements.

If your church does not yet use an online giving service, I would also consider doing a membership survey that could help pave the way for it. But don't survey your membership and simply ask them if they'd like to contribute via an online service. Instead, survey them to find out if they pay their bills online, or if they've made any online purchases over the last year. Once again, this type of information would go a long way in building your case for starting an online giving program.

If your church has a desire to reach out to the community, consider doing a survey of the residents of the community. For example, this could be a great way to introduce social networking opportunities to your church. If you can get a survey of your surrounding community and show a good percentage of them use social networking sites such as Facebook, you will go a long way in helping to make the case that your church should have a Facebook site as well.

We Really DON'T Have Any Money

Think back through the book and reflect on all of the ideas presented that actually didn't cost a single penny.

It wouldn't cost anything for your members to record their testimonies using a computer camera and microphone and post them on YouTube. You could make the entire process an event! Have a class on how to share your testimony, and then find a member with a computer with a built in camera and microphone (they are standard on most new notebooks sold today). You can record the video testimonies right there in the class and then post them. You could then post the links on your churches Web site and encourage others to check them out. Don't have a Web site? Post them in your bulletin and/or newsletter. Make flyers and post them around town encouraging others in your community to log in and watch!

And remember, Twitter is free. There is NO cost to setting up Twitter accounts and encouraging people to follow.

Many of the blog services I listed are free as well. It won't take a lot of time for your pastors or key lay leaders to post blogs and respond to comments and questions. Blogs can open up some fantastic doors for you to communicate with others in your church, your community and even with those around the world.

Remember the online discipleship classes offered by the Radio Bible Class at www.ChristianCourses.com? Of course, they have classes that require a fee, but I also provided you a long list of classes that cost NOTHING! I even outlined a way to use this service in a classroom environment within your church without having a live Internet connection.

Don't have a Web site? Remember that some of the Christian Web site services we discussed offer a simple brochure site for free. It's better than not having anything at all. And don't forget that social networking sites such as Facebook are free. There is no cost to set up a site and use it to tell others about your church. People in your community will find it if you have a site. Don't forget to make it open to the public. In addition, there are many online church directory services that are available which allow you to list information about your church. This makes it very easy for those seeking a church in your community to find the information they need to contact you.

As outlined earlier, it is easy and affordable to produce podcasts, and once you have them you can post them on a variety of sites, including iTunes for absolutely no cost. Besides recording your services and Bible or book studies, consider providing content that can be entertaining, yet evangelical at the same time (I really hope someone tries doing radio dramas and post them as podcasts. If you do, please contact me so I can give them a listen).

Use Your Imagination and Be Open to the Holy Spirit

Sometimes I run across unique examples of churches using technology for ministry that surprise even me. Let me share a few examples.

In 1996 I was invited to speak at a church in Phoenix, Arizona. I wish I could remember the name of the church, but I lost my contact information for it several years ago. During that time period, email was just beginning to take off as the newest technology tool. Since the church was in Phoenix, their membership consisted of many retirees who had moved to that area. These senior citizens had discovered, however, that their grandchildren were not interested in keeping in touch via letters. So the church started a ministry to help teach those in their community on how to use email. They encouraged local businesses to donate old computers and didn't concern themselves about access speed. Back then, most of the computers were accessing the Internet via modems anyway, so they were happy to get the castoffs that were slower than the current models ones being offered in the marketplace. I remember commenting to one of the ministers about this since most people I knew were constantly seeking faster connections. He pointed out that considering that most of his membership was retired, the one thing they had plenty of was time!

They showed me how they went about offering an email class to their members and the surrounding community as a ministry. They had a large area in their basement that had been converted into an email communication center. Throughout the week they even provided transportation between people's home and the church so people could come and access the computers and communicate with their friends and family across the nation via email. Back in 1996 computers were not cheap, and they were not in everyone's home like they are today. By offering this service they were providing a ministry opportunity to their community that opened the door for them to share the message of salvation in a loving way. Over time they reported many new members who had become a Christian and joined their church as a direct result of the email ministry service that had met a fairly vital need in the community.

In another example, a few years ago I was invited to speak at a computer users group that met at Willow Creek's church. The first time I spoke they asked me to address security and filtering concerns. I was more than happy to speak on the subject, but normally I am asked to address church groups and Christian leaders on subjects related to Bible software programs or other Christian-related technology issues. However, when I arrived the night before I was to speak, I realized that my talk was actually a part of a very important and exciting outreach effort. The "computer user group" at Willow Creek was not actually designed to help the members in their group use technology, but designed to work as a team to provide technology solutions to their community in the hopes that it would open the door for outreach and ministry. My speech had been promoted not to the church membership, per se, but rather to the community. And each member of the computer user group had used the opportunity to invite their unchurched friends. I was instructed to keep my talk on target and not to preach or make my talk too "church" related. They had a breakfast that preceded my talk, and this is where the ministry really took place. Each member of the computer user group was assigned their own table, and during the breakfast time they sought to create relationships they could build upon as they established an opportunity for life-style evangelism. It was fantastic!

Stay Informed

New technologies are constantly hitting the market. Keep your eyes and ears open. Watch what teenagers and young adults are "into." Pick a few sources you trust that can help you keep informed on technology trends. The church is going to have to figure out how to use new applications and programs that continue to be developed, such as location awareness services that will help us connect face-to-face using technology services such s BrightKite. Churches need to use Google Alert to monitor what others are saying on the Internet about their church and ministries, and they might need to use TweetBeep to monitor texts as well. Google's new Wave might change the way we do many things on the Internet in the area of connection, and the impact of mobile computing will become more and more important in the next few years.

Technology advancements continue to break each day, and when they impact the way we communicate and connect with each other, the church must stay informed and ready to adapt.

Index